S0-AZG-800

WEST BEND LIBRARY

PERSONAL FINANCE

A Guide to Money and Business

EDITOR

Stephanie Schwartz Driver

Marshall Cavendish
Reference

NEW YORK

WEST BEND LIBRARY

Copyright © 2010 Marshall Cavendish Corporation
Published by Marshall Cavendish Reference
An imprint of Marshall Cavendish Corporation

All rights reserved.

No part of this publication may be reproduced, stored in a retrieval system or transmitted, in any form or by any means, electronic, mechanical, photocopying, recording, or otherwise, without the prior permission of the copyright owner. Request for permission should be addressed to Permissions, Marshall Cavendish Corporation, 99 White Plains Road, Tarrytown, NY 10591. Tel: (914) 332-8888, fax: (914) 332-1888.

Website: www.marshallcavendish.us

This publication represents the opinions and views of the authors based on personal experience, knowledge, and research. The information in this book serves as a general guide only. The authors and publisher have used their best efforts in preparing this book and disclaim liability rising directly and indirectly from the use and application of this book.

Other Marshall Cavendish Offices:
Marshall Cavendish Ltd. 5th Floor, 32-38 Saffron Hill, London EC1N 8 FH, UK • Marshall Cavendish International (Asia) Private Limited, 1 New Industrial Road, Singapore 536196 • Marshall Cavendish International (Thailand) Co Ltd. 253 Asoke, 12th Flr, Sukhumvit 21 Road, Klongtoey Nua, Wattana, Bangkok 10110, Thailand • Marshall Cavendish (Malaysia) Sdn Bhd, Times Subang, Lot 46, Subang Hi-Tech Industrial Park, Batu Tiga, 40000 Shah Alam, Selangor Darul Ehsan, Malaysia

Marshall Cavendish is a trademark of Times Publishing Limited

All websites were available and accurate when this book was sent to press.

Library of Congress Cataloging-in-Publication Data

Personal finance : a guide to money and business.
        p. cm.
Includes bibliographical references and index.
ISBN 978-0-7614-7909-3 (alk. paper)
1.   Finance, Personal.
HG179.P3746 2009
332.024—dc22

                                                                  2009009461

Printed in Malaysia

12 11 10 09 1 2 3 4 5

Marshall Cavendish
Publisher: Paul Bernabeo
Production Manager: Michael Esposito
Development: MTM Publishing
Cover Design: Patrice Sheridan
Indexer: AEIOU, Inc.

Photo credits: Cover: Photo Edit/ Tony Freeman, **AP/Wide World**: 13, 15, 33, 40, 41, 48, 116, 120, 125, 154, 165, 166, 189; **Corbis**: 32, 81, AFP 89, 101, 143, James Amos 124, Bernard Annabique/Sygma 56; Bettmann: 14, 46, 55, 94, 153, 170, CB Productions 75, Duomo 17, Peter M. Fisher 73, Philip Gould 160, w161, Hulton 148, Raif Finn Hestoft 79, Howard Jacqueline 44, Joe McBride 62, Jean Miele 82, Jose Luis Pelaez 22, Mark Peterson 95, Photodisc Green 105, Premium Stock 131, Thierry Roge/Reuters 140, Charles Rotkin 136, Rob Rowan Progressive Image 134, Saba 18, Chuck Savage 16, 63, 107, Ariel Skelley 108, 128, Richard Hamilton Smith 35, Bill Varie 96, 97, Lee White 155; **Getty Images**: Creative 24, Digital Vision 43,144, Richard Elliot/Taxi 72, Don Emert/AFP 164, Hulton 9, Alan Kiehr 151, Mark Langridge 92, Win Mcnamee 119, David Paul Morris 144, Donna Ray 65, Taxi 90; **Library of Congress**: 6, 31, 61, 113, 159, 173; **Network for Teaching Entrepreneurship** 84; **Poole Archive** 137

Alphabetical Table of Contents

YA
332.024
P432d

Contributors

Editors

William R. Childs
Ohio State University

Scott B. Martin
Columbia University

Wanda Stitt-Gohdes
University of Georgia

Editorial Consultants

Judith Olson-Sutton
Madison Area Technical College

Don Wentworth
Pacific Lutheran University

Contributors

Stephanie Buckwalter; Nicole Cohen; Denise Davis; Will Drago, University of Wisconsin–Whitewater; Walter C. Farrell, University of North Caroline–Chapel Hill; Ken Friedman, Norwegian School of Management, Sandvika; Joseph Gustaitis; Carl Haacke, Skylight Consulting; John Keckhaver, University of Wisconsin–Madison; Renee Sartin Kirby, University of Wisconsin–Parkside; Andrea Korb, Union High School, New Jersey; David Korb, Ernst & Young, LLP; Laura Lambert; Angeline Lavin, University of South Dakota; Marilyn Lavin, University of Wisconsin–Whitewater; David Long, International Baccalaureate Program, Rufus King High School, Wisconsin; Rich MacDonald, St. Cloud State University; Lisa Magloff; Carl Pacini, Florida Gulf Coast University; Mark C. Schug, University of Wisconsin–Milwaukee; James K. Self, Indiana University–Bloomington; Mary Sisson, Crain's New York Business; Lois Smith, University of Wisconsin–Whitewater; Andrea Troyer, University of California–Irvine; John Troyer, Carlson School of Management, University of Minnesota; Phillip J. VanFossen, Purdue University; Randall E. Waldron, University of South Dakota; John Western, Administrative Resource Options

Introduction

The need for financial, economic, business, and entrepreneurial literacy is relevant not only on the personal level. It is also one of the keys to the financial strength of nations. As Alice M. Rivlin, former vice chair of the Federal Reserve board, said, "A free market economy works well only when the participants—producers, consumers, savers, investors—have the information they need to make intelligent decisions." In order for any country's economy to thrive, people need to understand the constituents of their economy. Informed consumers will hold their financial institutions to high standards, helping to ensure the soundness of the financial system and the growth of the economy.

The goal of *Personal Finance: A Guide to Money and Business* is to lead students toward a fuller understanding of those aspects of business and finance they will commonly encounter in their lives. This A-to-Z guide will provide guidance for students learning to manage personal financial affairs, from setting budgets and managing spending and borrowing to understanding their financial rights and responsibilities. It will also help them to put their personal economic lives in a national context, understanding the ways that broader economic trends, such as inflation or economic recession, affect their own options. In doing so it will give them the economic background they need to understand current events of national and global significance.

Personal Finance: A Guide to Money and Business recognizes that today's students are the foundation of tomorrow's national economic success. In response, it aims to give future entrepreneurs a grounding in the basics of running a successful enterprise, from crafting a business plan to understanding some of the nuances of contracts and intellectual property law.

Each article in this collection contains references for further research on the Internet so that students can independently take their reading to the next level. These online resources are from reputable institutions and will remain up-to-date in the context of a rapidly changing economic landscape.

—*Stephanie Schwartz Driver*

Accounting and Bookkeeping

Businesses use accounting and bookkeeping to identify, measure, record, and communicate information about their financial activities. Information provided through accounting and bookkeeping helps people—those working within a firm and those with whom the firm does business—make informed decisions about business operations and strategy.

Accounting as it is practiced today can be described as a cycle including the following steps:

1. Collect data.
2. Analyze data.
3. Enter data into journals.
4. Post to ledger accounts.
5. Prepare a trial balance.
6. Calculate adjustments and record adjusting entries.
7. Prepare adjusted trial balance.
8. Compile financial statements.
9. Close appropriate accounts and prepare post-closing trial balance.

In this cycle, the first five steps fall into the realm of bookkeeping; the final four steps, into accounting.

In 1943, an accountant totals the returns at the seed dealers, W. Atlee Burpee Company in Philadelphia.

Bookkeeping Functions

For as long as people have been engaged in commerce or trade, they have needed to do some form of bookkeeping. Before computers, records of business transactions were kept in journals or books (hence the term bookkeeping). Although the term has evolved to reflect technological advances (such data recording is now often referred to as record keeping or data processing), its purpose has remained the same: to document and preserve information about financial activity, thus providing information to be used in financial decision making.

Bookkeeping begins with a collection of data. Many events affect a business every day; however, only those activities that affect it financially qualify as sources of data for bookkeeping. Such activities are called transactions. Examples of transactions include purchases or sale of inventory or equipment, loans taken out or paid, and payment of employees' salaries. Documentation is gathered representing these transactions in the form of receipts, bank statements, invoices, and so on. Activities that cannot be documented in dollar amounts, such as the hiring and training of new employees or a competitor lowering its prices, do not qualify as transactions, even though they do affect the business.

After data are collected, they must be analyzed. The analysis involves business accounts in five main categories: assets, liabilities, owner's equity, revenue, and expenses. Revenue and expenses are considered part of owner's equity. The amount of money in each category, or the balance of each account, is recorded on an ongoing basis, and an analysis is done to determine the effect of each transaction on the accounts. For example, if a business uses $500 cash to purchase goods to sell, the analysis would show that, as the bill was paid in cash, the amount of cash (an asset) held by the business has decreased by $500. At the same time, the business gained goods to sell, increasing the amount of inventory (also an asset) by $500.

Once data are collected and analyzed, they must be recorded, or entered, in a journal. This is the third step of the accounting cycle. This third step reflects the basic accounting equation:

Assets = Liabilities + Owner's Equity

Every transaction is entered chronologically into a journal using the double-entry accounting system. This system reflects the fact that every transaction affects two accounts, which keeps the accounting equation balanced. For example, one entry can increase assets and another entry can decrease assets by the same amount; or assets can be increased and liabilities can be increased by the same amount. Both examples preserve the accounting equation.

Activity in each of the three types of account of the basic accounting equation is divided into debits and credits, representing increases and decreases. A debit is an increase in an asset account or a decrease in a liability or equity account. A credit is the opposite—a decrease in an asset account or an increase in a liability or equity account. Each transaction, following the double-entry accounting system, is entered twice: in one account as a debit, and in another as a credit.

Because the basic accounting equation must balance, the debit and credit for each transaction must be equal. If a business purchases supplies for $500 cash, a journal entry is made as a debit on the inventory account and a credit on the cash account, both in the amount of $500.

Once a transaction is recorded in the journal, it is transferred into the company's ledgers. This process, called posting, is the fourth step in the accounting cycle. A company typically uses a general ledger and a subledger. The general ledger shows each debit and credit from the journal—listed for each account on a single page of a book, with debits appearing on the left and credits on the right. The general ledger is usually maintained by computer; a subledger is maintained if more detail is required for a specific account than the general ledger provides.

The final bookkeeping responsibility, preparing a trial balance, is typically done every month. The trial balance is a report summarizing the general ledger; it lists all accounts in the general ledger with their corresponding

Steps in bookkeeping: (1) collecting data; (2) analyzing data; (3) entering data into journals; (4) posting to ledger accounts; and (5) preparing a trial balance.

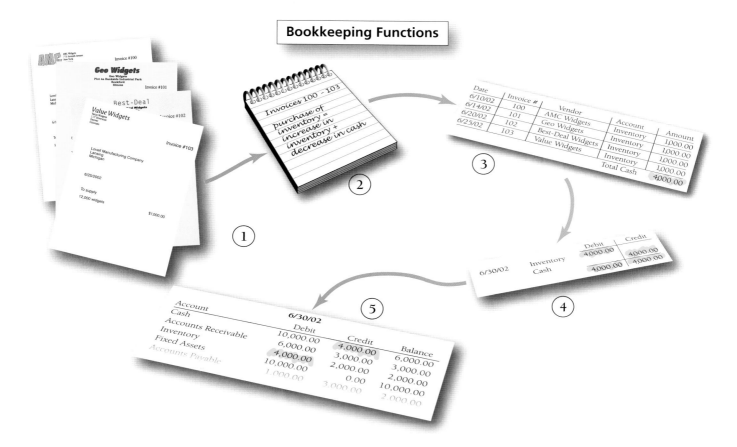

Bookkeeping Functions

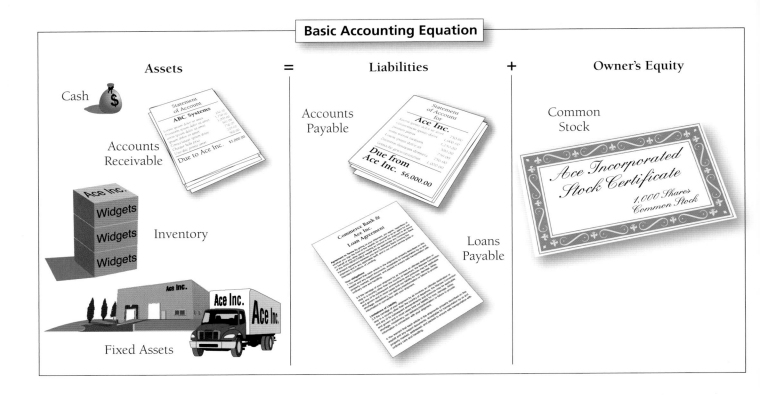

Basic Accounting Equation

Assets	=	Liabilities	+	Owner's Equity

Cash

Accounts Receivable

Inventory

Fixed Assets

Accounts Payable

Loans Payable

Common Stock

The basic accounting equation.

debit or credit balances, as well as the total amount of debits and credits. The trial balance is critical because it ensures that journal entries have been posted correctly. The total dollar debit amount must equal the total dollar credit amount; if it does not, the bookkeeper must go back through the previous four steps in the accounting cycle to find where the error was made. Once the trial balance is correct, the bookkeeper's work is done.

Accounting Functions

The general purpose of accounting is to use the bookkeeper's data to create reports that can be used internally (management reporting) and externally (financial reporting). Management reporting provides members of the company's management with information to help them understand the company's performance and to make decisions for improving it. Financial reporting enables people outside the company to understand how well or poorly the company is operating. To successfully create these reports, the accountant must complete the final four steps of the accounting cycle.

The accounting functions begin with the completed trial balance. Although the trial balance summarizes the important financial transactions that have taken place, it does not include other information such as interest earned but not yet received or prepaid expenses not yet recorded by bookkeepers that may have a significant economic impact on the company. Economic events like these must be calculated and adjusted in the sixth step of the accounting cycle.

After all adjusting entries are made, the accountant must prepare the adjusted trial balance. The adjusted trial balance is the same as the trial balance produced in the bookkeeping process, but it includes all of the accountant's adjusting entries. Again, the total dollar amounts of the debits and credits must be equal; if they are not, the accountant must review the adjusting entries for errors and correct them.

Once the adjusted trial balance is established, it can be used in the creation of financial statements, which is the eighth step of the accounting cycle. Four primary financial statements are used to convey account information: the income statement, statement of changes in retained earnings, balance sheet, and cash flow statement.

Income Statement. The income statement reports the profitability of the company for a specific period. It uses all of the revenue and expense accounts from the trial balance and summarizes them. For example, the company may have many expense accounts, but on the income statement they are reported on one line called "Other Expenses." The result is a net income figure (revenues minus expenses).

Statement of Changes in Retained Earnings. This report shows all transactions that affect retained earnings during the period. The report is created using the previous period's retained earnings, the net income from the income statement, and anything that decreases the retained earnings. The result is the current period's retained earnings.

Balance Sheet. The balance sheet shows the company's financial position at a single point in time. It uses all asset and liability accounts from the trial balance and summarizes them. For example, a company may have one account for office supplies, another account for cleaning products, and so on. These accounts may be reported in one line item called "Other Assets." The goal is to summarize the company's financial position clearly so people inside and outside the company can make informed decisions.

Cash Flow Statement. The cash flow statement summarizes the inflows and outflows of cash during a given period. The report is typically broken out into cash flows from operating activities, investing activities, and financing activities. The cash balance at the beginning of the period plus or minus the cash flows from these three activities equals the current cash balance in the trial balance and on the balance sheet.

When the financial statements are completed, the accountant must close the appropriate accounts and prepare the post-closing trial balance. This is the final step in the accounting cycle. Revenue and expense accounts are not cumulated over time. In each accounting period, revenues and expenses must start at zero to correctly generate the income statement for the next period. Therefore, the accountant must enter reversing entries to transfer revenue and expense

Computers play a key role in accounting.

account balances into owner's equity. For example, if interest expense had a debit balance of $500, an entry to credit interest expense and debit owner's equity must be made. Once all closing balances are made, a post-closing trial balance is generated to ensure that the debits still equal the credits.

In the same way that individuals need money to survive, so does every business organization. From local schools and hospitals to the largest, richest corporations, all institutions base their daily decisions on their financial status. Can they afford to buy the new equipment they need? Will a decline in revenue force them to lay off employees? The decisions institutions make determine their success, and accounting and bookkeeping inform those decisions.

Further Research
Association of Chartered Accountants in the United States.
www.acaus.org
Home page of the Association of Chartered Accountants; site also features an international history of accounting practices.
Bean Counter
www.dwmbeancounter.com
This site offers educational resources on bookkeeping and accounting.
Chartered Accountants of Canada
www.cica.org
Home page of the Canadian assocation
— *Andréa Korb and David Korb*

Bankruptcy

When individuals and businesses get into financial difficulty, they sometimes file for bankruptcy. In the United States, bankruptcy proceedings are governed primarily by federal law and, to a lesser extent, by state law. The law allows debtors—both individuals and businesses—to seek relief from existing debts; the purpose of relief, when it is granted, is to enable debtors to get a fresh start. The law also provides for the quick, equitable distribution of debtors' assets among creditors when claims against debtors are sustained.

One of America's founding fathers, Benjamin Franklin, once remarked that creditors observe "set days and times" and expect to be paid at agreed-upon times. Traditionally, debtors were subjected to punishment, including debtors' prison and involuntary servitude, for not paying debts. Today's legal system does not follow a punitive philosophy in its approach to bankruptcy.

Bankruptcy Law in the United States

Federal bankruptcy law is contained in Title 11 of the U.S. Code. Chapter 7 provides for liquidation proceedings (the selling of various assets and the distribution of proceeds to creditors). Chapter 11 governs reorganizations. In reorganization cases, creditors usually look to the debtor's future earnings as a source for repayment, whereas in liquidation cases creditors look to the debtor's property. Chapter 12 (applying to family farms) and Chapter 13 (applying to individuals) provide for the adjustment of debts of parties with income; that is, these chapters provide for repayment plans.

Chapter 7 governs what is called straight (or ordinary) bankruptcy. In straight bankruptcy proceedings, debts are liquidated; the debtor's assets are sold and proceeds are distributed to creditors. The debtor may be an individual, a partnership, or a corporation. (Railroads, insurance firms, banks, savings and loans, and credit unions cannot be debtors under Chapter 7.)

An illustration of a debtors' prison in England; the origins of U.S. bankruptcy law were partly inspired by the harsh treatment of debtors in Europe.

INTERIOR OF A DEBTORS' PRISON—THE FLEET, 1809

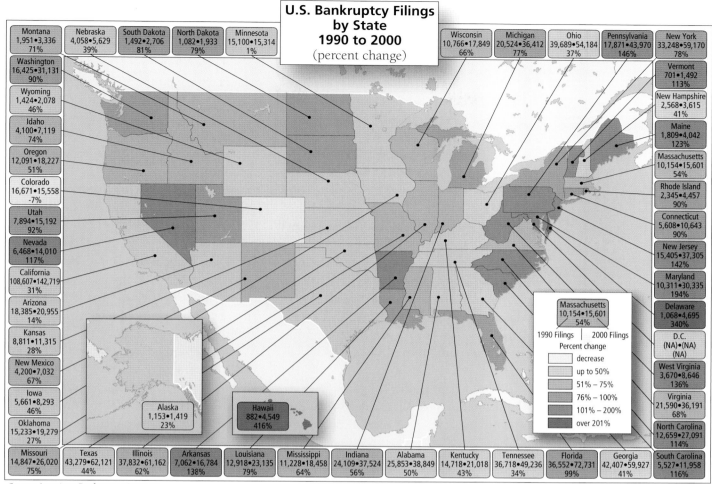

U.S. Bankruptcy Filings by State 1990 to 2000 (percent change)

State	1990 Filings	2000 Filings	Percent change
Montana	1,951	3,336	71%
Nebraska	4,058	5,629	39%
South Dakota	1,492	2,706	81%
North Dakota	1,082	1,933	79%
Minnesota	15,100	15,314	1%
Wisconsin	10,766	17,849	66%
Michigan	20,524	36,412	77%
Ohio	39,689	54,184	37%
Pennsylvania	17,871	43,970	146%
New York	33,248	59,170	78%
Washington	16,425	31,131	90%
Vermont	701	1,492	113%
Wyoming	1,424	2,078	46%
New Hampshire	2,568	3,615	41%
Idaho	4,100	7,119	74%
Maine	1,809	4,042	123%
Oregon	12,091	18,227	51%
Massachusetts	10,154	15,601	54%
Colorado	16,671	15,558	-7%
Rhode Island	2,345	4,457	90%
Utah	7,894	15,192	92%
Connecticut	5,608	10,643	90%
Nevada	6,468	14,010	117%
New Jersey	15,405	37,305	142%
California	108,607	142,719	31%
Maryland	10,311	30,335	194%
Arizona	18,385	20,955	14%
Delaware	1,068	4,695	340%
Kansas	8,811	11,315	28%
D.C.	(NA)	(NA)	(NA)
New Mexico	4,200	7,032	67%
West Virginia	3,670	8,646	136%
Iowa	5,661	8,293	46%
Virginia	21,590	36,191	68%
Alaska	1,153	1,419	23%
Hawaii	882	4,549	416%
Oklahoma	15,233	19,279	27%
North Carolina	12,659	27,091	114%
Missouri	14,847	26,020	75%
Texas	43,279	62,121	44%
Illinois	37,832	61,162	62%
Arkansas	7,062	16,784	138%
Louisiana	12,918	23,135	79%
Mississippi	11,228	18,458	64%
Indiana	24,109	37,524	56%
Alabama	25,853	38,849	50%
Kentucky	14,718	21,018	43%
Tennessee	36,718	49,236	34%
Florida	36,552	72,731	99%
Georgia	42,407	59,927	41%
South Carolina	5,527	11,958	116%

Legend:
Massachusetts 10,154 • 15,601 54%
1990 Filings | 2000 Filings
Percent change
- decrease
- up to 50%
- 51% – 75%
- 76% – 100%
- 101% – 200%
- over 201%

Source: American Bankruptcy Institute.

Certain debts, however, are not dischargeable under Chapter 7; the debtor cannot be released from them even if he or she has filed for bankruptcy. These include debts arising from customs duties and taxes, alimony, maintenance, or child support awards, fraud, embezzlement, larceny, or violation of a fiduciary duty (for example, the duty a lawyer owes to a client). Certain consumer debts and cash advances are also nondischargeable.

An ordinary bankruptcy proceeding is initiated by the filing of a voluntary or an involuntary petition. More than 99 percent of all bankruptcy petitions are filed voluntarily. Any person who is a debtor may file a voluntary petition and need not be insolvent to do so. (Insolvency is a financial condition in which an individual is unable to pay his or her debts as they come due or a condition in which liabilities exceed assets.)

A voluntary petition results in an automatic stay (a court order that suspends creditors' claims until the issues have been resolved). The petition must include a list of all creditors, a list of all property owned by the debtor, a list of property claimed by the debtor to be exempt, and a statement of those assets considered necessary for a fresh start. Precisely what is exempt from claims of creditors depends on state law. To be official, a bankruptcy petition must be given under oath and signed by the debtor. Concealing assets or knowingly supplying false information in a bankruptcy petition is a crime.

An involuntary petition under Chapter 7 occurs when creditors force a person (or a business) into bankruptcy. An involuntary petition cannot be filed against a farmer, bank, insurance company, nonprofit corporation, railroad, or a person who owes less than $10,775. If a debtor opposes an involuntary petition, the court must hold a hearing. If the court finds that legal grounds for involuntary bankruptcy exist, the court will order relief on behalf of creditors.

Chapter 13 of the bankruptcy law provides for adjustment of debts (repayment plans) of an individual with regular income, under specified conditions. After a debtor completes all or nearly all payments under a Chapter 13 plan, the court will grant a discharge of all debts (except alimony and child support, student loans, criminal restitution and fines, and debts requiring payment over a period longer than that of the plan). Even if the debtor does not complete the plan, a hardship discharge may be granted under certain conditions—for example, if failure to complete the plan was caused by circumstances beyond the debtor's control.

Chapter 11 Bankruptcy

When corporations fall into deep debt, they often use a Chapter 11 reorganization proceeding. In 2001, America's second-largest corporation, Enron, filed for Chapter 11 reorganization. This ranked as the largest U.S. bankruptcy until September 2008, when Lehman Brothers Holdings, an investment bank, and Washington Mutual, a commercial and retail bank, both filed for bankruptcy; General Motors, with assets of $91 billion, filed in 2009, the largest U.S. bankruptcy for an industrial company.

Chapter 11 reorganization allows debtors to restructure finances, the business to continue, and creditors to be paid. A bankruptcy case under Chapter 11 is started by the filing of a petition requesting an order for relief. Petitions may be voluntary or involuntary. A petition will result in a stay or suspension of creditors' actions against the debtor.

An individual or company filing for bankruptcy under Chapter 11 is usually allowed to operate as a debtor-in-possession (the debtor may continue to operate the business) unless a creditor or a party-in-interest (another party with a claim against the debtor) requests appointment of a trustee. A debtor-in-possession has 120 days after the order for relief to file a plan and 180 days to obtain acceptance before others can file a plan. After creditors have approved the plan, the court holds a hearing to confirm the approval, and the debts not provided for in the plan are discharged.

For many years, creditors have complained to Congress that current bankruptcy law permits debtors to avoid their debts too easily. Some of the more common objections are that debtors' homes receive too much protection, that businesses can stay too long in Chapter 11 reorganization, and that credit card debts are too easily discharged. By summer 2001, such complaints had generated strong support in Congress, and bills had been drafted to tighten bankruptcy procedures under Chapters 7 and 13. According to some proposed reforms, consumers also would have found discharging credit card debt more difficult. By the fall of 2001, however, leg-

Largest U.S. Bankruptcies 1980 to 2008			
	Company	Bankruptcy Date	Total Assets Pre-Bankruptcy
1.	Lehman Brothers Holdings Inc.	09/15/08	$691,063,000,000
2.	Washington Mutual, Inc.	09/26/08	$327,913,000,000
3.	WorldCom, Inc.	07/21/02	$103,914,000,000
4.	Enron Corp.	12/02/01	$65,503,000,000
5.	Conseco, Inc.	12/17/02	$61,392,000,000
6.	Pacific Gas and Electric Co.	04/06/01	$36,152,000,000
7.	Texaco, Inc.	04/12/87	$34,940,000,000
8.	Financial Corp. of America	09/09/88	$33,864,000,000
9.	Refco Inc.	10/17/05	$33,333,000,000
10.	IndyMac Bancorp, Inc.	07/31/08	$32,734,000,000
11.	Global Crossing, Ltd.	01/28/02	$30,185,000,000
12.	Bank of New England Corp.	01/07/91	$29,773,000,000
13.	Lyondell Chemical Company	01/06/09	$27,392,000,000
14.	Calpine Corporation	12/20/05	$27,216,000,000
15.	New Century Financial Corp.	04/02/07	$26,147,000,000
16.	UAL Corporation	12/09/02	$25,197,000,000
17.	Delta Air Lines, Inc.	09/14/05	$21,801,000,000
18.	Adelphia Communications Corp.	06/25/02	$21,499,000,000

Source: BankruptcyData.com, New Generation Research, Inc., Boston, http://www.BankruptcyData.com

islators were confronted with a steep downturn in the U.S. economy. As unemployment rates rose and business failures increased early in 2002, the movement for bankruptcy reform was eclipsed by congressional attention to issues of national security and proposals for stimulating economic recovery. However, in 2005, Congress passed the Bankruptcy Abuse Prevention and Consumer Protection Act of 2005, a major reform of the bankruptcy system as it pertains to individuals. Among its measures, the new law required mandatory credit counseling and education and tightened eligibility for Chapter 7 filings.

Bankruptcy reform issues again surfaced after 2008 as both corporations and individuals were affected by the economic recession and bankruptcy rates rose. Legislators continue to examine how best

to reconcile the legitimate interests of creditors with the public's interest in fostering resilience on the part of debtors.

—Carl Pacini

An employee of the bankrupt Pan Am Airlines passes baggage loaders and machines headed for the auction block in 1992.

Web Resources on Bankruptcy

www.BankruptcyData.com is the premier business bankruptcy resource Web site. It provides access to updated information on business bankruptcy filings.

www.abiworld.org, the Web site of the American Bankruptcy Institute, is a great resource for information on bankruptcy.

www.swiggartagin.com/lawfind provides information on all legal aspects of bankruptcy; it is maintained by the Boston law firm Swiggart and Agin, LLC.

www.nacba.com is the home page of the National Association of Consumer Bankruptcy Attorneys, serving the needs of consumer bankruptcy attorneys and consumer debtors in bankruptcy.

www.bankruptcy-expert.com, a service of the Moran Law Group in California, provides information on personal and business bankruptcies.

www.hg.org/bankrpt.html is a useful research guide to every aspect of bankruptcy law.

Better Business Bureau

The Better Business Bureau (BBB) was created by businesspeople to police business practices. Its 125 local offices in the United States and Canada, usually incorporated as independent nonprofit businesses, gather information on local businesses, handle millions of consumer complaints and inquiries each year, and monitor local advertising. These efforts provide consumers with information; indirectly, BBBs regulate advertising and sales practices—a feat all the more impressive because the BBB operates as a voluntary association with little means to punish those who violate its guidelines.

Local BBB offices in the United States are affiliated with the National Council of Better Business Bureaus. The council's National Advertising Division (NAD) monitors the accuracy of national advertisements. The council is a supporting member of the independent National Advertising Review Board (NARB), which examines advertiser appeals of NAD rulings.

Both locally and nationally, the BBB is supported by membership fees. Member businesses agree to follow BBB guidelines. Such participation is strictly voluntary; attempts to force businesses to follow BBB guidelines have been struck down in U.S. courts as violations of antitrust law.

The BBB arose from the "truth in advertising" movement of the early twentieth century in the United States. At the turn of the nineteenth century, advertising claims made for some products were so outrageous that several magazines refused to carry any medical advertising. Advertising professionals, fearing that the entire industry's reputation would be sullied beyond repair, began to push for reform. In 1912, a New York City association of advertising professionals formed a vigilance committee. The 33-member committee began investigating complaints about misleading advertising, turning fraudulent ads over to law enforcement officials. Although the committee was established only to investigate advertising, the members quickly found themselves handling complaints by consumers about the sales practices of retailers. This experience prompted the Associated Advertising Clubs of America to establish a National Vigilance Committee later that year. In 1921 the National Better Business Bureau of the Associated Advertising Clubs of the World was incorporated, becoming an independent entity in 1926. In that year, the BBB had 45 local offices; by 1962 the number had increased to 122.

Although the BBB provides consumer information, it differs from consumer organizations in important ways. It focuses narrowly on good business practices rather than consumer protection (although the two goals sometimes overlap). Thus, the NAD and NARB focus on the accuracy of claims made in national advertising, but whether an advertisement aimed at adults is in good taste is outside the purview of either organization. In addition, while the BBB sometimes makes recommendations regarding consumer-protection legislation, it is not a lobbying organization and generally avoids drafting laws and trying to influence policy.

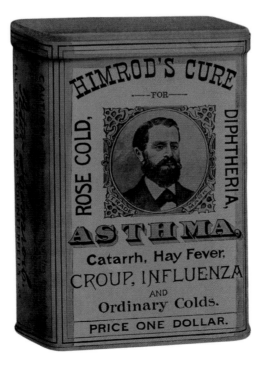

The BBB was created to protect consumers from fraudulent advertising like this nineteenth-century ad for Himrod's Cure, which promises to cure everything from hay fever to diphtheria.

James Bast, former president of the BBB, introduced the BBBOnline service, which helps customers evaluate businesses that advertise on the Internet.

The BBB also has no legal authority to regulate companies. It establishes guidelines for business practices but, unlike government agencies that issue regulations, has no way to enforce its guidelines. Occasionally a local BBB office will sue a business in court, but the main weapon in the BBB's arsenal is publicity. For example, if an advertisement is found by the NAD to be deceptive, the punishment imposed on the advertiser is simply that the division publishes a report of its findings. A local BBB office can also suspend the membership of a business that does not follow its guidelines; in such a case the office will usually issue a press release explaining its action to the local media, which tend to cover BBB suspensions and admonitions closely. These tactics often prove to be effective. Indeed, consumer organizations that strongly criticized the creation of the NAD and NARB in the early 1970s as simply a ploy by the advertising industry to avoid government regulation have largely dropped their opposition and now work with BBB organizations.

To preserve its influence, the BBB cultivates a reputation as an honest broker between businesses and consumers. Local offices have full-time staff and seek a wide range of business support to prevent them from becoming beholden to a single company. Businesses and business associations sometimes charge the BBB with going overboard in its efforts to be impartial. The BBB has maintained its support within business circles, however, because it is seen as protective of legitimate businesses and as a workable alternative to government regulation.

Further Research

Better Business Bureau

www.bbb.org

This site features product and policy news as well as consumer and business guidance.

Better Business Bureau in Canada

www.ccbbb.ca

The Canadian Council is the coordinating and licensing body for Canada.

—*Mary Sisson*

Basic Principles of Truth in Advertising

1. The primary responsibility for truthful and non-deceptive advertising rests with the advertiser. Advertisers should be prepared to substantiate any claims or offers made before publication or broadcast and, upon request, present such substantiation promptly to the advertising medium or the Better Business Bureau.

2. Advertisements which are untrue, misleading, deceptive, fraudulent, falsely disparaging of competitors, or insincere offers to sell, shall not be used.

3. An advertisement as a whole may be misleading although every sentence separately considered is literally true. Misrepresentation may result not only from direct statements but by omitting or obscuring a material fact.

—Better Business Bureau Code of Advertising

Brand Names

Brand names provide a means of identification of products, differentiation from competition, and assurance of a consistent level of quality. Without brand names, buyers would have to choose from individual products each time they shopped, as when they choose fresh meats or fish from a butcher's counter. Buyers reduce their shopping time as they easily identify familiar brands. At the same time, brands create financial value for the seller. Every time shoppers buy Campbell's Tomato Soup, they expect to see the familiar lettering on the red and white can. They are assured that the soup will taste the same each time they buy it and will be at the level of quality they have learned to expect.

A brand name is that part of a brand that can be spoken aloud, as contrasted to a brand mark that is a design or symbol. The word *Nike* is a brand name, while the swoosh design is a brand mark. Along with product performance, packaging, and advertising, brands help to create an image for products. Buyers identify some brands so closely with a particular product category that the brands are referred to as master brands. The Kleenex brand, for example, means facial tissues. The phenomenon of brand loyalty occurs when a buyer purchases one brand fairly consistently and has a positive attitude toward that brand. In some instances, the loyalty is so strong that buyers display brands prominently, in effect associating their own images with those of the brands. Harley-Davidson Motorcycle buyers sometimes go so far as to tattoo the Harley brand name and the eagle brand mark on their bodies.

What Makes a Good Brand Name?

When companies create new products, they usually spend considerable time choosing brand names that will convey the image they want. Brand names fall into a number of categories. Some brand names are people's names, such as Ford or Dell. Other brand names are made-up words

Many companies depend on the concept of brand loyalty to influence customers to choose one product over another, virtually identical, product.

such as Exxon or Kodak. Clean Shower and Windex illustrate the third category of brand names, those that show product benefits or describe products in some way.

Good brands typically have several characteristics. They are easy to say, spell, and remember. A shorter name is preferable to a longer one. The brand should also be readily differentiated from the competition. Brand names showing product benefits and contributing to a desirable product image are usually good choices. Finally, a good brand name should be appropriate to international markets. Tide brand laundry detergent is an example of positive brand name characteristics. The word *Tide* is easy to say, spell, and remember. It is short. When Tide is printed on the side of a box of detergent, its letters can be large and commanding on the shelf, fairly shouting at the supermarket shopper. The word *Tide* means water and sea, conjuring the image of waves washing in and out; the name

supports a positive, clean concept appropriate to a detergent. Intending to compete with the Tide brand, a newer laundry detergent made an obvious brand name choice with similar meaning when it chose the name *Surf*.

Brand names, whether they are for tangible or intangible products, may be legally registered. Once they have been registered, they are official trademarks, and the owners have the exclusive right to use of these brand names. The owner is responsible to police the trademark and to bring legal action against organizations that may be using the brand without permission.

Short History of Branding

The first kinds of companies to promote brand names heavily were those making consumer goods—products sold in supermarkets and discount stores. These consumable brands were followed by durable goods like appliances and automobiles.

Sports star Michael Jordan turned himself into a brand name, which enables him to have successful side businesses like his own cologne and this Chicago restaurant.

The late twentieth century saw an increased emphasis on branding in the marketplace. Historically, with the occasional exception of long-established brands such as Dole or Chiquita, produce tended not to have brand names, but now many fruits and vegetables like mushrooms and tomatoes come packaged with pronounced brand names and marks. Formerly, the only meats branded tended to be luncheon or processed meats. Now the shopper sees branded fresh poultry products and sometimes beef.

Competition exists not only between individual brands but also between kinds of brands. The "battle of the brands" is sales competition between manufacturer's brands, also known as national brands, and private or store brands. Manufacturer's brands carry a name chosen by the producer. Examples would be Sony, Kellogg's, or Oxydol. Private or store brands carry names chosen by wholesalers or retailers such as Gap, Kroger, or Sam's American Choice. Although manufacturers' brands still outsell private labels, these private brands are gaining sales in discount stores and supermarkets because of their good value. In clothing stores, private label brands provide the seller the advantage of exclusivity and usually higher profits. The only place to buy Old Navy clothing is at an Old Navy store.

Brand names are a means of identifying and differentiating products, of creating images, and of assuring buyers of a consistent level of quality and reliability. The movement in the marketplace is definitely toward placing more emphasis on brand names. The use of brand names has expanded beyond consumer goods to business-to-business markets and to services, government agencies, and not-for-profit organizations.

Some extremely successful brands are recognized the world over: Here, shoppers seek the Gap clothing brand at a store in Tokyo.

Next, companies aiming their products at businesses began to emphasize their brand names. Then services like financial institutions and not-for-profit organizations embarked on a process of creating images through emphasizing their brand names and marks. Educational institutions, government agencies, vacation locations, and even individuals have all realized the importance of creating brand identities. Michael Jordan, Madonna, and Martha Stewart are all people, but they are brand names as well.

Further Research
International Branding Association
www.internationalbranding.org
An online forum for professsionals and students.
Khermouch, Gerry, Stanley Holmes, and Moon
	Ihlwan. "The Best Global Brands." *Business Week,* August 6, 2007.

—*Lois Smith*

Budget

A budget is a plan detailing projected income and expenses for a specific period. Such documents are used by businesses, governments, and personal households to set financial goals and determine steps by which to achieve them.

To understand the purpose and importance of budgeting, think of an Olympian trying to break the world record in the long jump. To make the attempt, the athlete must know the record in advance and use it as a benchmark against his own performance. Without this benchmark, the Olympian would not know how much time to put into training or how close he is to achieving the world record. Like an Olympian, individuals and businesses are more likely to achieve a goal that is clear and concrete. A budget sets a path for achieving that goal.

Corporate Budgeting

Successful companies use budgets for every area of the business. They use budgets for every dollar they expect to earn or spend, for the amount of inventory they expect to hold, for the number of products they expect customers to return, and even for the number of products they expect to be

Income Statement
(in thousand dollars)

Revenues	Prior year	Current budget	Responsible manager
Northern sales	5.5	6.1	Northern regional sales manager
Southern sales	1.2	3.0	Southern regional sales manager
Eastern sales	5.8	5.5	Eastern regional sales manager
Western sales	9.7	10.0	Western regional sales manager
Total returns	−1.7	−1.5	Quality control manager
Total sales	20.5	24.6	
Expenses	Prior year	Current budget	Responsible manager
Cost of goods sold	−6.5	−7.0	Purchasing manager
Transportation costs	−1.2	−1.1	Transportation manager
Inventory loss	−.9	−.5	Operations manager
Salary expense	−5.2	−4.5	Human resource manager
Bonus expense	−1.2	−3.0	Human resource manager
Depreciation (M&E)	−1.5	−1.7	Operations manager
Depreciation (Plants)	−1.2	−3.0	Plant manager
Office supplies	−.4	−.2	Office manager
Insurance expense	−.1	−.1	Operations manager
Other expenses	−1.1	−.7	Operations manager
Total expenses	−19.3	−21.8	
EBIT	1.2	2.8	
Interest expense	−8	−1.3	Treasury manager
Taxes	−.2	−.2	Finance manager
Net income	.2	1.3	Chief executive officer

EBIT = Earnings Before Interest and Taxes.

A sample corporate income statement.

Balance Sheet (in thousand dollars)			
Assets	*Prior year*	*Current budget*	*Responsible manager*
Cash	2.1	3.5	Treasury manager
Inventory	4.8	2.4	Operations manager
Accounts receivable	3.5	2.0	Finance/treasury manager
Land, Plants	13.5	15.5	Plant/finance manager
Machinery, Equipment	7.2	10.0	Operations manager
Liabilities	*Prior year*	*Current budget*	*Responsible manager*
Accounts payable	1.2	1.5	Finance/treasury manager
Salaries payable	.3	.5	Human resource manager
Notes payable	9.5	7.5	Finance/treasury manager
Owner's equity	*Prior year*	*Current budget*	*Responsible manager*
Capital	15.0	15.0	Treasury manager
Retained earnings	5.1	8.9	NA

A sample corporate balance sheet.

stolen. In large companies, many managers control parts of each category. For example, the quality control manager works to achieve a low level of customer returns by ensuring that the company's products are acceptable. The higher the quality, the fewer returns and the more likely the product return category will be on budget. If the quality control manager's compensation is based on the actual return performance versus the budgeted or projected performance, the manager will try very hard to improve quality for each product. Improving the quality of its products is the company's goal: Determining a method by which to measure that quality makes the goal more obtainable.

Similarly, assume a particular salesperson is responsible for selling the company's product in a specific region. To achieve profitability, the company must sell 500 units in that region. Knowing this, the salesperson can put steps into place to achieve the goal. Without this benchmark, or budget, the salesperson's goal might be set randomly, either too low or unrealistically high.

The examples of the quality control manager and sales manager demonstrate some of the various budgeting strategies that can be used by a corporation. Budgets can be set on each section of the income statement, as well as on each section of the balance sheet and other financial statements. Each manager directs a team to work toward the planned budget daily. The manager must educate team members about what must be done to achieve budgetary goals in a given time. Team members must alert the manager about their performance, so the manager can make adjustments if necessary.

For example, if halfway through the period, a sales manager notices that her team has sales of only $2 million, knowing the budgeted goal is $5.5 million, the manager would need to implement new strategies to help the team achieve its goal. One solution could be to hire additional people to sell the product more aggressively. Another solution could be to offer prizes to the best salespeople in the second half of the period. Managers must know the budget variances at certain intervals during the period to give them more opportunities to realize their goals.

Personal Budgeting

Most individuals have one or more financial goals. A person might want to save for a house, a car, college, or retirement. A budget can help provide a solid understanding of what can be achieved. Usually, an individual knows what his or her income, or earnings, will be over a specified period. Even if an individual is paid per hour, the number of hours to be worked is usually known. Some expenses—rent, food, and utilities—are predictable; others are variable—money spent on entertainment or recreation, clothing, and medical services.

Consider the following budget for the Smith family. The Smiths earn an annual income of $100,000. The Smiths want to buy a house in one year but need $25,000 as a down payment. The Smiths have only $1,000 in the bank at the beginning of the year. The Smiths put together an annual budget to help them achieve their goal. At the end of the period, the Smiths also record the actual amount in each budget category.

The Smiths developed a budget to save $24,300 (including expected salary and subtracting all expected expenses for the year). Therefore, the Smiths expected that by the end of the year they would be able to buy their house ($1,000 already in savings + $24,300 to be saved this year = $25,300). However, looking at the actual results at the end of the year, the Smiths had saved only $18,500. They did not meet their goal and, therefore, were unable to buy a home.

The budget information at the beginning of the year is very valuable. If the Smiths were serious about buying a house at the end of the year, they certainly would not have taken an extra vacation or eaten out as much. By controlling these two expenses throughout the year, the Smiths would have had no problem achieving their goal of saving $25,000. If they wanted to save even more, they could have done many things to lower expenses, such as shop less or move to a less expensive apartment. This shows how critical and valuable creating budgets and taking the time to monitor variances are for individuals as well as for corporations.

Setting Budgets

The most difficult part of the budget process is the actual setting of the budget: Once a budget is set, the actions to be taken are fairly straightforward. Typically, managers and individuals use historical data to set the current budget. For example, if the average sales over the last few years were $2 million, the budget should

		Smith Family Budget		
Budget item	Budget	Actual	Reason for variance
Salary	$100,000	$103,000	Additional bonus
Living expenses			
Taxes	−$35,000	−$36,500	Higher salary
Rent	−$19,000	−$19,000	
Utilities (phone, heat)	−$2,800	−$2,900	Cold winter, more heat needed
Car	−$3,600	−$3,600	
Insurance	−$2,000	−$2,000	
Gas for car	−$800	−$500	Drove car less than expected
Drug store expenses	−$3,000	−$3,000	
Grocery expenses	−$2,000	−$2,000	
Entertainment expenses			
Restaurant expenses	−$500	−$3,500	Ate out more this year
Vacations	−$3,000	−$7,000	Took one extra vacation
Shopping	−$4,000	−$4,500	Bought a new wardrobe
Savings	$24,300	$18,500	

A sample family budget.

Making a family budget involves reviewing expenses and setting future goals.

estimate sales at close to $2 million. Next, the manager typically considers the latest developments and adjusts estimates. For example, if the company expects to hire more salespeople, the manager would expect sales to increase this year. Also, if customers tell the manager they expect to buy more this year, the manager will raise the budget by an appropriate amount.

Above all, however, the budget should be realistic. Failing to meet the budget could lead to major problems (for instance, a low salary for the manager or no house for the individual). Budgeting is an important activity, not only for a corporation, but also for families and individuals. Goals

help people achieve success, and budgets help set those goals.

Further Research
Budget worksheet
http://financialplan.about.com/cs/budgeting/l/blbudget.htm
A useful template for setting up a personal budget.
Free Management Library
managementhelp.org/finance/fp_fnce/fp_fnce.htm
This section of a very useful Web site provides information on financial management for small for-profit enterprises.
Bankrate.com
www.bankrate.com/brm/news/Financial_Literacy/Jan07_budgeting_howto_a1.asp
Seven steps to creating a budget.

—*Andréa Korb and David Korb*

Bundling

Bundling is a strategy of selling goods and services by offering them together in a single package. Bundling can vastly improve a company's bottom line, or it can alienate customers and spark antitrust investigations. Determining what kind of bundle to offer and how to offer it can be quite complex. While a business selling items singly must determine at which price to offer the items, a business selling bundles must also figure out what combination of items should be priced as a bundle.

Sometimes bundles are priced at a premium, as when a book dealer offers a complete set of first editions of *The Wizard of Oz*. More often, a bundle is offered at a discount to what the items would cost if purchased separately. Even with a discount, well-designed bundles can increase revenues and profits. For example, consider the "value meals" offered at fast-food restaurants like McDonald's. A value meal is a combination of a drink, fries, and a burger or a sandwich that costs slightly less than the three items would if they were purchased separately. Despite the discount, value meals increase revenues because many budget-minded customers who might otherwise buy just a burger—leaving out the fries and drink as an unnecessary expense—instead buy a value meal. Selling more fries and drinks is good for McDonald's because profits on those items are higher than profits on even an undiscounted burger.

Just like the value meal encourages the average McDonald's customer to buy more food, another popular kind of bundle—bundles of several options on a new car—encourages car buyers to purchase more options. As with the value meal, the discount is essential: A customer who might buy just two options will buy four if they are in a discounted bundle because the customer believes he is getting a deal. To the customer, the bundle is well worth buying—he is spending more, but he is getting more for his money. To the car manufacturer, the bundle is well worth offering because the average customer will spend more per car. In addition, offering standard bundles on car options can cut manufacturing costs because certain options are manufactured more economically when produced at the same time.

Another advantage of bundling is that it sometimes allows a company to raise the prices of the individual components. For example, a person who really wants call waiting on her home telephone but does

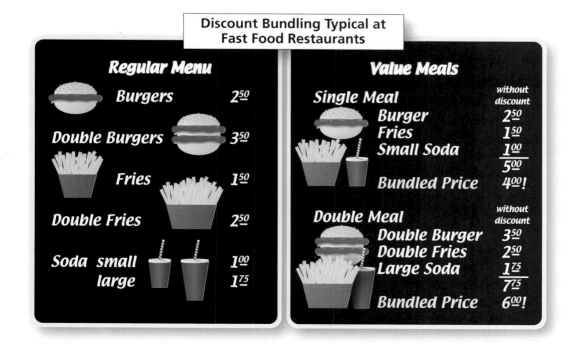

Discount Bundling Typical at Fast Food Restaurants

Regular Menu

Burgers	2⁵⁰
Double Burgers	3⁵⁰
Fries	1⁵⁰
Double Fries	2⁵⁰
Soda small	1⁰⁰
large	1⁷⁵

Value Meals

Single Meal — without discount
Burger	2⁵⁰
Fries	1⁵⁰
Small Soda	1⁰⁰
	5⁰⁰
Bundled Price	4⁰⁰!

Double Meal — without discount
Double Burger	3⁵⁰
Double Fries	2⁵⁰
Large Soda	1⁷⁵
	7⁷⁵
Bundled Price	6⁰⁰!

The basic economics of the bundling strategy can be seen in fast-food restaurants.

Auto dealerships commonly use bundling in selling new cars.

not want any of the other available services probably cannot afford to miss calls for a good reason. Thus, she is probably willing to pay more for call waiting as a stand-alone service. On the other hand, if she mildly wants call waiting but is not willing to pay a lot for it, she may also mildly want any number of other services and could easily be sold a bundle—especially when she sees the discount the bundle offers over buying two or three stand-alone services.

Bundling can also be used to sell supplies or services associated with the use of the device sold. Cellular phones are often sold at a very low price if customers also purchase a contract for a year of phone service. Likewise vendors of copy machines often sell servicing contracts and supplies of toner along with the machines. Such bundles are popular because consumers tend to focus on the up-front, one-time costs of the item and give less thought to the future regular charges for the service or goods.

Bundling services with goods can ease the introduction of new technology as customers feel they will not be stuck by

themselves trying to figure out how to work the device. For example, a company might sell a new inventory-tracking software system bundled with the services of consultants who can help install and run it.

Bundling does not always help make sales. When the telecommunications industry was largely deregulated in 1996, many observers thought that consumers would be eager to purchase bundles of telephone, Internet, and cable television service from a single provider. Consumers, however, did not see much advantage to such bundles and did not particularly mind using different providers.

Sometimes bundles are used to encourage a person to buy something he or she does not particularly want—a toiletries manufacturer who makes a popular shampoo and an unpopular body wash might bundle the two together to promote the body wash or at least get it out of inventory. If an unwanted service or good is bundled with something that people must buy, and the person cannot opt out of the bundle, that practice is called tying. For example,

Bundling Products and Services

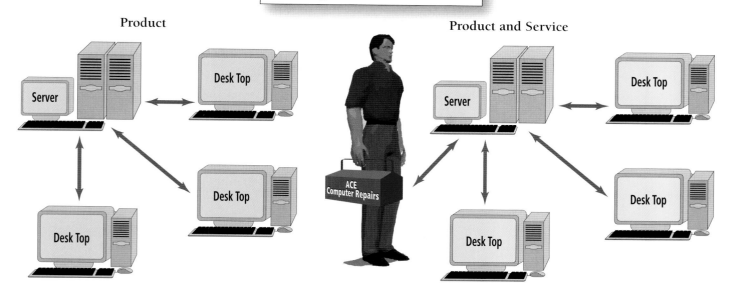

Product

Local Area Network (LAN) equipment

Product and Service

LAN equipment plus installation and maintenance contract

until the practice was banned in the early 1960s, movie studios forced movie theaters to book groups of movies. If a theater wanted to show a hit film by a particular studio, it also had to pay for some flops from the same studio.

Tying tends to run afoul of antitrust laws because monopolies can use it to expand their monopoly into new areas. For example, in the early twentieth century IBM controlled most of the market for tabulating machines that ran on punch cards. The machines were complicated, and very few companies made them. The punch cards themselves, in contrast, were easy to make, and many companies could have made them. IBM, however, would not sell its machines to a company unless that company promised to buy the punch cards from IBM as well. IBM used tying to leverage its domination of the tabulating-machine industry into a domination of the punch-card industry until 1936 when the U.S. Supreme Court banned the practice.

The antitrust suit brought by the U.S. Department of Justice against Microsoft focused on tying. For years Microsoft bundled different kinds of software with its Windows operating systems, which were

used on roughly 90 percent of desktop computers and often came installed with the computer—another type of bundling. The antitrust suit alleged that these were anticompetitive practices and argued that computer makers had no choice but to buy the additional software when they bought Windows and that Microsoft was attempting to leverage its operating-system monopoly into other kinds of software. Ultimately, the courts forced Microsoft to discontinue some of its most anticompetitive practices but allowed the bundling to continue. Bundling has helped Microsoft enter new software markets—further evidence of the power that can be tapped through this marketing and pricing strategy.

Further Research

Carney, Dan, and Mike France. "The Microsoft Case: Tying It All Together." *Business Week,* December 3, 2001, 68.

Department of Justice

www.usdoj.gov/atr/public/hearings/single_firm/ comments/219224_e.htm

A detailed article by a legal professional about the business practices of tying and bundling and the need for antitrust modernization in the U.S.

—*Mary Sisson*

Bundling services, like user support with computers, can be an effective way for customers to get both the technology they require and the help they need to use it.

Business Plan

A business plan is a formal document designed to attract investment in or capital resources to a start-up business or an established business that wants to expand. Such a document takes a reader from a general idea (or business concept), to a perceived opportunity, to the presentation of a plan for the practical operation of a business. A business plan summarizes potential limitations and obstacles and proposed strategies for overcoming them. It forecasts costs, profits, and overall values. In many ways, a business plan is to an entrepreneur what a term paper is to a student: a research paper that presents and defends a new concept.

Business plans vary greatly depending upon the authors and their businesses. For example, Lamar Muse and Herb Keller of Southwest Airlines wrote a business plan for a low-fare airline that concentrated on a narrow market (Texas) with a special emphasis on customer service. Of course, Southwest Airlines has grown beyond its original business plan to service areas outside its initial market. However, the other two foundations of its initial business plan—low fares and customer service—remain core principles of the airline today.

Elements of a Business Plan

Like a term paper, a business plan begins with an introduction. Frequently titled "Executive Summary," this section is commonly described as one of the two most important components of a business plan (the other, "Financials," comes at the end). The executive summary is intended to capture a reader's attention by presenting clearly and concisely the product or service being offered, the market, and the operational strategy behind a business. Its general purpose is always the same: to attract the attention of the audience and to make readers want to continue reading.

Most business plans follow the executive summary with a "Company Description." This section offers general information about the business without including overwhelming amounts of detail. Commonly provided details include (but are not limited to) the company's name,

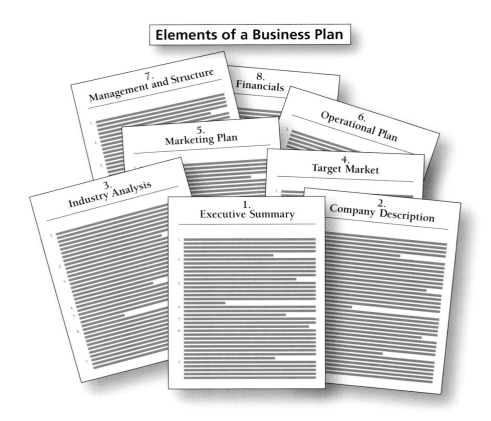

Elements of a Business Plan

7. Management and Structure
8. Financials
6. Operational Plan
5. Marketing Plan
4. Target Market
3. Industry Analysis
1. Executive Summary
2. Company Description

location, product(s) or service(s), mission statement, legal status, and ownership. The mission statement describes, in a sentence or two, what a business does and how its employees execute their business. A business's legal status may be, for example, a partnership, a corporation, or a non-profit organization.

The next section, "Industry Analysis," describes other businesses that provide similar products or services and other businesses that supply critical resources. This information is typically followed by a brief summary of industry trends and examples of how the business concept being presented addresses a market opportunity. Supporting information in this section may include industry growth rates, size and market share of likely competitors, short-term obstacles to entering into the market, and long-term opportunities described by the business plan.

The "Target Market" section identifies the group of customers (or client base) of the business. In its simplest form, this section addresses and briefly quantifies the market's demand. An investor always wants to know that a product or service to be offered will not change fundamentally within a few weeks or months of its initial offering. Short-term reactive changes in a product or service might show an entrepreneur's poor understanding of the market, the product, or the service. This section must demonstrate a clear understanding of the target market and explain how the product or service will fill a need in that market.

The next section of a business plan is usually the "Marketing Plan." Based upon market surveys and forecasts of trends within the industry, the marketing plan demonstrates that a quantifiable, long-term opportunity exists and that the potential benefits of investment in this opportunity outweigh all of the associated costs. Details in the marketing plan should describe the market opportunity (sometimes referred to as the "strategic position"), a sales strategy, and the limitations

---

Reasons for Creating a Business Plan

- Tests feasibility of business idea.
- Becomes business's resume for lenders and outside investors and for attracting employees.
- Creates a timetable for operations.
- Serves as a modeling tool that helps evaluate variable factors affecting the business.
- Establishes a vehicle for tracking business progress.
- Provides benchmarks against which to adjust operations to achieve business goals.
- Is the starting point for future planning.

(sometimes referred to as "risk assessment") associated with the business.

The "Operational Plan," which may later serve as the outline for a procedures manual, summarizes how the entrepreneur intends to conduct a functioning business. It describes resources and assets that are critical to the success of the business; it tells when those resources and assets will be needed; and it explains how the proposed company will distinguish itself from the competition. Frequently, this section also addresses production and cost-effectiveness. What kind of labor force will be required? How will the business measure cost, productivity, quality, efficiency, and capacity?

Web Resources for Business Plans

www.sba.gov/smallbusinessplanner/index.html is part of the Small Business Administration Web site, which offers a wealth of free resources. It provides a step-by-step guide to writing a business plan and a detailed outline of what a business plan should include.

www.bplans.com provides electronic resources to help write a business plan as well as sample plans.

www.businessplans.org, home page of the Center for Business Planning, provides a variety of resources for writing a successful business plan.

enterpriseforum.mit.edu/mindshare/planning/index.html, established by the MIT Enterprise Forum, provides an extensive bibliography of business plan resources. The Forum provides educational programs on entrepreneurship worldwide. focusing on technology.

www.bizplanit.com is the home page of a consulting firm that provides advisory services for writing business plans.

www.business-plan.com is the home page of a publisher of business books and business plan software.

www.cbsc.org/ibp is a Canadian-sponsored, interactive aid for writing business plans.

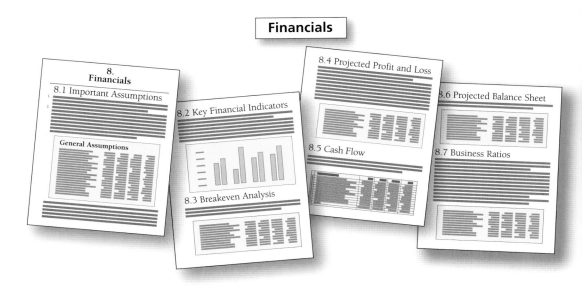

The operational plan should flow smoothly into the section describing the "Management and Structure" of the business. Through short biographical sketches, this section should introduce those employees who are most important to the business and explain why their presence is critical to its success. A brief overview of any advisory bodies, for example, board of directors, consultants, or committees, is commonly given. Organizational charts that show a business's reporting structure (telling who reports to whom within the organization) are also commonly provided in this section.

Business and financial professionals agree that the two most important sections of a business plan are the first and last: the "Executive Summary" and "Financials." The financial section of a business plan must quantify the vision presented in the "Executive Summary." The figures presented in this section include the anticipated profits, the anticipated costs, and the anticipated value of the business as a whole. Typically, a business plan forecasts these figures for three to five years. Investors can and do hold an entrepreneur to the numbers presented in the financial section—a fact that makes careful research throughout all preceding sections critical to the success of a business plan and indeed to the success of the business as a whole.

A well-researched and well-written business plan is essential to the creation of a new business or the expansion of an existing business. In many cases, a start-up business or an expansion requires additional capital or investment that goes beyond what is readily available. A business plan presents the business case for capital investment in a perceived opportunity. Should an automobile manufacturer, for example, invest in the development of alternative-fuel vehicles or should it strive to make future models with greater fuel efficiency? A business plan can provide quantifiable answers to such questions for entrepreneurs and investors alike.

Further Research
Business Canada
www.canadabusiness.ca/gol/cbec/site.nsf/en/index. html
A guide to small businesses from Business Canada, a service of the Canadian government, which includes an interactive business planner and links to information about starting a small business in Canada.
Entrepreneur.com
www.entrepreneur.com/businessplan/
Articles and other resources about business plans from *Entrepreneur* magazine.
Southwest Airlines: The Hottest Thing in the Sky
www.mutualofamerica.com/articles/Fortune/March 04/fortune.asp
An article from *Fortune* magazine about the Southwest's business plan and strategy.
—*John Western*

Cash Flow

Cash flow is a measurement used by companies to indicate how much ready money is created and consumed by a particular project or by the company as a whole. A company's overall cash flow is considered to be a particularly revealing indicator of its ability to survive—even more than whether the company is profitable. Cash flow is so vital that all publicly owned companies in the United States, as well as in countries that have adopted international accounting standards, must analyze cash flow for their shareholders (in a form similar to the sample at the right) along with revenue and profits).

As the name suggests, cash flow is all about cash. In the world of business, *cash* does not mean actual bills and coins but rather so-called liquid assets, or assets that can be used right away to pay invoices, salaries, or other obligations. A shortage of cash can lead to what is called a liquidity crisis.

People and even countries can also have liquidity crises. Consider this example: a man has no savings and a job at a fast-food restaurant. The job barely pays the rent of $600 a month on his apartment, which he must pay in cash at the end of every month or he will be forced out. His car breaks down; he needs $300 to have the car repaired, but payday is several days away. The man now has a cash-flow problem.

The next day, he buys a winning lottery ticket worth $20 million. He goes down to the lottery office to turn in his ticket. The lottery officials tell him that he will receive several million dollars in cash but not for 18 months, since it will take that long to process the paperwork. How is he going to get the car fixed?

Just as the future lottery payout will not pay the mechanic, a business's buildings, equipment, and long-term investments will not pay landlords, suppliers, and employees—only cash will do that. While the lottery winner probably will not have too much trouble convincing someone to lend him rent money, the loan will cost him, as it would a company that found itself in a similar situation. A company could also attract additional investors, swapping ownership

Sample Consolidated Cash Flow Statement

Consolidated statements of cash flow
(in millions of euros)

	2007	2008	2009
Cash flows from operating activities			
Net income (loss)	(4,963)	1,324	644
Minority interests	5	3	37
Adjustments to reconcile income before minority interests:			
– Depreciation and amortization, net	1,279	1,189	1,050
– Amortization of goodwill and purchased R&D[1]	1,937	597	800
– Changes in reserves for pension obligations, net	41	24	(116)
– Changes in other reserves, net	2,001	(32)	(146)
– Net (gain) loss on disposal of non-current assets	(943)	(915)	(862)
– Share in net income of equity affiliates (net of dividends received)	88	(47)	(133)
Working capital provided (used) by operations	**2,143**	**1,274**	**(555)**
Net change in current assets and liabilities:			
– Decrease (increase) in accounts receivable	1,117	(2,147)	(453)
– Decrease (increase) in inventories	1,186	(3,330)	(333)
– Increase (decrease) in accounts payable and accrued expenses	(1,203)	2,089	588
– Changes in reserves on current assets (including accrued contract costs), net[2]	–	–	–
Net cash provided (used) by operating activities	**545**	**(1,245)**	**1,076**
Cash flows from investing activities:			
– Proceeds from disposal of fixed assets	182	107	191
– Capital expenditures	(1,748)	(1,834)	(1,224)
– Decrease (increase) in loans	299	(962)	(20)
– Cash expenditures for acquisition of consolidated companies, net of cash acquired, and for acquisition of unconsolidated companies	(743)	(834)	(2,173)
– Cash proceeds from sale of previously consolidated companies, net of cash sold, and from sale of unconsolidated companies	3,627	1,579	750
Net cash provided (used) by investing activities	**1,617**	**(1,944)**	**(2,476)**
Net cash flows after investment	**2,162**	**(3,189)**	**(1,400)**
Cash flows from financing activities:			
– Increase (decrease) in short-term debt	(1,401)	(889)	(352)
– Proceeds from issuance of long-term debt	1,744	2,565	1,756
– Proceeds from issuance of shares	8	1,490	110
– Dividends paid	(567)	(508)	(391)
Net cash provided (used) by financing activities	**(216)**	**2,658**	**1,123**
Net effect of exchange rate changes	7	(4)	59
Net increase (decrease) in cash and cash equivalents	1,953	(535)	(218)
Cash and cash equivalents at beginning of year	3,060	3,595	3,813

(1) R&D = research and development

Cash and Telecommunications

In the late 1990s, the telecommunications market was deregulated, and the industry began to expand rapidly. New companies were entering the market, challenging the local telephone companies that had once operated with no competition.

Investors became enamored of the sector. In 1999 and 2000, U.S. telecommunications companies raised an average of $2 billion every month by making initial public offerings of stock. Many of these new telecommunications businesses took on an enormous amount of debt to build expensive networks.

In 2000, the stock market crashed and investors began to avoid telecommunications stocks, making it very difficult for the upstarts to raise cash by issuing and selling stock. Such companies generally did not have enough customers to get lots of cash from them, and, as they had already borrowed so much money, they could not borrow more. Telecommunications upstarts—even the profitable ones—began to have trouble making the cash payments on the large loans they had taken out in the late 1990s. Many went into bankruptcy, while others were bought out.

Who did the buying? The stodgy, old-fashioned local telephone companies that investors had ignored but that had lots of cash, thanks to the millions of customers who paid their local phone bills every month. Even a relatively small player like Alltel Corp., which mainly offered local service in rural areas, generated $2 billion in cash from business operations in 2001. Such companies were able to buy faltering competitors and pay for other expansions with cash, rather than by borrowing money or selling stock. As the established telephone companies did not have to pay interest on loans, they were more profitable, and, more important, they survived the industry shakeout.

of the company for cash. Sometimes, however, a company in a liquidity crisis cannot raise the cash it needs. In that case, the company may go bankrupt.

Liquidity crises are all the more disturbing because revenue and income statements may not indicate that one is approaching. A fast-growing company with strong profits may face a liquidity crisis because it is expanding so quickly that even its growing revenues are not enough to cover the additional costs of more personnel, equipment, and supplies.

In addition, the way that revenues and income are calculated can conceal serious problems. Under standard accounting principles, accounts receivable—payments due for products that have been sold to a customer—are counted as revenues. Customers that owe a company money may not actually pay it, however. Customers may be about to enter bankruptcy, in which case the company may never get paid or get only a small fraction of what it is owed.

Cash flow is designed to help investors and companies spot a potential liquidity crisis before it wipes a company out. Cash flow is very focused on the here-and-now, as opposed to income and revenue, which tend to be more influenced by what has happened in the past and what might happen in the future.

For example, accounts receivable cannot be counted as positive cash flow. Cash flow reflects only money that has actually been received from customers. If a firm is owed a lot of money by its customers but is not actually collecting much money, that tells investors and executives that something is wrong—either the company's main customers are all in serious trouble or the company is not doing a very good job of collecting its debts.

Cash flow and income figures account for major purchases in different ways. In an income statement, the money spent on a factory or expensive piece of equipment must be depreciated, or averaged out, over the expected lifetime of the purchased item. Cash flow simply records how much cash was spent to make the purchase at the time it was made.

Cash flow has limitations. It can be highly volatile; the purchase of, for example, an expensive factory can result in sharply negative cash flow, even if the purchase was a wise long-term business decision. Nevertheless, cash flow provides companies with a valuable planning tool, allowing them to anticipate potential liquidity problems and secure financing in advance. Cash flow also gives investors a method to determine whether the company in which they are investing is likely to be around in the future.

Further Research
Cash Flow Calculator
www.bplans.com/business_calculators/cash_flow_calculator.cfm
This useful and free online tool helps small businesses to predict the effects of sales, inventory, credit terms, and other variables.
Monthly Cash Flow Calculator
http://www.bygpub.com/finance/CashFlowCalc.htm
A cash flow calculator designed for young people.

—*Mary Sisson*

Chambers of Commerce

A chamber of commerce consists of business leaders who join together to promote business interests in a community, state, or nation. Its primary goal is to promote the development and continued success of its members while making the area attractive to visitors, investors, and the workforce. It provides a place for members to discuss and act on important business issues and exerts influence in the legal arena by participating in discussions of and action about legislation, regulation, and court rulings.

Chambers of commerce can be found at all levels: international, national, state, and local. Most chambers focus on business and legal issues at their level but can extend their influence to higher levels of government when it serves their interests. Each chamber of commerce exists independently; for example, the U.S. Chamber of Commerce is not an umbrella organization for state and local chambers. However, a local chamber can join a state chamber of commerce, and both local and state chambers can join the U.S. chamber.

The U.S. Chamber of Commerce, located in Washington, D.C., works for businesses on the national level. Established in 1912, it advocates for U.S. business interests before regulatory agencies, all three branches of the government—Congress, the White House, and the courts—and in the media. In 2009 it represented three million businesses, as well as state and local chapters and industry associations, and 112 American chambers of commerce abroad. In addition to tracking bills in Congress, the U.S. Chamber of Commerce represents business interests in areas like

Members of the local chamber of commerce in Brooklyn, New York, pose with President Calvin Coolidge (fifth from right) in 1929.

Sign outside office of the Chinese Chamber of Commerce in San Francisco.

interests in the local community both legally and economically, local chambers may provide community bulletin board information, visitor and relocation information, maps, and a business directory. Other projects can include improving streets, public works, emergency services, schools, and recreational and tourist facilities. Their goal is to unify business interests for the good of the community. Many times the Convention and Visitors Bureau is part of the chamber of commerce.

State chambers of commerce work on business and legal issues at the state level of government. They ensure that employers' opinions are heard in legislative, regulatory, and judicial battles. Issues of concern might include taxation, business and environmental regulation, education and workforce training, technology, and development. State chambers also provide workshops and seminars (both classroom and online), benefits programs like health insurance and discounts on goods and services, and a variety of other services to help businesses stay competitive. Joining the state chamber of commerce allows members to network with similar businesses across the state.

Chambers of commerce abroad are called American Chambers of Commerce (AmChams). There are more than 100 AmChams in various foreign countries, all affiliated with the U.S. Chamber of Commerce. Local companies of the host country can outnumber American companies in membership. In most, if not all, cases, AmChams are privately funded, receiving no money from host countries. AmChams concentrate on foreign trade and investment opportunities for U.S. companies abroad. This could include developing services to promote commerce, representing American interests to the host country's government, businesses, and general public, or keeping abreast of current business practices and trends. They work with both U.S. and host country governments to create a mutually favorable trade environment.

Other kinds of chambers of commerce include the U.S. Junior Chamber of Commerce (Jaycees), which is dedicated to developing future business leaders through community service and leadership training.

economic and tax policy, education and workforce training, legal reform, privatization and procurement, transportation, retirement and Social Security, e-commerce and technology, defense, and immigration.

Membership offers benefits: discounted goods and services, retirement plans and insurance, information on business policy issues, and a variety of resources for business owners, especially small businesses. The U.S. Chamber of Commerce does not distribute lists of its members nor does it endorse organizations or provide references for its members.

Local chambers of commerce focus on building the community economically and improving the quality of life in the community. In addition to representing business

Local chambers of commerce often organize events to attract tourists. The Hollywood Chamber of Commerce runs the Walk of Fame, a five-acre stretch of bronze stars commemorating members of the entertainment industry. Actor Jackie Chan, center, received a star, surrounde by, from left, honorary mayor of Hollywood Johnny Grant, actor Owen Wilson, Chan, director Brett Ratner, chairman of the board of the Hollywood Chamber of Commerce Russ Joyner, and Leron Gubler, president of the Hollywood Chamber of Commerce.

Founded in 1920 in St. Louis, Missouri, the Jaycees focuses on education, networking, and career advancement in addition to community service, encouraging young people to develop skills that will serve them in their professional lives. The national organization promotes nationwide service projects while local chapters of the Jaycees are involved in community service projects. Jaycees around the country have built parks, playgrounds, and housing for the elderly, and raised millions of dollars for charity. The organization also partners with other advocacy groups, including the "Support our Troops" program, the American Cancer Society, and and the government-sponsored Citizens Corps.

The United States Hispanic Chamber of Commerce is specifically concerned with Hispanic-owned businesses, business interests, and networking. In addition to offering support on business development and legislative issues, this organization works with Latin American countries to foster favorable trade agreements. The National Black Chamber of Commerce represents black-owned businesses and has chapters across the United States and abroad. Its primary purpose is to empower black communities and promote participation in the free enterprise system.

The idea of businesspeople banding together for their common good also extends to the Internet. Several Web chambers of commerce serve the interests of companies that do business on the World Wide Web. Some of the Web chambers require adopting a set of Internet business ethics; others focus on issues related to doing business on the Web.

When businesses band together, they gain the advantage of numbers in the legal and economic arenas. Although the main purpose of chambers of commerce is to promote members' business interests, most recognize the importance of giving back to the community, both directly through community projects and information and through improved economic strength. A healthy local or state economy can attract even more businesses to an area, bringing increased opportunity, employment, and tax revenues.

—*Stephanie Buckwalter*

Chambers of Commerce on the World Wide Web

Canadian Chamber of Commerce. **www.chamber.ca**

International Chamber of Commerce. **www.iccwbo.org**

National Black Chamber of Commerce. **www.nationalbcc.org**

United States Chamber of Commerce. **www.uschamber.org**

United States Hispanic Chamber of Commerce. **www.ushcc.com**

Junior Chambers of Commerce

Canada Junior Chamber. **www.jcicanada.com**

Junior Chamber International. **www.jci.cc**

United States Junior Chamber (Jaycees). **www.usjaycees.org**

Commodities

In broad terms, commodities are any products that can be traded and that are used for commerce. More narrowly, commodities are products that are traded on an authorized commodity exchange. Major commodities of this kind include wheat, rice, corn, pork bellies, oilseeds, sugar, coffee, cocoa, tea, oil, natural gas, cotton, wool, jute, sisal, rubber, copper, zinc, lead, and tin.

The practice of buying and selling commodities in an open marketplace began in ancient times. The Agora in Athens and the Forum in Rome were originally commercial marketplaces; medieval fairs were their successors. These regional fairs were gradually replaced by the establishment in cities of specialized trading centers. In Japan, commodity exchanges arose in the eighteenth century. In these markets the purchase of commodities was generally made on the basis of immediate delivery ("spot" trading). Gradually, however, the merchants developed the practice of forward contracting, or futures, which is today one of the most crucial functions of a commodity exchange.

Commodity futures, which are contracts for delivery of specific commodities at a stated price at a specified future date, perform several important functions. The buying and selling of futures tends to even out price fluctuations (caused, for example, by seasonal availability) by allowing the market to mirror expectations about future harvests (or other variables in supply) and changes in demand. Futures are not usually employed for the buying or selling of the actual commodity, but for hedging price fluctuations. Hedging is a method by which individuals or businesses gain protection against future price changes.

For example, say that a coffee dealer knows that six months down the line he will buy 10,000 pounds of coffee to send to a processor, and he has promised to sell that coffee to the processor at a certain price. To protect himself, the coffee dealer buys coffee futures contracts representing 10,000 pounds of coffee. If the price of coffee is higher six months later, the value of the futures contracts rises too. By selling the futures at a higher price than he paid for them, the coffee merchant offsets the extra money he has to pay for the coffee. Hedging thus not only helps to even out gains and losses incurred by fluctuating prices, it also helps contribute to an even flow of business.

The number of commodity markets is not fixed. There are major commodity markets in more than twenty countries. In addition to the Chicago Board of Trade, major commodity markets include the Chicago Mercantile Exchange, the New York Cotton Exchange, the New York Commodity Exchange, the New York Mercantile Exchange, the New York Metal Exchange, the New York Sugar Exchange, and the London Metal Exchange. Important commodity markets are located in Winnipeg, Canada (rye, barley, and oats); Brazil, India,

Kinds of Commodity Futures	
Livestock / meat products	• Propane
Examples:	• Unleaded gas
• Cattle	**Financial and index futures**
• Hogs	Examples:
• Pork bellies	• Dow Jones industrial average futures
Grains, cereal / oilseed	
Examples:	• NASDAQ 100 index futures
• Canola	• NYSE composite index
• Corn	• S&P 500
• Cotton	**Currencies**
• Flaxseed	Examples:
• Oats	• Australian dollar
• Rice	• British pound
• Soybeans	• Canadian dollar
• Wheat	• Japanese yen
Metals	**Miscellaneous commodities**
Examples:	Examples:
• Copper	• Butter
• Palladium	• Cocoa
• Silver	• Coffee
Soft commodities / energy	• Lumber
Examples:	• Milk
• Heating oil	• Orange juice
• Natural gas	• Sugar

The interior of the Chicago Board of Trade.

and Egypt (cotton); and Australia, New Zealand, and South Africa (wool).

Most commodities do not pass through commodity exchanges but are sold by direct contact between exporter and importer, who agree on a contract. Commodity exchanges are of great global importance, nevertheless. Commodity markets are the hubs where buyers and sellers trade information and opinions, and their mutually reinforcing expertise tends to determine world prices of a particular commodity. The basic function of a commodity exchange is to ensure the regular and reliable flow of commodities by establishing accepted markets and determining current prices. Properly organized commodity markets strive to establish prices that are in line with demand and that do not fluctuate widely; in addition, as commodities often must be transported great distances from their point of origin to their point of use, commodity markets make certain that products are delivered reliably. Commodities markets are probably best known as the places where futures contracts are traded.

The futures market relies on individuals who are willing to accept risk. Futures attract speculators, persons who usually have no direct contact with the specific commodity but who get into the market in the hopes of making a profit by buying low and selling high. Because of the high risk and great potential profits of their activities, speculators have often been considered as buccaneers who add little value to business. Yet speculators play an important role in the commodities world. They are willing to bear the risk that hedgers seek to avoid and thus act as a kind of insurance underwriter.

Further Research
Chicago Board of Trade
www.cbot.com
Home page of the Chicago Board of Trade offers
    stock performance information, news, and
    market data.
New York Mercantile Exchange
www.nymex.com
The home page of the largest commodities futures
    exchange.
TFC Commodity Charts
futures.tradingcharts.com
This site provides performance measures as well
    as educational resources.

—Joseph Gustaitis

Compound Interest

Becoming a millionaire is fairly easy for those who start saving early in life. If Michael, a 20-year-old, begins to deposit $22 every week in an account that earns 10 percent interest and continues to invest $22 every week until he is 65, he will accumulate $1 million. Compound interest is the key.

What is interest? Interest is the cost of borrowing money. If a customer borrows money to buy a car, the bank will charge the customer interest on the amount borrowed. Bank customers also may earn interest. If a customer puts money into a savings account, the bank will pay interest on the amount deposited. Interest thus encourages both lending and saving. It compensates lenders for the risk they take when they make loans, and it compensates savers for giving up consumption today in exchange for the ability to have more money and be able to purchase more goods in the future. Although bank savings accounts rarely offer 10 percent interest, a 10 percent return on other investments may be attainable. According to the *Stocks,*

Bonds, Bills, and Inflation 1999 Yearbook™ published by Ibbotson Associates, Inc., the average annual return on investment in large-company stocks between 1926 and 1998 was 13.2 percent.

Simple interest and compound interest differ. Simple interest is interest earned on the original principal (that is, the amount saved) only. Compound interest is interest earned on the original principal and on interest reinvested from prior periods.

For example, 50 years ago Phoebe invested $100 in a savings account at 5 percent simple interest rate. Today, that $100 is worth $350 because Phoebe earned 5 percent, or $5 per year, on the account for 50 years. The ending value of her investment is the original $100 principal plus $250 simple interest. If Phoebe had deposited her $100 in an account paying compound interest at a rate of 5 percent, however, her account would be worth $1,146.74 after 50 years. That is $796.74 more than she earned from the simple interest account; the difference is explained by compounding, or interest earned on interest.

To gain the most from compound interest, one should invest early and often. The more frequently individuals make investments, the sooner the money will be available

In the first year simple and compound interest are the same because the amount of interest earned on interest is $0. However, in the twenty-fifth year, interest earned on interest is $11.13; and, in the fiftieth year, interest earned on interest totals $49.61.

Compound Interest vs. Simple Interest				
Year	Beginning Value of Investment Account	Annual Compound Interest	Ending Value of Investment Account	Annual Interest Earned on Interest *(Compound interest minus simple interest of $5 per year)*
1	$100	.05 x 100 = $5	100 + 5 = $105	5 – 5 = $0
2	$105	.05 x 105 = $5.25	105 + 5.25 = $105.25	5.25 – 5 = $0.25
3	$110.25	.05 x 110.25 = $5.51	110.25 + 5.51 = $115.76	5.51 – 5 = $0.51
25	$322.51	.05 x 322.51 = $16.13	322.51 + 16.13 = $338.64	16.13 – 5 = $11.13
50	$1092.13	.05 x 1092.13 = $54.61	1092.13 + 54.61 = $1146.74	54.61 – 5 = $49.61

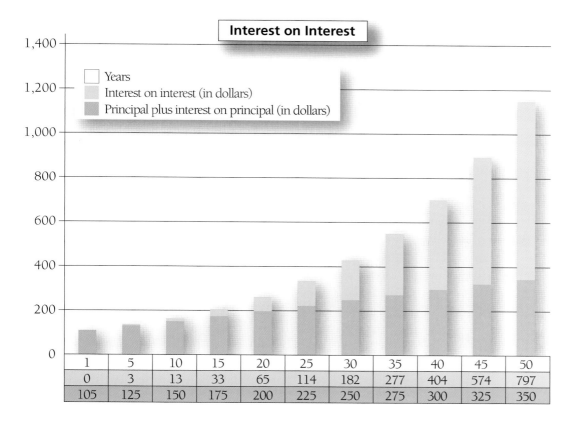

Interest on Interest

	1	5	10	15	20	25	30	35	40	45	50
Years	0	3	13	33	65	114	182	277	404	574	797
	105	125	150	175	200	225	250	275	300	325	350

Legend:
- ☐ Years
- Interest on interest (in dollars)
- Principal plus interest on principal (in dollars)

Earning interest on interest greatly increases wealth over time.

for the accumulating effects of compound interest. In other words, investing regularly throughout a given time period, say a year, is preferable to waiting to invest a lump sum at the end of a year, because the incremental investments start earning compounding interest immediately.

Returning to the millionaire example: if Michael does not start investing $22 per week until age 30, he will accumulate only $366,130 by age 65. He pays a $633,870 penalty for waiting 10 years to begin investing. If he waits until age 30 to begin investing, and he still wants to accumulate $1 million by age 65, he will need to invest $60 per week at 10 percent. If he waits until he is 40 to start saving, he will need to invest $172 per week to become a millionaire by age 65.

If Michael waits until age 30 to begin investing and wants to invest only $22 per week, he will need to earn 13.72 percent on his money to accumulate $1 million by age 65. Although a 13.72 percent return on investment may be feasible, it will require investment in riskier assets than investing for a 10 percent average return.

The key to earning compound interest is to reinvest interest payments rather than spend them. The primary benefit of forgoing consumption today in return for future consumption is the overall increase in earnings gained. Compound interest provides savers with an opportunity to assert control over their financial future.

Further Research

Brain, Marshall. "Understanding and Controlling Your Finances." BYG Publishing. http://www.bygpub.com/finance/finance0.htm.

Compound Interest Calculator

www.moneychimp.com/calculator/compound_interest_calculator.htm

This calculator also has links explaining the compound interest formulas with interactive graphs.

Financial Web

www.finweb.com/investing/compound-interest.html

The magic of compound interest, presented by an independical finance portal with information about all aspects of personal finance.

Fool.com

Motley Fool's Web site features investment data and advice, discussion boards, and portfolio tracking features.

—*Angeline Lavin*

Consumer Protection

Everyone is a consumer. From food, medicine, and shelter to the latest gadgets and toys, the market economy of the United States revolves around the production, sale, and consumption of goods. The responsibility for protecting consumers from false advertising, unsafe products, and other marketplace dangers falls on numerous federal, state, and private organizations. Individuals have frequently played a role in shedding light on product shortfalls as well. The snake-oil salesmen of the 1800s may have vanished, but protecting the consumer remains an ongoing battle. Sometimes unwary and occasionally susceptible to telemarketing scams and pyramid schemes, consumers are, at least, not alone in their unceasing efforts to get what they paid for.

Who Protects the Consumer?

Many federal agencies and organizations have consumer protection duties in the United States, including the U.S. Consumer Product Safety Commission, the National Credit Union Administration, the Office of Thrift Supervision, and the Federal Reserve. Three others that directly address consumer issues and that have significant and far-reaching responsibilities are the Federal Trade Commission (FTC), the Food and Drug Administration (FDA), and the National Highway Traffic Safety Administration (NHTSA).

The Federal Trade Commission, an independent agency established in 1914, is responsible for keeping markets competitive. The FTC's Bureau of Consumer Protection oversees a variety of products and industries, and has several tools at its disposal. It issues consumer alerts warning potential buyers of possibly dangerous products and deceptive claims by manufacturers. Along with the Department of Justice, the FTC investigates business mergers to ensure that no single company gains a monopoly in its particular industry. Monopolies limit consumer choices. The FTC also looks into abusive lending practices, false advertising, and other issues that threaten to limit consumers' freedom of choice in the marketplace.

Another key federal consumer protection organization is the Food and Drug Administration. The FDA is charged with overseeing the food, medication, and cosmetics industries. The FDA regulates the food industry by making sure that all ingredients used are safe. When a food producer wants to introduce a new additive to a product, the additive must pass a series of safety tests before the product gains FDA approval for sale to consumers. The FDA covers most food products, but meat and poultry are under the jurisdiction of the United States Department of Agriculture (USDA). Medicines and medical products are regulated by the FDA and must be proven safe and effective before they can be used.

The FDA also approves the labeling of these products. For example, medical equipment must be labeled with clear instructions for its use. The FDA also handles cosmetics, but its regulation of cosmetics differs from that of food and drugs. The FDA monitors cosmetics to make sure they are safe and are properly labeled, but these products are not reviewed before they are placed on the market, and they do not

---

Key Areas of Consumer Concern

- ✔ Advertising
- ✔ Credit
- ✔ Information
- ✔ Labeling
- ✔ Pricing
- ✔ Quality
- ✔ Safety
- ✔ Selling

Lemon Laws

"Lemon laws" protect consumers who have bought vehicles that unexpectedly require significant repairs soon after purchase (in other words, from buying a real "lemon"). In 1982, Connecticut passed the first "lemon law"; now every state in the United States has some form of lemon law.

Although the specifics of these laws differ from state to state—some cover used cars and motorcycles, for example, while others do not—some basic features are common from state to state. Most establish a warranty period of one or two years during which the defects have to arise. Most define how significant the needed repairs must be and provide that the manufacturer, not the dealer, is responsible for them. Typically, after a number of unsuccessful attempts are made to repair a defect, the vehicle is considered a lemon and its owner is entitled to a refund or a replacement. In about half of the states, consumers may even recover attorneys' fees if they have had to take the manufacturer to court. While smart consumers will closely inspect any vehicle they are considering purchasing, lemon laws provide some protection against significant defects undisclosed and undiscovered at the time of purchase.

Federal Drug Administration	Federal Trade Commission	National Credit Union Administration	National Highway Traffic Safety Administration	U.S. Consumer Product Safety Commission
✓ Sets standards for drugs and cosmetics ✓ Ensures foods are safe, wholesome, and sanitary ✓ Forbids distribution of adulterated products ✓ Requires honest labeling	✓ Prohibits monopolistic practices ✓ Sets requirements for food, drug, clothing, and cosmetics labeling ✓ Requires advertisers to substantiate claims ✓ Issues consumer alerts on dangerous products or deceptive claims	✓ Supervises and insures 6,000 federal credit unions ✓ Cultivates the safety and soundness of federally insured credit unions ✓ Works to improve credit union service ✓ Encourages credit unions to extend credit to all Americans	✓ Sets safety standards for motor vehicles and motor vehicle equipment ✓ Investigates safety defects in motor vehicles ✓ Sets and enforces fuel economy standards ✓ Provides grants to state and local government to conduct safety programs	✓ Develops and enforces product safety standards ✓ Bans consumer products if no feasible standard can protect the public ✓ Initiates the recall of products ✓ Conducts research on potential product hazards

require safety testing. Part of the FDA's responsibility for products and ingredients it must approve prior to being placed on the market is to test and approve or disapprove them in a timely manner. The FDA, then, through its administrative rules, must balance the safety and effectiveness of products against the financial need for businesses to get new products out the door.

The National Highway Traffic Safety Administration is responsible for automobile safety. The Highway Safety Act of 1970 established the NHTSA. Its mission at that time was to carry out safety programs under federal legislation passed in the late 1960s. In 1972, the Motor Vehicle Information and Cost Savings Act was passed and charged the NHTSA with additional consumer protection duties. The agency is now responsible for reducing injuries, deaths, and financial losses caused by motor vehicle crashes. The NHTSA attempts to accomplish its mission by setting and enforcing safety performance standards for motor vehicles and motor vehicle equipment. The NHTSA also assists local and state governments by providing grants for highway safety programs and provides consumers with information on a wide range of vehicle safety topics including air bags and the proper use of child car seats and safety belts.

Augmenting these federal efforts, every state government in the United States has some form of consumer protection organization. The state of New York, for example, has a wide array of governmental agencies and departments responsible for protecting the consumer. They produce a consumer help

Thalidomide

Thalidomide is a sedative that was used to relieve morning sickness and nausea in pregnant women. Considered so safe that it was available over-the-counter in many countries, thalidomide was widely adopted for use around the world after its introduction in Germany in 1958. The application to market thalidomide in the United States arrived at the Food and Drug Administration in September 1960. FDA officer Dr. Frances Kelsey found troubling inconsistencies and incomplete data in the thalidomide application, and she delayed approval of the drug pending further review.

That decision saved thousands of American children. In November 1961 a German physician linked the use of thalidomide to an upswing in several rare birth defects, including facial abnormalities and the absence of arms and legs. Some 10,000 children would be born with birth defects caused by thalidomide before the drug was removed from most markets by the fall of 1962. In the United States, thanks to Dr. Kelsey, only 17 such children were born.

Inspired by the close call that averted an American thalidomide disaster, in the early 1960s Congress passed the Kefauver–Harris Bill, which lengthened the approval process for new drugs. Then hailed as a model of concern for consumer safety, the FDA would later come under fire from AIDS and cancer activists for delaying approvals and preventing patients from obtaining experimental drugs. In an ironic twist, one of the experimental drugs in demand by activists was thalidomide. Bowing to activist pressure, in 1998 the FDA approved thalidomide for use in AIDS, cancer, and leprosy patients.

—Rebecca Sherman

manual covering everything from state regulations on pawnbrokers to landlord–tenant relations. Consumers are told how to file utility complaints, what travel agent practices are prohibited, and informed about the various kinds of warranties that accompany products. New York handles consumer protection through agencies like the state attorney general, the Public Service Commission, the Banking Department, the Department of Health, the Governor's Office of Regulatory Reform, and the Empire State Development Corporation. Cities and counties in New York also host consumer affairs offices, like the Better Business Bureau.

Private citizens and organizations have played an important role in uncovering unsafe products and in bringing misleading marketing to light. Ralph Nader is perhaps the best-known consumer advocate of the twentieth century. He became famous in 1965 with his blistering critique of automobile safety in his book *Unsafe at Any Speed*. Nader argued that the automobile industry was focused more on profits than on driver and passenger safety. The National Traffic and Motor Vehicle Safety Act of 1966 was at least partly the result of the public outcry stemming from Nader's accusations. The act established important safety standards for new cars. Nader later formed the consumer advocacy organization Public Citizen, Inc. Since the 1960s he has addressed consumer protection issues in several other industries, including health care and energy, as well as taking on tax and campaign reform.

Tools Used to Protect the Consumer

The tools used by those concerned with and responsible for consumer protection vary widely. Individuals and private consumer advocacy groups often use the media to expose marketplace dangers. They write articles and books, talk to community organizations, and attempt to influence legislators.

For government agencies and departments, the tools at their disposal depend in large part on the specific industry under their

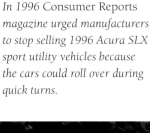

In 1996 Consumer Reports *magazine urged manufacturers to stop selling 1996 Acura SLX sport utility vehicles because the cars could roll over during quick turns.*

Michigan attorney general Jennifer Granholm displays a mailing from Publisher's Clearinghouse that was judged deceptive to consumers. As a result of a lawsuit brought by Michigan and 25 other states, Publisher's Clearinghouse agreed to pay $19 million in restitution to customers and to stop using phrases like "guaranteed winner" in its mailings.

jurisdiction. For example, the Food and Drug Act of 1906 laid the foundation for modern food and drug laws. The law was enhanced in 1938 with the Federal Food, Drug, and Cosmetic Act. The FTC also accomplishes its mission primarily through enforcement of federal statutes. Examples are the Fair Packaging and Labeling Act, the Consumer Leasing Act, and the Telemarketing and Consumer Fraud and Abuse Prevention Act.

In many nonfood and drug markets, industry standards offer what consumer protection exists. These nonstatutory standards do not have the force of law. Recommendations for industry standards, covering, for instance, the safety of electric kitchen appliances, are made with manufacturer input and even approval. A seal or symbol may be placed on the product alerting the consumer to the product's compliance with the industry safety standard. Whether these measures affect consumer choices is open to debate. Nor do the standards always address actual product effectiveness or ineffectiveness.

Complete protection of the consumer is not possible. The properly labeled medical device, for instance, must still be correctly operated by a trained professional, and the long-term effects of food additives are sometimes difficult to ascertain during a typical testing period. The American consumer receives a lot of attention, however. Agencies and offices at all levels of government, private organizations, and even dedicated individual advocates look out for their well-being. Consumer alerts notify potential buyers of faulty products and deceptive advertising. Significant federal statutes authorize government agencies to monitor and regulate whole industries, and industry standards offer some protection in areas that are difficult to address with legislation.

Further Research

Federal Trade Commission

www.ftc.gov/bcp

The FTC's Bureah of Consumer Protection home page offers a range of useful information.

Consumers Union

www.consumerreports.org

Consumer Reports is published by the Consumers Union, an independent, nonprofit organization that provides consumer information.

—*John Keckhaver*

Contracts and Contract Law

A contract is an agreement consisting of reciprocal promises that the law will enforce. Contract law is the body of law that oversees that enforcement. In a typical commercial contract, Party A promises to provide goods or services to Party B in exchange for a consideration, for example, a promise to pay a sum of money.

Contracts take many different forms: they can be as simple as verbal agreements between individuals and as complicated as 20-page signed documents. Written contracts between corporations, for instance, often involve detailed terms that account for the time and manner in which the goods or services will be delivered, the expected quality of the goods or services, and what happens if a breach of the contract occurs (expectations are not fulfilled). In this way, companies can set limits on their liability and come to an agreement about what remedies a party can expect if the contract's terms are not satisfied.

Contracts are used by everyone, not just businesspeople. Even the purchase of something as simple as a movie ticket creates a contractual relationship with the movie theater, with the promise being that the purchaser will be allowed to enter the theater and watch the movie, and the consideration being the price paid for the ticket.

In the United States, contracts must meet a number of requirements to be considered legally binding. One requirement is legality of object: The purpose of a contract must not be against the law; a contract for a drug deal, for example, would not be legally enforceable. Another requirement is consideration. Both parties must offer something; contract law does not enforce agreements where goods or services have been promised but no counter-promise has been made, as in the case of gifts or charitable donations. Contracts also require mutual agreement, often represented by the signature of both parties on a written contract. Finally, both parties must have contractual capacity—the legal ability to enter into a contract. A mentally ill person might be found by a judge to lack contractual capacity. Minors have limited capacity.

Why Are Contracts Essential?

Consider the following: Company A agrees to supply Company B with 100 widgets, which Company B needs to build its product. Company A fails to provide the widgets, which results in the inability of Company B to complete production on time. Imagine, now, that Company B has no recourse because the law does not require Company A to pay damages for its failure. While over time Company A may gain a reputation for being untrustworthy, and hence go out of business, Company B has still incurred a loss in the present. Because it cannot complete production in a timely manner, B's sales may suffer, and it may even be forced into bankruptcy. Nor does the tarnished reputation of Company A help Companies C, D, and so forth, which in turn relied on Company B's product being completed by the projected time.

Requirements for Legally Enforceable Contracts

Mutual assent

Consideration

Contract

Legality of object

Capacity

Written contracts are usually signed by both parties, showing mutual agreement to the terms listed.

Considering all the many individuals, companies, governments, and countries that rely on each other's goods and services, imagine the chaos that would ensue if they could not trust that promises would be fulfilled—or that the law would intervene if the terms of their agreements were not satisfied. No market society could function smoothly without clear legal rules governing contracts. Accordingly, countries all over the world have created systems of contract law to facilitate trade within and between their borders.

Indeed, versions of contract law have existed for thousands of years, ever since early civilizations began to trade with one another. The ancient Romans had the principle *Consensus ad idem:* a meeting of the minds between parties where each understands the commitments made by the other—a basic principle in contract law even now. In the 1700s, as market societies emerged, England and France developed complex contract law systems that form the basis of the modern legal system.

Contracts are so essential to the smooth functioning of business that the founding fathers protected them in the U.S. Constitution. As Article 1, section 10 states, "No State shall . . . pass any . . . Law impairing the Obligation of Contracts." In other words, the government cannot create laws that void legal contracts or that render legal contracts illegal or unenforceable after the fact. Hence, in the United States, contracts are protected from the government as much as they are protected by it.

How Are Contracts Enforced?

Samuel Goldwyn, the Hollywood movie mogul, famously remarked that "A verbal contract is as worthless as the paper it's written on." This is not necessarily true: a verbal contract is just as enforceable under law as a written contract. A case like *Main Line Pictures v. Basinger* (1993) illustrates the validity of verbal contracts: in an infamous court decision, the actress Kim Basinger was ordered to pay $7 million in damages to Main Line Pictures because she was found to have breached a verbal agreement to star in the company's film *Boxing Helena*. Although this decision was ultimately overturned by an appellate court on

Actress Kim Basinger was sued for breach of contract when she backed out of a verbal agreement to star in the film Boxing Helena. *The role was eventually played by Sherilyn Fenn, pictured here supine on the set.*

a technicality, it effectively changed the way Hollywood did business.

A verbal contract is never as reliable as a written contract because it depends on the contracting parties' memories and versions of events, which often differ. At their best, written contracts prevent misunderstandings about the terms of the agreement and leave very little open to interpretation. Some kinds of contracts must be in writing to be enforceable. These contracts are specified by an area of law called the statute of frauds, and include real estate and marriage contracts, contracts whose terms of performance extend for more than a year, and contracts involving sales of goods of $500 or more.

Even written contracts are subject to a court's interpretation, however. A court may find that the terms of the contract were unreasonable. For instance, sometimes a party will attempt to limit liability

for breach of contract by building in a contractual clause that protects against such a claim. The court, however, may still find the party liable. In other words, the court has the final say in interpreting the level of protection the contract offers and the fairness of the contract's terms.

Alternatively, a court may find that the purpose of the contract itself is illegal or otherwise against public policy. For instance, in the notorious "Baby M" case, Mary Beth Whitehead entered into contract with Richard Stern to carry his child to term and release the baby to him and his wife at birth; upon delivery of the baby, Whitehead was to receive $10,000 plus money for any extra medical costs incurred because of the pregnancy. When Whitehead changed her mind and refused to give up the baby, Stern filed suit in the state of New Jersey for breach of contract. Although New Jersey had no specific law governing surrogacy contracts, the appellate court of New Jersey ruled that the contract was against public policy because it amounted to an attempt to circumvent New Jersey's adoption laws, which do not allow payment for babies. Although the court decided to grant Stern custody of the baby, Whitehead was not held liable for breach of contract.

When a court finds that a breach of contract has occurred, the suffering party is often awarded remedies like the $7 million in compensatory damages awarded to Main Line in *Main Line Pictures v. Basinger*. Why $7 million? Because Main Line argued that the film would have been that much more profitable had Basinger starred in it.

An Ever-evolving System

In the Middle Ages, the sale of a property was conducted through a verbal contract. The sale was symbolically closed when a clump of dirt from the purchased land was delivered to the buyer. In the absence of a written contract, this delivery of dirt—called the *livery of seisin*—served as evidence of the transfer of property. As more and more people began to own property and a merchant class emerged, such transactions needed clearer guidelines and documentation. Such a transfer of property is now evidenced by written documents, facilitated by lawyers and real estate agents, and enforced by the courts if the agreement is disputed.

In the late twentieth century, as businesses crossed national borders to develop a global marketplace, new contract law questions emerged: Which nation's law would apply to the contract? Where would litigation take place in the case of a breach of contract? In recognition of these uncertainties, in 1980 the United Nations instituted the Convention on Contracts for the International Sale of Goods, which established a set of uniform rules governing commercial contracts between parties in participating countries.

New demands on contract law have since surfaced in response to the emergence of electronic business. The U.S. Uniform Computer Information Transactions Act, passed in 1999, was intended to allow states to adopt uniform laws that take into account the unique aspects of e-business, but concerns, including the perception that it weakened consumer protection, prevented its acceptance. Today, no clear international guidelines governing e-business exist. Organizations like the Business Software Alliance urge governments worldwide to develop a new set of guidelines to ensure the smooth functioning and development of this growing industry.

As much as contract law influences business and industry, business and industry influence contract law. Systems of contract law are always evolving to accommodate our ever-growing—and ever-more-complicated—global marketplace.

Further Research

**Australian National University Faculty of Law,
    Contract Law On-Line Information Network**
law.anu.edu.au/colin
 A clear introduction to contracts and contract law
    from an Australian university.
Business Software Alliance
www.bsa.org
The Business Software Alliance is a nonprofit trade
    organization promoting safety and security in
    the digital world.

—Andrea Troyer and John Troyer

The Uniform Computer Information Transaction Act

Although the principles of contract law are old, debate still rages about how those principles should be applied in specific situations—especially regarding the information economy. In 1999 the Uniform Computer Information Transactions Act (UCITA) was designed to standardize contract law for products such as computer software, databases, and online and multimedia products. In particular, the law covers what are known as shrink-wrap licenses, the licenses that all users must accept before they are allowed to install software.

The UCITA was opposed by a wide variety of groups, including the American Library Association, the Association for Computing Machinery, and the attorneys general of 26 states. These groups felt that the UCITA was poor legislation for a number of reasons, including the fact that the UCITA permitted companies to change the terms of a license after the product has been purchased. As originally written, the UCITA allowed companies to deny responsibility for product shortcomings or damage their products might cause to users' computers. Furthermore, the UCITA permitted companies to prohibit users from publicly criticizing software they had bought. The UCITA was revised in 2002 to address some of the complaints. Opponents felt that the adjustments did not go far enough to protect consumers, however, and only two states, Maryland and Virginia, have passed the law.

Copyright

Copyright is an author's exclusive right to reproduce, publish, and sell works of literature, music, or art. Copyright is defined by law and protects both the content and the form of the work.

Knowledge before Copyright

Before the invention of copyright, knowledge was considered to be a general common good that belonged to anyone who could learn it. In a sense, knowledge belonged to the person who knew it. He or she could keep it, share it, sell it, or transmit it in any form at all. It was the form and not the content of knowledge that mattered.

The invention of the printing press led to the need for copyright laws. This illustration of an early printing press is from the title page of Hegesippus, *a book published in 1511.*

Once a manuscript or an idea left its author, it was free for all to use.

Anyone who wished to profit from knowledge was required to protect it as proprietary information, much as trade secrets or proprietary processes are protected today. Material goods could be protected by walls and guards, but knowledge could be protected only by secrecy. The knowledge of the guilds, the arts, and sciences was jealously guarded. Manuscripts, maps, formulas, and other documents were protected as carefully as jewelry or coins. In many places, certain forms of protected knowledge were classified as state secrets. Sharing these forms of knowledge constituted an act of treason, punishable by death.

The shift from feudal society to early modern society that gave rise to the new humanism and the birth of science also gave birth to new attitudes about knowledge. This change was connected to the invention of the printing press and to the growth and expansion of universities. With this shift came two forms of recognition about knowledge: first, knowledge is a common good that grows only through use and social interaction; second, individual knowledge creators require incentives to generate and share knowledge, and they require the ability to protect the profits of their knowledge even while sharing it widely.

The Concept of Intellectual Property

While copyright laws were an innovation of the age of printing, they had three predecessor forms. One was the royal patent, or monopoly, over any useful trade, art, or practice. A second was the royal license of printing. The third was the early modern intellectual property law that began with the Venetian patent laws of 1474.

Property rights are the legal rights that govern the ownership and control of property. Intellectual property was an odd form of property in a world that looked on property as tangible goods. The appearance of books and the book trade played an important

- Literary works
- Musical works, including any
  accompanying words
- Dramatic works, including any
  accompanying music
- Pantomimes and choreographic works
- Pictorial, graphic, and sculptural works
- Motion pictures and other audiovisual
  works
- Sound recordings
- Architectural works

role in shaping the idea of knowledge as a good. In reality, knowledge cannot be separated from the active human knower. Once externalized, it becomes information. When knowledge is externalized as information, it becomes tangible. This shift suddenly emphasized the role of knowledge and information as goods rather than as intangible human properties or attributes.

Before Johannes Gutenberg revolutionized book production, books were scarce, costly, and difficult to obtain. The birth of the printing press led to a dramatic increase in available books. In the 1450s, Gutenberg launched his printing revolution. By the first decade of the 1500s, more than eight million books had been printed—a greater number than all the handwritten manuscripts created in human history.

In addition to the Bible and the classics, Europe saw the development of the first best-selling authors with the work of scholars like Erasmus. During this era, only authorized presses operating under royal license legally produced books. The printing industry and the publishing industry were identical, and printer–publishers controlled all rights in the new book trade. Before long, this monopoly created problems.

Information versus Knowledge

The solution was to switch ownership of the contents of a book to its author, granting control over content and control over the right to license production in any physical form. By granting an author complete control over the work for a limited period, an author could profit from writing. Authors thus had incentive to create new content for the growing book trade while helping to increase the stock of information that individuals could turn into knowledge as they read and retained the information that would lead to new learning and generate knowledge. Economist Adam Smith saw this as one of the few cases of monopoly that serves the public good.

The first copyright law was the Statute of Anne passed by the British Parliament in 1710. The purpose of copyright then, as now, was to serve the public good by protecting an author's interests in his or her work. The stated goal of copyright law was "the encouragement of learning." Granting copyright to authors gave authors an incentive to create knowledge.

U.S. copyright law is also based on that premise. Copyright was one of the first issues that the founders addressed when they framed the Constitution of the United States. In Article 1, section 8, Congress is charged with making laws "to promote the progress of science and useful arts, by securing for limited times to authors and inventors the exclusive right to their respective writings and discoveries."

Modern Copyright Law

The Statute of Anne was but a beginning. Today, three principles of intellectual property and common good form the public policy basis of copyright laws.

The first principle is that knowledge builds on prior knowledge. The second principle is that no one can finally own knowledge—it is a common property that grows through circulation while shrinking with disuse. The third principle is that knowledge grows incrementally. In science, literature, the arts, philosophy, and in every field of work, new knowledge must account for and embrace what is already known.

Before copyright protection, the ideas and words of an author could be used by

A shop in Malaysia is decorated with antipiracy posters as part of a nationwide campaign to stamp out pirated software and DVDs.

anyone who gained access to them. While printing presses were controlled under license, any licensed printer could print any book for which he had a text. Anyone able to reach a market first gained the full benefit of an author's work while returning no profit to the creator. Copyright laws secured the legitimate interests of creators in the fruits of their work. These laws now distinguish between legitimate and illegitimate uses of copyrighted material, and the law distinguishes between theft and proper acquisition.

Rights Granted by Copyright

- To **reproduce** the work;
- To prepare **derivative works** based upon the work;
- To **distribute copies** of the work to the public by sale or other transfer of ownership, or by rental, lease, or lending;
- To **perform the work publicly**, in the case of literary, musical, dramatic, and choreographic works, pantomimes, and motion pictures and other audiovisual works;
- To **display the copyrighted work publicly**, in the case of literary, musical, dramatic, and choreographic works, pantomimes, and pictorial, graphic, or sculptural works, including the individual images of a motion picture or other audiovisual work; and
- In the case of **sound recordings, to perform the work publicly** by means of a **digital audio transmission**.

Modern copyright laws cover all kinds of creations. Copyright covers the content of works and whatever forms they take or media they use. Copyright governs the literary, musical, and artistic content of works like books, magazines, Web sites, plays, films, and musical products, as well as artworks and architecture. Rights of performance, broadcast, and publication are linked to copyright control.

Copyright law is subject to specific constraints. For example, the contents of books can be copyrighted but book titles cannot. A title must be trademarked. Copyright covers the specific expression of an idea, but not the idea itself.

One of the interesting facts of copyright law is that the work of an author—however large or small—is automatically copyrighted and protected until it is published or made public. A grocery list, love letters, personal correspondence, and study notes are protected, along with any poem or drawing or manuscript an individual might create. They remain under the creator's control until he or she gives permission to publish them or transfers the rights to a publisher.

If a work protected under this form of copyright is released to the public—that is, published—without proper copyright notice, it falls into the public domain unless ownership of copyright is proclaimed. This is why it is important for an author, artist, or composer to place a copyright declaration on any work before it is released or shown in public. A copyright declaration takes the form of a statement of the author's name, claim of copyright, the copyright symbol, and the year of publication. If a work is illegally or inadvertently published, a creator must act swiftly to assert copyright to avoid the loss of copyright to the public domain.

The new information technologies like the World Wide Web, e-mail, and a world of new media developments place the concepts and functions of copyright in a new light. In the so-called knowledge economy, where so much business is based on the transaction and sale of information, copyright is more important than ever.

Digital technology makes easy the copying and redistributing of works without quality degradation. Previous copying technologies like photocopiers and tape recorders invariably diluted the quality of each copy. Napster, the online music-swapping service that made copies of music recordings available for free, is a key example. It came under fierce legal attack by the recording industry for copyright infringements and has been used to justify further strengthening of copyright protections in the digital age.

The 1998 Digital Millennium Copyright Act (DMCA) extended legal protections for software and content producers by forbidding unauthorized copying of digital works. In certain circumstances, making or selling devices that are capable of either copying or circumventing the protections of copyrighted works is also a crime under the DMCA. The law provides some exemptions for libraries, archival databases, and educational institutions.

Whatever its intent, the DMCA sparked controversy among civil liberties groups, digital-device manufacturers, and content users. Critics argue that the law does not merely extend previous copyright protection to digital media, but that

Copyright Registration[1] by Subject Matter 1995 to 2007
(in thousands)

Subject matter	1995	2000	2007
Monographs[2]	196.0	169.7	198.6
Semiconductor chip products	0.8	0.7	–
Serials	88.7	69.0	52.6
Sound recordings	34.0	34.2	53.6
Renewals	30.6	16.8	1.4
Musical and dramatic works	163.6	138.9	130.6
Visual arts[3]	95.5	85.8	89.3
Total	609.2	515.1	526.1

[1] Claims to copyrights registered with the U.S. Library of Congress for both U.S. and foreign works.
[2] Includes software and machine-readable works. [3] Two-dimensional works of fine and graphic art, including prints and art reproductions; sculptural works; technical drawings and models; photographs; commercial prints and labels; works of applied arts, cartographic works, and multimedia works.
Source: The Library of Congress, Copyright Office, Annual Report, Washington, D.C.

Peer-to-Peer File Sharing and Copyright

Companies that market file-sharing software over peer-to-peer networks, such as Napster and Grokster, have been sued by major entertainment companies, alleging that they induce copyright infringement.

The music file-sharing computer service Napster is universally recognized for launching peer-to-peer (P2P) networking into the mainstream. While its foes argued that Napster facilitated copyright violations on a monumental scale, supporters call it a bellwether program that will be remembered as the beginning of a revolution. College freshman Shawn Fanning began work on what would become the Napster program in his Northeastern University dorm room in January 1999. Fanning set about creating a system that would allow users to swap songs in the MP3 computer file format directly from one to another, without having to go through a Web site. Users who launched the program while connected to the Internet were plugged into Napster's central computer system, and the MP3 files they had designated to share were added to Napster's continuously updated index of files available at that moment. Napster did not store MP3s but only indexed files that were stored on its users' own computers. If users disconnected from Napster, their files were no longer available and were removed from the index.

The music industry, which had been steadily losing ground in its fight to halt unauthorized MP3 trading, saw Napster as a formidable threat. In December 1999, the Recording Industry Association of America (RIAA), a trade group representing the major music companies, sued Napster, charging that the company facilitated piracy. Recording artists chose sides in the debate. Hard-rock band Metallica and rapper Dr. Dre filed their own piracy suits against the company, while rapper Chuck D defended Napster, and rap-metal band Limp Bizkit embraced the company as a sponsor. By 2001 Napster had been driven out of business by legal problems.

The entertainment industry continued to pursue copyright infringement over P2P networks; by 2006 the RIAA had sued more than 20,000 individuals for sharing music over P2P networks. Using a power of supoena embedded in the Digital Millennium Copyright Act (DMCA), the RIAA was able to force ISPs to reveal the names and addresses of clients using P2P networks. In 2005, another peer-to-peer network, Grokster, closed down after being sued by a consortium of 28 major entertainment companies led this time by a film studio, Metro-Goldwyn-Mayer (MGM). The case reached the Supreme Court, which ruled in favor of MGM. In the wake of legal action, P2P file sharing is largely limited to works in the public domain.

However, the legality of such behavior is, in fact, brought into question by provisions of the DMCA. The DMCA provides severe punishment: fines range as high as $500,000 and five years in prison for a first offense, up to $1 million and 10 years in prison for subsequent offenses.

Not everyone is concerned about the threat DMCA poses to civil liberties. Analyst P. J. McNeely, for instance, has suggested that a free market will eventually determine the limits of the DMCA. If copyright protection and legal sanctions are enforced beyond the public's tolerance, McNeely told the Newsbytes News Network in 2001, consumers will simply refuse to buy new digital media products and continue buying older products—opting to purchase paperbacks instead of e-books, for example. They will, in short, "vote with their wallets," McNeely says.

Another future battleground will likely be the issue of copyright extension. In 1998 Congress passed the Sonny Bono Copyright Extension Act to extend the terms of copyright protection, bringing U.S. law into line with European laws. However, critics such as Lawrence Lessig have argued that the law protects corporate interests at the expense of individual users.

Further Research

Creative Commons

creativecommons.org

Creative Commons is a nonprofit organization that provides licenses that work alongside copyright to facilitate sharing in the public domain.

Electronic Frontier Foundation

www.eff.org

The EFF is a nonprofit organization that promotes the public interest in debates over digital rights.

Stanford University Libraries: Copyright and Fair Use

fairuse.stanford.edu

This Web site offers overviews of copyright law and practice as well as primary documents.

U.S. Copyright Office

www.copyright.gov

The home page of the Copyright Office provides essential information as well as links to register copyright.

—Ken Friedman

it supersedes old copyright protections and, in some cases, cancels the public's traditionally guaranteed rights to fair use of copyrighted material. Fair use is a legal doctrine that allows individuals to duplicate copyrighted material without compensating the copyright holder if the copied material is used for education, research, criticism, or certain other purposes. The fair use doctrine suggests that such common acts as making copies of software programs to use on a second household computer or "ripping" tracks from CDs to make compilations for personal listening would be protected.

Cost of Living

Young people often hear older people talk about the "good old days" when gasoline cost a nickel a gallon and new homes sold for under $20,000. Did people in previous generations have a higher standard of living because they paid prices that seem low compared with the prices we pay today? Absolute prices (prices measured simply in dollars, unadjusted for the effects of inflation or changes in income levels) were lower in the past. The real question is whether relative prices (prices adjusted for inflation and income) were lower. Economists use a cost-of-living index to answer this question.

Cost-of-living indexes are mechanisms for measuring and comparing how much income (or money) is needed to acquire a specific quantity of goods and services over a given time, or to achieve a certain standard of living in a specific country or area. Thus, cost of living compares income at a given time to average prices at a given time. For example, if, on average, a smaller percentage of a family's income is needed to buy a house today than the percentage needed to buy a house in an earlier time, the cost of living may be lower today than it was during the "good old days," even though houses cost more in absolute or unadjusted dollars.

Because cost of living is a ratio of average prices to average income level, it is closely linked to inflation (the changes in the average price of goods and services over time). The cost of living is often represented by a price index like the Consumer Price Index (CPI). The CPI in the United States has been compiled by the Bureau of Labor Statistics (BLS) since 1890. It measures the changing cost of a specific market basket of goods and services (a loaf of bread, a pair of jeans, and a movie ticket, for example) that many consumers need and purchase. An increase in the CPI indicates that the cost of this market basket of goods and services has increased, and so, too, has the cost of living (unless average incomes have increased at the same rate). Thus when the CPI rises, consumers tend to pay more.

Changes in the CPI are often used to determine cost-of-living adjustments (COLAs) to people's salaries and to other income payments. The BLS estimates that CPI-based COLAs affect the income of about 80 million individuals, including food stamp recipients, military and federal Civil Service retirees and survivors, and more than two million private-sector workers. In 2001, for example, 48.4 million Social Security beneficiaries received a CPI-based COLA.

Cost of living is also linked to the concept of purchasing power (the amount of goods and services that can be purchased with a given amount of money). Purchasing power declines as prices rise. Because rising inflation indicates higher prices, inflation leads to falling purchasing power. When purchasing

Social Security payments include automatic benefit increases to adjust for increases in the cost of living. These increases, also known as cost-of-living adjustments (COLAs), have been in effect since 1975.

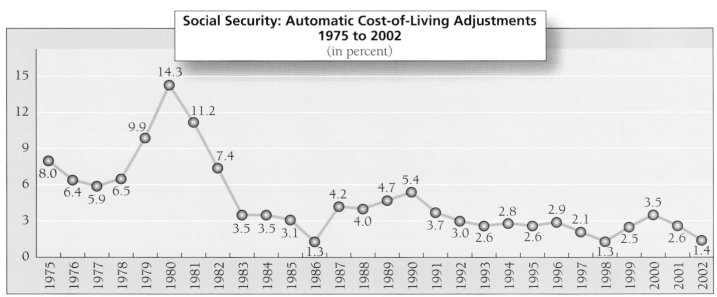

Source: Social Security Administration.

Basket of Goods: 1930 versus 2001

Item	1930 retail price[1]	Hours of labor needed (1930)[2]	2001 retail price[3]	Hours of labor needed (2001)[4]	Percent change in retail price	Percent change in hours of labor needed
Men's wool suit with vest	$23.50	42.73	$169.99	10.88	623.36%	−74.55%
Men's leather oxford dress shoes	4.95	9.00	65.00	4.16	1213.13%	−53.79%
Set of golf clubs (3 woods, 9 irons)	32.85	59.73	199.00	12.73	505.78%	−78.68%
Living room set (sofa, two chairs)	130.70	237.64	1,199.00	76.71	817.37%	−67.72%
Refrigerator (18.5 cu. ft.)	45.25	82.27	449.95	28.79	894.36%	−65.01%
Upright vacuum cleaner (12 amps)	29.95	54.45	149.95	9.59	400.67%	−82.38%
Gallon interior paint (semi-gloss enamel)	2.70	4.91	16.99	1.09	529.26%	−77.86%
Bayer® aspirin (100 tablets)	.98	1.78	5.79	0.37	490.82%	−79.21%
Orange juice (48 oz.)	.59	1.07	2.59	0.17	338.98%	−84.55%
Extra-virgin olive oil (16 oz.)	.45	0.82	3.99	0.26	786.67%	−68.80%
Cookies (1 lb. box, assorted)	.29	0.53	3.39	0.22	1068.97%	−58.87%
Package of chewing gum	.03	0.05	.59	0.04	1866.67%	−30.80%
Box of chocolates (mixed)	.59	1.07	4.79	.31	711.86	−71.43%
Totals for basket	**$272.83**	**496.05**	**$2271.02**	**145.30**	**732.39%**	**−70.71%**

Notes: [1] 1930 retail prices taken from the 1930 Sears, Roebuck catalog. [2] Hours of labor—at 1930 average wage rate of $0.55/hour—needed to earn the retail price of item. [3] 2001 prices taken from Sears.com Web site or other similar retail outlet. [4] Hours of labor—at 2000 average wage rate of $15.36/hour—needed to earn the retail price of item.
Sources: U.S. Department of Labor Bureau of Labor Statistics, *National Compensation Survey: Occupational Wages in the United States, 1999*, Washington, D.C., 2001.
U.S. Department of Labor Bureau of Labor Statistics, *Employment, Hours, and Earnings: United States, 1909–1984*, Washington, D.C., 1985.

To assess changes in the cost of living from one year to the next, we need to compare prices for a similar basket of goods commonly purchased by a typical family. In the table, the prices for such a basket are compared for 1930 and 2001. Prices for goods in this particular basket were more than seven times higher in 2001 than they were for the same goods in 1930.

However, cost of living is a ratio of average prices to average income level. Therefore, to compare the cost of living in 2001 with that of 1930, we must also account for changes in the average income level over this time. According to the U.S. Bureau of Labor Statistics (2001), the average wage paid to workers in 1930 was $0.55/hour. By 2000, the average wage had risen to $15.36/hour, a nearly 28-fold increase over 1930 wages.

In measuring the cost of living, changes in prices and changes in wages can be accounted for by determining the number of hours a worker would have to work to earn the income needed to purchase a specific good or service. Although the prices for the goods in this basket rose steeply between 1930 and 2001, the amount of work (in hours) needed to purchase the basket fell by more than two-thirds. Thus, despite price increases, U.S. consumers in 2001 can buy the same basket of goods for less effort than was required in 1930. The real cost of living has dropped.

power falls, the cost of living tends to rise: if one dollar buys less than it used to buy (has less purchasing power), then a consumer will need more dollars to buy the same basket of goods and services.

The cost of living varies from city to city and from state to state. In the United States, for example, Alaska has the highest cost of living; Arkansas has the lowest. The American Chamber of Commerce Researchers Association

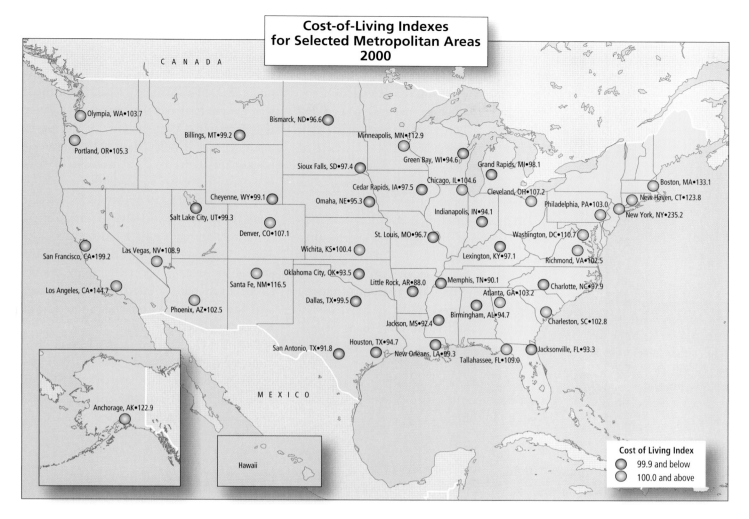

Cost-of-Living Indexes for Selected Metropolitan Areas 2000

Olympia, WA•103.7
Portland, OR•105.3
Billings, MT•99.2
Bismarck, ND•96.6
Minneapolis, MN•112.9
Green Bay, WI•94.6
Grand Rapids, MI•98.1
Boston, MA•133.1
Sioux Falls, SD•97.4
Cedar Rapids, IA•97.5
Chicago, IL•104.6
Cleveland, OH•107.2
New Haven, CT•123.8
Cheyenne, WY•99.1
Omaha, NE•95.3
Philadelphia, PA•103.0
New York, NY•235.2
Salt Lake City, UT•99.3
Indianapolis, IN•94.1
San Francisco, CA•199.2
Las Vegas, NV•108.9
Denver, CO•107.1
Wichita, KS•100.4
St. Louis, MO•96.7
Washington, DC•110.7
Los Angeles, CA•144.7
Lexington, KY•97.1
Richmond, VA•102.5
Santa Fe, NM•116.5
Oklahoma City, OK•93.5
Little Rock, AR•88.0
Memphis, TN•90.1
Charlotte, NC•97.9
Phoenix, AZ•102.5
Atlanta, GA•103.2
Dallas, TX•99.5
Birmingham, AL•94.7
Charleston, SC•102.8
Jackson, MS•92.4
San Antonio, TX•91.8
Houston, TX•94.7
New Orleans, LA•99.3
Jacksonville, FL•93.3
Tallahassee, FL•109.0

Anchorage, AK•122.9

Hawaii

Cost of Living Index
○ 99.9 and below
○ 100.0 and above

(ACCRA) sets the cost-of-living index. For purposes of comparison, ACCRA sets the median state's, New Mexico, cost of living index to equal 100. Thus, the cost-of-living index in Alaska for the year 2000 was 125.7, or 25.7 percent higher than the cost of living in New Mexico. For Arkansas, the cost-of-living index for 2000 was 92.3. Thus to maintain the same standard of living, an accountant from Arkansas who wants to take an accounting job in Alaska must be prepared to negotiate a higher salary for the Alaska job; to maintain her standard of living (to acquire the same basket of goods), the accountant will have to negotiate a salary in Alaska that is nearly 40 percent higher than her current salary in Arkansas.

Cost of living varies widely around the world. Some countries with significantly lower costs of living than the United States include Colombia and Hungary; countries with significantly higher costs of living than the United States include Switzerland and Argentina. While many factors contribute to these higher (or lower) costs of living, the basic question is still the same: What is the relative price of the same basket of goods in one country compared with another?

The standard of living for a person or a nation depends upon that person's or nation's capacity to consume goods and services. That capacity is determined, to a large extent, by the average relative prices facing that person or nation. The higher the average relative prices, the less consumption possible—all other things, including income, being equal. As economic growth is dependent on consumption, economists need to measure trends in the cost of living to determine and analyze growth trends.

Further Research
Bureau of Labor Statistics: Consumer Price Index
www.bls.gov/CPI

—Phillip J. VanFossen

In addition to preparing cost-of-living indexes (COLIs) for states, the American Chamber of Commerce Researchers Association also reports COLIs for selected metropolitan areas.

Credit

In the simplest terms, credit is a promise to pay. Sometimes credit is extended based on collateral, which is a tangible asset like a car or a house. Other times, credit is extended based on earnings potential of a business or individual. In both cases, credit is extended on the basis of character—that is, how likely a borrower is to repay the loan.

When a lending institution extends credit, it creates both an asset and a liability on its balance sheet. The asset is the interest it hopes to receive on the amount lent. The liability is the amount of money given to the borrower. In an ideal world, borrowers would repay their loans in full, including the interest. In the real world, borrowers default, go bankrupt, and get behind in payments. Lending institutions must balance the risk of lending with the reward of profit.

Brief History of Modern Banking

Originally, banks were independent operations. They could practice investment banking alongside commercial banking, and many did. Their primary lending business was commercial paper. Commercial paper is a short-term loan (usually 30–90 days) made to businesses. These loans are used to pay for items like an increase in seasonal inventory. Banks used other available funds for investing in bonds and the stock market. Banks were legally prohibited from making real estate loans because real estate loans were not considered liquid enough to sustain normal banking operations. Each bank issued its own money, and the money was only as good as the bank that issued it.

During the Civil War, the federal government stepped in and created a national currency (National Currency Act, 1863) and a national bank (National Bank Act, 1864). The purpose for creating these was to sell

An illustration from the Civil War era. Inside the U.S. Treasury, then located on Wall Street in New York City, people buy the first-ever U.S. bonds, which were issued by the government to raise money for the war.

In 1930 worried customers line up to withdraw their money from the Bowery Savings Bank in New York City.

bonds to finance the war. In effect, the nation's debt was tied to its currency—a relationship that still exists and influences inflation, interest rates, credit, and the amount of money in circulation.

Although the national currency could be cashed in (for gold) at any national bank or at the national Treasury, there was no federal guarantee of the solvency of those banks. Such guarantee would come in 1933, with the creation of the Federal Deposit Insurance Corporation (FDIC). Prior to 1933, if a bank made bad decisions on extending credit, the bank would have to close when it ran out of funds.

Before the creation of the FDIC, the Federal Reserve Act of 1913 had established a system of 12 federal banks that functioned as a central banking system. These banks were to hold the idle reserves of national and county banks as a backup for banks in crisis. These 12 banks were located across the nation so that all other banks were within one day's travel of a Federal Reserve bank. If customers wanted their cash from a bank that did not have enough cash on hand, that bank could take its commercial paper and cash it in within 24 hours.

During and after the Great Depression, the economy came to a standstill because consumers were afraid to spend money, borrow money, or to put money in banks. By 1933, business had recovered somewhat, but consumers were still reluctant. The FDIC was created in 1933 to boost consumer confidence and to get people borrowing and spending again. Even with the guarantee that the federal government would back up money in any member bank, people still held on to their money. Not until after World War II did consumer borrowing and spending rise enough to rejuvenate the economy.

Another early piece of legislation that shaped credit in the United States is the Banking Act of 1935. This act changed the financial structure of the country by centralizing power within the Federal Reserve Board in Washington, D.C.; until then, most of the banking powerhouses were located in downtown Manhattan. The move marked the evolution from private banking to public banking and moved the Federal Reserve (often called the Fed) from banking into a regulatory function. The Fed now controlled interest rates, cash reserves, and some aspects

Lines of consumer credit can be accessed via credit cards.

of investment banking. Meanwhile the Banking Act loosened the requirements for real estate lending, marking a move from short-term, liquid lending to longer-term lending on hard-to-move assets.

The post–World War II era brought another round of changes in the lending environment. By 1950, Diners' Club had come out with the first modern credit card. No-down-payment loans became popular, along with federally guaranteed home mortgages (amortized to make them profitable for the lending institution), and personal loans with easier terms. In the second half of the twentieth century, this relaxation of lending terms resulted in much higher debt burdens, both for the consumer and commercial interests. The economy benefited because mass production requires mass consumption. As consumers bought more homes, cars, and products, businesses had to expand, hire more people, and buy more supplies to keep up with the demand. Both businesses and consumers needed loans to manage those increases. The economy picked up and, even though it has experienced a few recessions, has continued to grow into the early twenty-first century. The availability of easy credit has fueled much of this growth.

The Gold Standard

The ready availability of credit is partly attributable to the switch from the gold standard to our current system. From 1879 to 1932, all U.S. money was tied to the gold standard. Gold backed the currency and could be bought at a set price: $20.67 per ounce. At any time, individuals could go to a bank and demand their money in gold. When the gold was taken out of the banks and ultimately the Treasury, interest rates rose, causing the country to go into a recession.

In 1932, the United States switched to a gold-exchange standard. Instead of the dollar being backed only by gold, it was now backed by both gold and commercial paper. Using commercial paper, or short-term loans, for collateral, implied that good loans were the same as "money in the bank," or in the Federal Reserve, to be exact. This expanded the amount of currency available in the United States, but the international markets still held to a semblance of the gold standard. A foreign government could still convert its dollars into gold from the Treasury. Gold was still leaving the country, decreasing the federal reserves.

In 1971 President Richard Nixon signed a bill that halted the conversion of dollars into gold, even for foreign countries. This, in effect, ended any ties to the original gold standard. From that point on, the dollar has been backed by the solvency of the U.S. government; the dollar is legal tender simply because the government says it is. Its value expands and contracts with the economy. This enables the Federal Reserve to control the amount of money in circulation by extending or restricting the extension of credit.

Commercial Lending

The U.S. economy is strong because of the nation's industrial supremacy. However, industrial supremacy depends on mass production, which depends on mass consumption, which depends on mass credit—to both businesses and the consumer. Supply (production) and demand (consumption) working together properly lead to more jobs, which may result in more potential borrowers.

The corporate tax structure of the United States heavily favors debt financing over equity capital. For example, interest paid on corporate debt is tax deductible but dividends paid out are not only taxed, but also taxed twice, first to the corporation and then to the shareholder who receives them. In other words, it pays to be in debt.

Debt can take many forms—commercial paper, construction loans, business loans, or bonds. Lending institutions must decide how much risk is involved in lending to a particular business. In the past, that risk was determined by past financial performance or a close examination of a company's finances, particularly for small businesses. Lenders have now turned to risk ratings of business owners. Personal credit history is a good indicator of how a small-business owner will pay the company's bills. Risk ratings compare personal credit history against other borrowers who fit the same profile. These profiles are created by companies that specialize in risk ratings. Lenders can purchase risk ratings on anyone with a personal credit history. Lending with this method gives the bank a better idea of the potential risk and eliminates the need for extensive study of a company's financial statements.

Companies can also become borrowers by issuing bonds. They sell bonds to investors at a specific interest rate. When the bonds mature, the company redeems the bonds at the stated rate. Bonds give companies the opportunity to raise capital without using a lending institution. The interest paid is determined by the current interest rate. The main issue for the company is convincing investors that the company is a good risk.

Consumerism, Credit, and the Economy
In one sense, consumer spending drives the economy. As evidenced by the economy's virtual standstill during the Great

Credit Time Line

1863–1864 National Currency Act and National Bank Act are passed to help finance the Civil War.

1913 The Federal Reserve Act creates a central banking system.

1929 The stock market crash signals the onset of the Great Depression.

1932 United States switches to a gold-exchange standard; the dollar is backed by both gold and commercial paper (short-term loans).

1933 In the wake of mass bank failures, the Federal Deposit Insurance Corporation (FDIC) is created.

1935 The Banking Act centralizes financial power within the Federal Reserve.

1950 Diners' Club issues the first modern credit card.

1971 Nixon administration terminates the gold standard.

Web Resources on Credit

www.ncua.gov, Web page of the National Credit Union Administration, is an independent federal agency that charters and supervises federal credit unions.

www.equifax.com, the home page of one of the largest credit reporting services; it also provides global financial services.

www.nfcc.org, the home page of the National Foundation for Credit Counseling, the largest nonprofit credit counseling service provider in the United States.

www.ftc.gov/os/statutes/fcra.htm features the complete text of the Fair Credit Reporting Act, which requires accuracy and fairness in credit reporting.

www.farmcredit.com, the home page of an agency that provides credit and financial services to farmers and ranchers.

Depression and for more than a decade after, consumer spending and borrowing depend on consumer confidence in the financial future. When fear sets in, people stop spending. When consumers stop spending, the economy slows and finally grinds to a halt. Banks actually see an increase in deposits as people begin saving for an uncertain future.

In the early twenty-first century, the amount of money Americans spend far outweighs the amount of money they take home in a paycheck or in investment income. The reason they can do so is credit. Credit comes in a variety of forms—mortgages, car loans, personal loans, student loans, and credit cards. Over time, lending institutions and the federal government have eased the requirements for extending credit by offering easy terms and requiring little or no down payment. The federal government's backing of loans gives confidence to both the borrower and the lender. Credit profiling permits easier identification of potential financial deadbeats. More credit has been and can be extended to more people.

Credit issuance was central to the economic downturn that began in the United States in 2008. During a "credit boom" in 2006 and 2007, mortgage and other consumer loans were issued to many people who eventually defaulted on their payments. In the wake of mass defaults, banks stopped their lending, which meant that American consumers curtailed their spending, particularly on high-priced items such as automobiles. The Federal Reserve responded by launching programs to encourage banks to resume consumer lending, in part by offering government backing for consumer loans.

The question arises: Why would so many people go into debt so easily? The short explanation is the American Dream—the dream of owning a home, nice cars and furnishings, and to have money for leisure activities. Many Americans have come to view this dream as their rightful heritage. More and more, that dream is within reach through credit.

The perceived upside of consumer credit is that it allows individuals to increase their social status through the accumulation of more and better goods. If consumer credit is managed well by using it for investment purposes, for example, purchasing a home, it can increase a person's net worth. Once the loan is repaid (provided the homeowner remains in possession long enough to see the home's price increase), the home becomes an asset with real value.

However, if consumer credit is used to purchase consumable goods, it actually decreases a person's net worth. Automobiles, which appear to be an asset, depreciate rapidly. As a car ages, it becomes a liability as repairs are more necessary and more frequent. The amount of interest paid on those kinds of loans increases the price of those goods tremendously and with little or nothing to show for it in the end.

Credit is a double-edged sword. On the one hand, easy availability entices consumers to borrow and spend, which increases demand, which turns the wheels of production and boosts the economy. This upward cycle points to prosperity all around. On the other hand, unwise use of credit can turn prosperity to poverty for some when individuals or businesses overextend themselves to the point of financial ruin. The wisest use of credit is to increase net worth while borrowing at the lowest interest rate possible.

—*Stephanie Buckwalter*

Credit Cards and Debit Cards

Credit cards are used in millions of transactions each year. Consumers use credit cards to buy all kinds of goods, to buy food, and for large purchases like appliances and travel. Businesses also rely on credit card transactions for purchases and sales. A whole industry has developed focused on credit cards, debit cards, and electronic transfers of funds. Companies in this industry offer, manage, and manufacture the products and services used in the credit card industry.

What is a credit card? It is a small plastic card containing a means of personal identification and account information. The card authorizes the person named on it to charge purchases using his or her account. Each month, the holder of the card receives a bill based on those charges. Most credit cards are issued by banks, retail stores, or gas companies. Visa and MasterCard are the largest of the bank-card companies. Sears offers the Discover Card. Not-for-profit organizations and even professional baseball and football teams have begun to issue credit cards.

Plastic Money?: The Nature of Credit Cards

Some people refer to credit cards as plastic money. When they do, however, they are making a mistake. Credit cards are not money. One characteristic of money is that money is a medium of exchange. By itself, a credit card is not a payment for a good or service; it is a promise to pay. A credit card transaction is most often a loan made by the card issuer to the cardholder. Like other loans, credit card loans must be repaid. After a grace period (often 25 days) during which interest is not charged, consumers pay interest on the balance they owe until it is paid off.

It is common today for young people as well as adults to use credit cards. Many teenagers about to enter college receive unsolicited credit cards in the mail. Parents often want young people to learn about credit cards, but they also worry about the potential for abuse. Secured credit cards are popular with people who are new to using credit cards and with those who have a bad credit history. A secured credit loan involves making a deposit to a bank or other financial institution. The credit limit of the credit card may equal the amount deposited.

Credit limits are among the several factors to consider when obtaining and using a credit card. A higher credit limit gives the cardholder increased flexibility but can also lead to high balances owed, which can be difficult to pay off. Other considerations include the interest rates charged on the unpaid balance and other fees imposed by the credit card issuer.

Interest rates can vary from card issuer to card issuer by several percentage points. Some credit card companies offer a low annual percentage rate (APR) of interest for the first few months of card use and then increase the rate. Card users likely to keep a high balance on their accounts should consider shopping for a low APR.

However, interest rates may be related to fees. Obtaining a low interest rate might require payment of a high annual fee to the card issuer. Card users who pay their balance in full every month might benefit from using a higher-interest card if it comes with a low annual fee or no fee. Other fees may include charges for late or missed payments, charges for exceeding credit limits, and charges made for cash withdrawals.

Choosing a Credit Card

Credit cards differ in kinds of services. Variations to consider when choosing a card include:
1. Interest rates on purchases and cash advances;
2. Whether an annual membership fee is required;
3. The number of merchants who accept the card;
4. Length of grace period before interest is charged;
5. Rewards for the cardholder including cash-back payments, gifts, frequent flyer miles, or discounts on certain purchases;
6. Travel services like covering the insurance deductible on rental cars, discounts on hotels, travel life insurance, or check cashing privileges.

Protection and Regulation

Credit cards contain valuable information, including the cardholder's name, account number, and the card's expiration date. This information can be misused if it falls into the wrong hands. Some people discover after loss or theft of a credit card that it has been used within hours to purchase thousands of dollars worth of goods. Cardholders are advised, accordingly, to use their cards carefully—never giving account information to a telephone solicitor or to people or organizations (online or in person) with whom they are not familiar—and to report lost or stolen cards promptly.

To further protect consumers, credit card loans are regulated by state and federal laws. The Equal Credit Opportunity Act, for example, was passed to ensure that all consumers have an equal chance to receive credit. The Equal Credit Opportunity Act makes it illegal to discriminate against credit applicants on the basis of sex, marital status, race, national origin, religion, age, or because they receive public assistance.

The Truth-in-Lending Act requires that creditors disclose the cost of credit in simple terms. The lender must state the percentage costs of borrowing in terms of the annual percentage rate (APR). The Truth-in-Lending Act also protects against unauthorized use of credit cards. If your card is lost or stolen, you are liable for not more than $50 of unauthorized charges, provided you report the lost or stolen card promptly. After notification, you cannot be held responsible for any unauthorized charges.

History of the Credit Card Industry

During the 1920s some individual firms, oil companies and hotels among them, began issuing credit cards to customers for direct purchases of goods and services. These early credit cards simply extended the revolving charge accounts many businesses had offered to customers. Use of credit cards increased greatly after World War II as more Americans began to travel. Credit cards were a convenience to consumers who purchased goods and services from large national hotel chains and oil companies.

The next step was to introduce universal credit cards; a universal card was one that could be used with different, unrelated businesses. The first credit cards were actually charge cards. Charge cards require the holder to pay off the balance in full each billing cycle. The cardholder paid an annual fee to use the card, but did not pay interest if the bill was paid on time. In 1950 the Diners' Club issued a charge card that could be used in different restaurants, not merely those owned by one company. The American Express Company soon followed, establishing a major universal charge card in 1958. American Express contracted with businesses whereby participating merchants agreed to pay a service charge to American Express for credit card transactions. In turn, participating merchants hoped that the convenience of using the card would attract additional customers to their businesses.

The credit card industry changed dramatically when banks entered the picture. People in the banking industry took note of the success of American Express and other credit card firms. Bankers recognized that credit cards could become the

---

The Equal Credit Opportunity Act

The Equal Credit Opportunity Act was passed in 1974 to abolish discriminatory practices in consumer lending. For example, in deciding whether to extend credit to an individual, a company may not:

- Consider gender, race, marital status, national origin, or religion;
- Consider the race of the people in the neighborhood where the applicant wishes to buy, refinance, or improve a house with borrowed money;
- Consider age, unless
  (a) the applicant is under 18
  (b) the applicant is over 62 and the creditor will favor the applicant because of age
  (c) it is used as part of a valid scoring system to determine overall credit (for example, if an applicant is close to retirement age, his income might be expected to drop);
- Refuse to consider public assistance income the same way as other income;
- Discount income because of sex or marital status. For example, a creditor cannot count a man's salary at 100 percent and a woman's at 75 percent. A creditor may not assume a woman of childbearing age will stop working to raise children;
- Discount or refuse to consider income because it comes from part-time employment or pension, annuity, or retirement benefit programs;
- Refuse to consider regular alimony, child support, or separate maintenance payments.

basis for making highly convenient and widespread loans to consumers. Banks began issuing credit cards and soon formed associations to act as clearinghouses for transactions and to promote their own card brands. Banks are now consolidated into two major associations of card issuers, Visa and MasterCard.

The process of credit card transactions has changed greatly since the 1950s and 1960s. Originally a small metal plate similar to the license you might find on the collar of a dog was embossed with the name, address, and account number of the customer. Businesses purchased machines that would imprint the customer information onto charge slips. This technology has been replaced for the most part by the magnetic stripe on credit cards. Cards with magnetic stripes permitted merchants and eventually cardholders to register a transaction simply by swiping a credit card

The Truth-in-Lending Act

Originally enacted in July 1969 as part of the Consumer Protection Act, the Truth-in-Lending Act (TILA) requires that lenders clearly and accurately disclose the terms of the credit they extend. The law also provides consumers with a chance to back out of certain loans within a certain time frame.

The most important aspect of TILA for consumers is probably Regulation Z, which covers credit cards, personal loans, home mortgages, and other forms of consumer debt. Under Regulation Z, lenders must disclose the following information:
- Finance Charge, or the amount charged to the consumer for the credit;
- Amount Financed, or the amount that is being borrowed;
- Total of Payments, or the total amount of the periodic payments required;
- Total Sales Price, or the total cost of the purchase on credit, including the down payment and periodic payments;
- Annual Percentage Rate (APR), or the cost of the credit on a yearly basis.

The APR is important because it enables consumers to easily compare one credit offer with another. Companies that do not comply with the TILA can be sued by consumers. If a TILA violation is proven in court, sizable fines can be imposed.

through an electronic recording-and-transfer device. The magnetic stripe contains the account number of the cardholder. It allows merchants to enter and verify

Actress Anna Maria Alberghetti points to oversized Diners' Club card being held by Jules Podell, the director of the Copacabana nightclub (left), and Diners' Club chairman Ralph Schneider.

Credit Cards and Debit Cards   61

Boys buying sports gear with a credit card.

account numbers rapidly and accurately. Magnetic stripes offer three key advantages: They reduce transaction costs by reducing paperwork; they increase the number of transactions that can be handled; and they reduce the danger of credit card fraud.

The expansion of electronic transfers of funds has continued to bring changes and growth to the credit card industry. A major change came with the introduction and proliferation of automated teller machines (ATMs). ATMs had originally been a convenient service for people living in urban areas. When systems were developed to provide automated teller services in remote locations, people in small towns, rural areas, and travelers abroad gained access to ATM services.

Since 1989 the number of Americans with at least one credit card has increased steadily.

General Purpose Credit Cards 1992 to 2004

Year	Percent of families with general purpose credit card	Median number of cards	Median balance	Percent who:		
				Almost always pay off the balance	Sometimes pay off the balance	Hardly ever pay off the balance
1992	62.4	2	$1,100	53.0	19.6	27.4
1995	66.4	2	$1,800	52.4	20.1	27.5
1998	67.5	2	$2,200	53.8	19.3	26.9
2004	71.5	2	$2,100	55.7	20.3	24.0

Note: General purpose credit cards include MasterCard, Visa, Optima, and Discover cards. Excludes cards used only for business purposes. All dollar figures are in constant 1998 dollars.
Source: Board of Governors of the Federal Reserve System.

Debit Cards

As more and more merchants came to accept credit cards and ATMs became more widely available, the stage was set for the emergence of the debit card, a recent arrival on the plastic card scene. A bank issues a debit card to provide consumers with electronic access to the funds in their accounts. The procedure for using a debit card closely resembles the procedure for using a credit card. In each case, consumers hand the card to the cashier or swipe it themselves through the card-reading device.

Two important differences exist between credit cards and debit cards. First, a debit card allows a consumer to pay for a purchase through an immediate deduction from his or her checking account. Using the debit card is thus very similar to writing a check. In fact, debit cards are rapidly replacing checks as a method of payment. Debit cards are generally more convenient because they are more widely accepted than personal checks. Debit cards can also be used to withdraw cash from ATMs.

The second difference is that, unlike credit cards, debit cards do not provide consumers with the advantage of a "float" on their money. Float refers to the period between the time when a check is written and the time when it is cashed (the money would earn interest in that interval). Credit-card holders receive float for the 25 days they are not charged interest on purchases. As payment for the debit card transaction is withdrawn immediately from a checking account, there is no float in a debit card transaction.

Are debit cards plastic money? When consumers use debit cards for purchases, they are basically instructing the banks involved to transfer money directly from their checking accounts to the stores' bank accounts. Use of a debit card does not create a loan, as is usually the case in a credit card transaction; in effect, debit card account money is checking account money. In this respect, debit cards really are plastic money.

The credit card and debit card industry will almost certainly continue to expand and change. International use is widespread. E-commerce on the Internet has opened new opportunities for online merchants to accept credit cards and new challenges for banks and processors to provide secure and compliant transaction services.

A woman pays for groceries with a debit card; she inputs her personal identification number (PIN) on the keypad, just as she would if she were taking money out of an ATM.

Further Research

Creditcards.com

www.creditcards.com

A free online resource that compares credit cards and debit cards from various issuers and provides news and advice.

Federal Reserve

www.federalreserve.gov/consumerinfo

The government agency provides information about consumer credit and collects statistics about credit card and debit card use.

—*Mark C. Schug*

Credit History

Anyone who has filled out a credit application has a credit history. The information on credit applications is sent to a credit reporting agency (CRA) to verify the information submitted and to acquire any additional information about a requestor's ability to take on debt. If no information currently exists on that requestor, a credit file is created for future use, even if the credit application is not approved.

The credit file serves two purposes. First, it gives basic information about the requestor, salary and address, for instance. The next time a credit application comes through, it will be checked to see if any information has changed. If so, the CRA tracks those changes. The second purpose benefits only the CRA. CRAs sell information to third parties from their databases. Legally they are not allowed to sell credit payment information, but the basic "header" information is fair game. Header information typically includes full name, birth date, current and previous employer, position, current and two previous addresses, marital status, and spouse's name.

This information can be sold to anyone who wants to pay for it, including direct marketing firms, information brokers who resell it to others, lawyers, or private detectives.

In addition to the header, a credit file contains payment history information. Most of the payment information is from lenders who are paid monthly, for example, credit and charge card issuers and lending institutions that hold mortgages or any other kind of loan. The information provided by the lender includes how long the borrower takes to make a payment—30, 60, 90, or 120 days. When the borrower is involved in a bankruptcy or dispute, that becomes part of the credit file, too. Other kinds of businesses may file a report with the CRA for a borrower who is seriously delinquent in paying or when the account is turned over to a collection agency. These include local merchants, landlords, utility companies, medical and other professional service providers, and child support delinquencies in excess of $1,000.

Two more items go into a credit file: the names of creditors and others who have requested a copy of your information and public record information. Although public records are just that—information that is available to anyone—CRAs pay other companies to collect that information to include in credit files. The public records searched relate to a potential borrower's ability to repay loans. Public records include liens, bankruptcies, foreclosures, criminal records, divorce, and legal judgments.

The Importance of Credit History

What does all this information mean and who looks at it? The primary audience for a credit history report is lenders. Lenders want to know how safe it is to lend money. Bad loans mean lost revenue. Although a borrower does not have to have a perfect credit history to get a loan or receive credit, the lender has to balance the good credit risks against the bad ones. The bad credit risks will have a harder time getting credit, but will not be shut out entirely.

Increasingly, employers and insurance companies are requesting, and being granted,

Fair Credit Reporting Act

Key Provisions

- People can find out what is in their files
- People must be told if information in their files has been used against them
- People can dispute inaccurate information
- Inaccurate information must be corrected or deleted
- Outdated information may not be reported
- Access to files is limited
- Consent is required for reports that are provided to employers or reports that contain medical information
- People may choose to have their information excluded from CRA lists for unsolicited credit and insurance offers
- People may seek damages from violators

Credit cards should be used prudently, since a bad credit report can cause problems in the future.

access to credit files. Employers use the information to judge personal integrity and the risk of illegal activity from desperate debtors. Insurance companies use the credit histories to check for information on any major medical problems.

Consumers have three major national credit bureaus: Equifax, Trans Union Corporation, and Experian (formerly TRW). Almost all local credit bureaus are members of or are affiliated with one of these three.

Lenders and other parties can request a report from one or all three credit bureaus. Each bureau collects information independently of the others. Their reports differ in format, but all contain the same kind of information. However, each may collect different pieces of information. For example, a bankruptcy report may include a long list of debts. The credit bureau may not record all of them, and the three credit bureaus may not record the same debts.

In 1968 Congress passed the Consumer Credit Protection Act to protect individuals with a credit history. The specific subchapter of the act related to credit history is the Fair Credit Reporting Act. The two major tenets of the act are that credit reports must

Credit Report Problems

Possible Problems with Credit Reports

- Inaccurate credit information
- Out-of-date credit information
- Incorrect personal information, such as name, address, marital status, birth date
- Crossed information from consumers with similar names
- Information left on report that should have been removed
- Identity theft

be accurate and that the CRA must protect the privacy of the consumer. The Fair and Accurate Credit Transactions Act of 2003 allows consumers to obtain a free annual credit report.

Most credit history problems relate to inaccurate or out-of-date information. When this occurs, consumers can clean up their credit reports by contacting the CRA directly and asking for a review of items under question. Credit repair organizations offer to do the same for a fee. However, these organizations are bound by the same laws as the consumer. To ensure compliance, the Credit Repair Organizations Act lays out the requirements for the practice of credit cleaning plus the relationship between the consumer and the repair organization. The repair organization must provide a written contract that states the services offered and that the repair organization will not try to remove any accurate information from the consumer's credit history, even if it is negative. The contract must also contain a "buyer's remorse" clause that gives the consumer 72 hours to cancel the contract without penalty.

Some of the more common problems not related to actual bad credit are wrong header information, crossed information from consumers with similar names, and information left on the report that should have been removed. Bankruptcy information remains on a credit report for 10 years, most other information for seven years. Some information stays longer because of state statutes. Other entries—criminal records and lawsuits—may remain indefinitely.

One problem with the relatively free flow of information is identity theft. Consumers should regularly review their files to clean them up and to check for unauthorized use of their names or credit. Identity theft occurs when someone collects personal data like that found in the header of a credit file and uses it to assume that person's identity or to request that additional credit cards be sent to a new address. The credit card industry has no standards or regulations to stop identity theft; thus it is important that consumers check their credit reports regularly.

Business Credit History

Businesses develop a credit history in much the same way as do individuals, especially small businesses that establish a credit history by acquiring a credit card in the name of the business or corporation. All the same rules apply. In addition to the credit bureaus tracing business credit cards, business credit is tracked by CRAs like D&B (formerly Dun & Bradstreet).

D&B is the largest of the business reporting agencies, with information on 70 million companies worldwide. It tracks credit history including payment habits, collections, and public information. It also tracks sales, assets, liabilities, and profits. D&B then produces reports based on its data to help other businesses, lenders, and investors make decisions based on the total financial picture of a business. This allows others to gauge their risk in dealing with or investing in a company.

In both the personal and business credit reporting industry, a trend toward creating what is commonly called credit scoring, risk scoring, or a risk rating is evident. This process produces a single number, or score, that predicts the borrower's payment habits. The higher the number, the lower the risk involved in extending credit. The score is obtained by comparing a large sample of borrowers and identifying the profiles of low-risk borrowers. No one-size-fits-all

YOUR CREDIT REPORT
As of October 10, 2003

Personal Information
Jane Doe
555 Main Street
Small Town, CA 99999

Social Security Number: 555-55-555

Date of Birth: January 1, 1980

A credit report contains not only current information about where the subject lives but also previous addresses going back several years.

Previous Address(es)
2 South Road
Small Town, CA 99999

Employment History
CyberWidgets
Silicon Valley, CA 99999

Employment Date: May 2000

Some credit reports (not all) give employment history.

Widgets Online
Silicon Valley, CA 99999

Employment Date: September 2002

Public Records
No bankruptcies on file
No liens on file
No foreclosures on file
No judgments on file
No marital status on file

A credit report includes publicly available information collected from federal, state, and local courts. This may include bankruptcies, court judgments, foreclosures, and even marriages.

Collections Accounts
No collections on file

If a debt is not repaid and the debtor turns the account over to a collection agency, this is noted in the credit history.

Credit Information

There are several different kinds of accounts: a credit card is a revolving account; a college loan is an installment account.

Company Name	Account Number	Date Opened	Last Activity	Type of Account and Status	Credit Limit	Balance	Amount Past Due
American Express	99999999999999	04/1999	09/2003	Revolving PAYS AS AGREED	$6,000	$2,466	0

Prior Paying History
30 days past due 04 times; 60 days past due 02 times; 90 + days past due 00 times

This section notes the number of times the debtor has been late with payments.

Company Name	Account Number	Date Opened	Last Activity	Type of Account and Status	Credit Limit	Balance	Amount Past Due
MasterCard	55555555555555	01/2002	05/2003	Revolving PAYS AS AGREED	$2,000	$1,100	0

Prior Paying History
30 days past due 01 time(s); 60 days past due 00 time(s); 90 + days past due 00 time(s)

Company Name	Account Number	Date Opened	Last Activity	Type of Account and Status	Credit Limit	Balance	Amount Past Due
Auto Finance International	G204576KR	11/1999	1/2001	Installment REPOSESSION	$13,500	$6,755	$300

Prior Paying History
30 days past due 09 time(s); 60 days past due 06 time(s); 90 + days past due 03 time(s)
AUTO REPOSSESSED

Loans that are not repaid are reported on the credit report, even, as in this case, when the car has already been repossessed.

Company Name	Account Number	Date Opened	Last Activity	Type of Account and Status	Credit Limit	Balance	Amount Past Due
California Student Loan Corporation	222222222222 INDIVIDUAL ACCOUNT	10/1998	02/1999	Installment PAYS AS AGREED	$3,800	$0	

Prior Paying History
Paid Account. Zero balance

Repaid loans and closed credit cards remain on the credit report.

Additional Information

Companies that Requested Your File

October 10, 2003	Check YR Credit Corporation
April 23, 2003	Friendly Cell Phone Co.
November 13, 2002	Home Furnishings Warehouse
January 4, 2001	MasterCard Co.

Consumers have the right to know who has been checking up on them. Credit reports list requests for credit history information, which might occur when someone sets up a new cell phone account, requests a line of credit from a store, or gets a new credit card.

Identity Theft

Although the Internet has done much to make consumers' lives easier, it has also made the lives of thieves easier. Identity theft, wherein a thief gains access to someone's personal information (Social Security number, credit card account numbers, and so on) and runs up charges on the innocent person's accounts, is on the rise.

The Federal Trade Commission (FTC) recommends taking the following steps to limit the chances of identity theft.

- Order a credit report from each of the three major credit bureaus once a year. One of the most common ways that consumers find out that they have been victims of identity theft is when they try to make a major purchase, like a house or a car. The deal can be lost or delayed while the credit report mess is straightened out. Knowing what is in a credit report allows time to fix problems before they jeopardize a major financial transaction.
- Place passwords on credit card, bank, and phone accounts. Avoid using easily available information like birth date, mother's maiden name, or a series of consecutive numbers. Many businesses still have a line on their applications for mother's maiden name; use a password instead.
- Ask about information security procedures in the workplace. Find out who has access to personal information and verify that records are kept in a secure location. Ask about the disposal procedures for those records.
- Secure personal information at home, especially if you have roommates, employ outside help, or are having service work done in your home.
- Do not give out personal information on the phone, through the mail, or over the Internet unless you initiated the contact. Identity thieves may pose as representatives of banks, Internet service providers, and even government employees. Before sharing any personal information, confirm that you are dealing with a legitimate organization.
- Deposit outgoing mail in post office collection boxes or at your local post office rather than in an unsecured mailbox. At home, promptly remove mail from the mailbox.
- To thwart an identity thief who may pick through trash or recycling bins to capture personal information, tear or shred charge receipts, copies of credit applications, insurance forms, physician statements, checks and bank statements, expired charge cards, and credit offers received in the mail.
- Before revealing any personally identifying information (for example, on an application), find out how it will be used and secured, and whether it will be shared with others. Ask if there is a choice about the use of the information. Can one choose to have it kept confidential?
- Do not carry a Social Security card; keep it in a secure place.
- Give out Social Security number only when absolutely necessary. Ask to use other kinds of identifiers when possible.
- Carry only the identification information and the number of credit and debit cards that are actually needed.
- Pay attention to billing cycles. Follow up with creditors if bills do not arrive on time. A missing credit card bill could mean an identity thief has changed the billing address.
- Be wary of promotional scams. Identity thieves may use phony offers to get personal information.
- Keep purses or wallets in a safe place at work.

Of course, not every instance of identity theft can be prevented. The FTC recommends that all consumers order copies of their credit reports at least once a year to verify that no one else is incurring debts in their name. Any false information should be immediately reported to the credit report issuer so that it can be investigated and corrected. The FTC maintains a Web site for more information about identity theft (http://www.consumer.gov/idtheft/index.html).

model for extending credit exists. Models vary depending on the kind of loan and the collateral. Some companies specialize in creating these models and selling the results. Large financial institutions may develop their own statistical models.

Risk rating does not replace credit history. Rather, the risk rating is based on the analysis of a large sample of credit files. The risk rating is not actually part of the credit file available to the consumer. The CRA owns the rating and is not legally required to disclose it to the borrower. A risk rating cannot be used as a reason for refusing credit. Refusal must be tied to specific items in the credit file.

Consumer credit bureaus have used risk ratings for years, but the business credit industry has begun their use relatively recently. This development is particularly important for small businesses. With credit scoring, the labor-intensive analysis and tracking of business plans and financials are reduced. Statistical models allow lenders to use objective data to predict payment habits. Low-risk business applicants can be pre-approved with no personal interaction up front and little monitoring.

With credit history, time is on the borrower's side. Most negative information eventually rolls off the report, usually in seven to 10 years. In the meantime, individuals and businesses should review their credit reports annually as part of managing their finances, correct any errors promptly, and work to guard against identity theft.

Further Research
Annual Credit Report

www.annualcreditreport.com

Sponsored by the three national credit reporting companies, this Web site provides free annual credit reports to all consumers, mandated by the Fair and Accurate Credit Transactions Act.

Equifax

www.equifax.com

Experian

www.experian.com

TransUnion

www.transunion.com

—*Stephanie Buckwalter*

Debt

Debt is a legal obligation to pay. A lender presumes that the debtor will enjoy a flow of cash in the future, that an indebted business will grow, and that investments will pay off. In the business world, debt involves using someone else's money to generate revenue with the intent to repay lenders and reward investors. This money can be used to fund the start of a business or expand an existing business. When debt is used constructively and managed properly, it can increase the value of a company over time.

Categories of Debt

However used, for start-up or expansion, debt falls into two broad categories: operating debt and investment debt. Operating debt is money borrowed to finance the daily or seasonal operation of a business. Investment debt pays for purchases like equipment, machinery, computers, and vehicles. Investment debt also includes payments made to bondholders—investors who have purchased promissory notes not secured by specific assets.

Individual debts can be short-term, as in commercial paper (30 to 90 days), which is used to fund inventory until it is sold, or long-term (years), often used to purchase office equipment or a building. Debts can be liquid or static. Liquid debts are those that can be converted to cash easily. For example, debt acquired from the purchase of office furniture is considered liquid because the furniture can be readily sold. Real estate and inventory are considered static.

Debt can be secured with assets, called collateral, or it can be unsecured. Examples of secured debt are mortgages and inventory stores. Examples of unsecured debt are bonds. Bonds are an investment in the business as a whole; therefore they are not tied to specific assets.

Debt Ratios and Cash Flow

Debt is a key element in the financial statements of a business. How debt falls on the balance sheet determines solvency, or whether a business has enough money to cover its debts. A balance sheet has two sides: liabilities (whatever takes money out of the business) and assets (whatever generates cash or retains value). Debt is a liability because money is going out of the business. If the debt is tied to a specific asset, the debt will show up on the liability side, and the amount of the asset that is paid for will show up on the asset side

---

Analyzing Debt: Liquidity Ratios

- Liquidity ratios compare net worth to liabilities
- Liquidity ratios relate to ability to repay short-term debts
- The higher the ratio, the better the company is doing
- Banks are interested in the trend of these ratios over time
- Also of interest to short-term lenders like vendors and suppliers

Current Ratio

$$\frac{\text{Current assets}}{\text{Current liabilities}}$$

Company A

$$\frac{2,000,000}{1,000,000} \Bigg] = 2{:}1 \ (\$2.00 \text{ for every } \$1 \text{ of debt})$$

Company B

$$\frac{5,000,000}{4,000,000} \Bigg] = 1.25{:}1 \ (\$1.25 \text{ for every } \$1 \text{ of debt})$$

> *Both companies have $1 million of working capital; working capital equals current assets minus current liabilities. However, Company A has a better financial picture because it has a higher liquidity ratio.*

Acid Test Ratio

- Eliminates least liquid assets, including inventories and prepaids

$$\frac{\text{Current assets} - \text{inventories and prepaids (expenses \& taxes)}}{\text{Current liabilities}}$$

Company A

$$\frac{2,000,000 - 800,000}{1,000,000} \Bigg] = 1.2{:}1$$

Company B

$$\frac{5,000,000 - 800,000}{4,000,000} \Bigg] = 1.05{:}1$$

> *However, when inventories and prepaids are taken into account, Company B is very close to Company A in its ability to pay its short-term debts.*

```
┌─────────────────────────────────────┐
│        Analyzing Debt:              │
│        Debt Ratios                  │
└─────────────────────────────────────┘
```

- Debt ratios compare liabilities to other aspects of the financials
- Debt ratios relate to ability to repay long-term debts
- The lower the ratio, the better the company is doing
- Debt ratios are usually of interest to the company and its investors

Debt to Net Worth

$$\frac{\text{Total debt (current liabilities + long-term debt)}}{\text{Net worth}}$$

Company A

$$\frac{100,000 + 75,000}{225,000} \Biggr\} = 0.78{:}1$$

Company B

$$\frac{330,000 + 80,000}{500,000} \Biggr\} = 0.82{:}1$$

Debt to Total Capital

$$\frac{\text{Long-term debt}}{\text{Total capitalization (long-term debt + net worth)}}$$

Company A

$$\frac{75,000}{75,000 + 225,000} \Biggr\} = 0.25{:}1$$

> *Company B has a much better ratio when looking at total capital.*

Company B

$$\frac{80,000}{80,000 + 500,000} \Biggr\} = 0.14{:}1$$

of the balance sheet. Traditional assets include real estate, inventory, furniture, fixtures, equipment, accounts receivable, and marketable securities.

Debt is weighed against various parts of the financial statement—operating expenses, interest, and taxes—to determine the ratio of debt in relation to assets, income potential, and equity. These ratios are called leverage ratios. Investors look at the leverage ratio to determine the viability of the company and the potential for return on their investment. A high ratio could mean that the business is about to go into default.

Other kinds of ratios are useful for debt management. Liquidity ratios give a point-in-time snapshot of a business's ability to convert assets into cash to cover its debts. Activity ratios are used to determine the rate of cash flow and are used to determine if a company generates enough cash to pay its obligations. Profitability ratios compare different categories in the balance sheet to determine how efficiently a company generates profits. Some of these comparisons will indicate whether a company is carrying too many assets or too much inventory, even if the company is profitable in general. Too many assets or inventory indicate that money is sitting idle and could be used elsewhere to generate more profit.

Business owners, lenders, and investors use debt information to determine risk and to monitor their investments. By analyzing the ratios, accountants can tell how well a business is doing at any point in time. When debt ratios are out of proportion on the negative side, the company may have problems meeting its financial obligations. If investors and lenders are not willing to bail the company out, a business may shut down or file for bankruptcy. Bankruptcy may include a pardon of debts or a restructuring of the debt to pay it back on different terms than originally agreed to.

Claims Structure

Debt gives lenders and investors a claim on the business's income and assets when a company cannot meet its financial obligations. One consideration in taking on debt is the claim structure of the lenders and investors. This structure is especially important to understand if the bondholders are family and friends who invested because of personal relationships.

Creditors have the first claim on income and assets. Those debts secured with specific assets give the lender specific claims. For example, a mortgage or debts to a vendor for special equipment are considered creditors with specific claims. This kind of lender typically plays no role in management when something goes wrong. They simply repossess their asset. Some creditors, for example, bondholders, have a general claim. Bonds

Home purchase	70.2%
Other loans	0.6%
Education	3.0%
Goods and services	6.0%
Vehicles	6.7%
Investment (real estate)	9.5%
Investment (excluding real estate)	2.2%
Home improvement	1.9%

Source: Federal Reserve, *Federal Reserve Bulletin*, 2007.

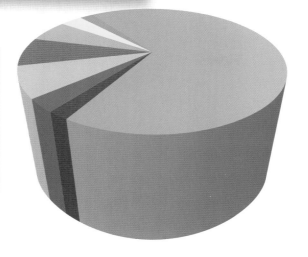

The vast majority of debt held by American families relates to home ownership; a mortgage is considered good debt because property gains value over time.

are not tied to specific items in the business. Bondholders can step into a management role in the case of problems with payment.

Stockholders have second and third claim to income and assets. Preferred stockholders have second claim; common stockholders have third claim. Although creditors and preferred stockholders have a higher claim on assets, common stockholders usually make more money on return on investments when the company prospers.

Alternatives to Debt

Often a business needs to avoid debt yet needs more capital to grow or fund research and development. The various alternatives all need to be balanced against cash flow, tax implications, time commitment to secure the funds, and existing debt structure.

One option for obtaining furniture, fixtures, and equipment is lease financing. For example, a business may choose to lease computer equipment with the option to buy at the end of the lease. The issue here is ownership. As of 1987, if a leasing company includes an option to buy in the lease, then it is treated as a traditional loan in which the business leasing the equipment owns the equipment. If that clause is not included, then the leasing company retains ownership. Although the equipment will end up costing more than if bought with a traditional loan, the business

gains the advantage of having the lease listed as a liability, but not as a debt.

The same advantage exists with renting versus owning real estate. A rental lease is a liability, but not a debt. A mortgage is a debt where the business retains ownership of the property and all its inherent liabilities. Once again, the issue is ownership: a mortgage, over time, leads to a substantial asset. However, if a company is already near its debt limit, then renting is a good option.

Another option is bartering. With bartering, a business will exchange its goods or services for the goods or services of another business. For example, a graphics firm could produce made-to-order advertising materials for a builder in exchange for carpentry work. This transaction has tax implications and must be recorded as if it occurred in cash. The taxes related to the transaction may actually need to be paid in cash to make bartering worthwhile. Businesses that barter can be found through trade associations or the local chamber of commerce. Professional bartering associations charge a fee for providing the point of contact between the parties.

Grants, tax credits, and venture capital are also viable options for raising capital without going into debt. Federal and state grants are available to some kinds of businesses and some industries. Competition is intense for limited funds, so much time and effort must be expended to win grant

Unsecured consumer debt— money owed to credit card companies—is considered bad debt because it lowers a person's net worth. High levels of consumer debt can cause stress if more money is going out than is coming in.

money. Some companies use professional grant writers to write the proposals and fill out the paperwork. Some cities, counties, or states offer businesses tax credits for locating in a particular area, for example, in an inner-city revival area. If a company has a product that is unique or on the cutting edge of science, medicine, or technology, it may be a candidate for venture capital. During the 1990s, many Internet start-ups ran on venture capital.

Partnerships can be used to steer clear of debt, too. A limited partnership has a silent partner who puts up money but leaves the business side alone. A limited partner will expect a return on the investment in the form of dividends.

Business versus Personal Debt

In business, debt is considered normal. It can be used to start a business, to expand it, for capital improvements, for inventory, and for many other reasons. From a tax standpoint, debt is desirable because the interest is tax deductible, whereas equity is taxed. Business owners are accountable to their lending institutions and investors for the amount of debt they incur in relation to the value of their business. They constantly

monitor their debt against their assets to maintain solvency.

Personal debt has some similarity to business debt. Personal debt falls into many of the same categories as business debt, including long-term or short-term, liquid or illiquid, secured or unsecured. As with businesses, some kinds of personal debt, such as a home mortgage, can be economically wise in the long run.

However, many consumers get into trouble with debt when they overextend themselves in the area of unsecured consumer debt—that is, with credit cards. Credit purchases of consumable goods that retain little or no value once purchased are a major departure from business debt. Credit card debt is rarely used to increase a person's net worth, whereas in business the idea is to use debt to increase the value of the business and make a profit.

Further Research
National Foundation for Credit Counseling
www.nfcc.org
The home page of the largest nonprofit credit counseling service in the United States.
National Venture Capital Association
www.nvca.org
The trade association of the U.S. industry.

—*Stephanie Buckwalter*

Demographics

Demographics describe the characteristics of a specific population, using such categories as age, income, sex, education, geographic location, and so on. The baby boom generation, for instance, is a demographic group comprising individuals born between 1946 and 1964, a generation that came of age during the turbulence of the 1960s and the Vietnam War. The baby boomers make up almost 30 percent of the U.S. population.

Demographics play a pivotal role in marketing strategies for businesses. Companies spend much of their financial resources studying a demographic group in the hopes of fulfilling its consumer needs. For example, prompted by demographic studies of their fans, in the mid-1990s major sports organizations, which had largely ignored the female market in the past, launched advertising and marketing campaigns to introduce women's apparel. Retail sales of women's sports apparel in 1996 were $13.2 billion, with women accounting for 36 percent of the $12 billion athletic footwear market. Since then, sales to women have held up consistently, even when men's apparel sales have fallen.

Women are not the only consumer demographic group to be targeted. American teenagers, sometimes referred to by marketers as Generation Y, constitute an even more powerful demographic, with tremendous spending potential. A study by Teenage Research Unlimited projected that young adults aged 12 to 19 would spend $159 billion in the year 2005 alone. A huge variety of businesses have attempted to capi-

Teenage shoppers are a key demographic group for many industries, including fashion and music.

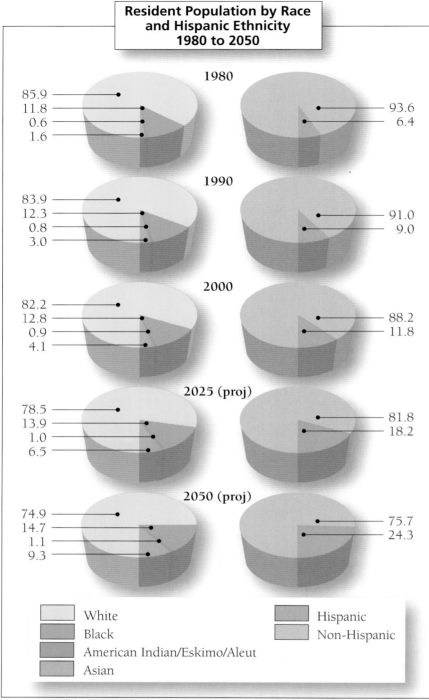

Resident Population by Race and Hispanic Ethnicity 1980 to 2050

1980
85.9
11.8
0.6
1.6

93.6
6.4

1990
83.9
12.3
0.8
3.0

91.0
9.0

2000
82.2
12.8
0.9
4.1

88.2
11.8

2025 (proj)
78.5
13.9
1.0
6.5

81.8
18.2

2050 (proj)
74.9
14.7
1.1
9.3

75.7
24.3

White
Black
American Indian/Eskimo/Aleut
Asian

Hispanic
Non-Hispanic

Note: Persons of Hispanic ethnicity may be of any race.
Source: Statistical Abstracts, 2001.

various demographic categories. For example, in the late 1990s Nike conducted a targeted marketing campaign to reach young, urban, southern California consumers with a specific interest in extreme and alternative sports. The more specific the demographic, the more customized the marketing strategies must and can be.

Demographics are not static. The desires of demographic groups change—what young, urban, southern Californians are shopping for today may not be what they shop for tomorrow. Similarly, as the powerful baby boom demographic continues to age, the products and services they seek will shift. Furthermore, demographic groups are themselves always subtly shifting. Businesses that sell products directly to consumers invest significantly in demographic research because keeping abreast of these delicate shifts is key to success.

Demographic Shifts in the United States

The United States is experiencing dramatic demographic changes. Projections show that by the middle of the twenty-first century, the United States will be a pluralistic nation in which no racial group is in the majority. Even more significant than population growth will be the cumulative effects of immigration. By 2050 the U.S. population will include 82 million people who arrived in or were born to people who arrived in the country after 1991. This group of immigrants and their children will account for 21 percent of America's population. These demographic changes are certain to profoundly affect the way business is conducted.

Unlike the immigrants of the nineteenth century, contemporary ethnic minority immigrants often attempt to maintain their cultural identities. They are slower to assimilate into mainstream American culture compared with their earlier counterparts. The view of the United States as one giant melting pot has given way to a vision of a quilt of varied American cultures. Businesses will have to employ distinct regional and ethnic marketing strategies to

talize on the teen market, ranging from specialty magazines like *Sports Illustrated for Kids* to clothing lines, from teen-targeted snack foods to boy bands.

In addition to studying specific age or gender demographics, businesses, in an attempt to tailor a product to consumers, may conduct market research that combines

U.S. businesses study demographic changes, for example, the increase in interracial marriages, to make their advertising appealing to their customers.

sell their products to an increasingly diverse population base.

In addition, businesses will have to be attentive to a changed and changing labor pool: everyone will belong to a minority group. White men will constitute less than half of the labor force; more than one employee in four will come from an ethnic minority group. Hispanics will far outstrip other groups as the nation's largest minority, and immigrants will become more important to U.S. population growth than natural increase. Using the right products and messages will be imperative when targeting these diverse groups.

The American family underwent profound changes in the second half of the twentieth century, and this trend is expected to continue well into the twenty-first century. Full-time homemakers will approach extinction as more than 80 percent of women age 25 to 54 will be in the labor force, and most children will never know a time when their mothers did not work outside the home. Businesses and other institutions will be increasingly dependent upon women's skills and will have to adapt to keep them on the job. Parental leave and child care at the workplace are expected to eventually become the norm for all but the smallest organizations.

In addition, business will have to reorient its view of the traditional family. Married couples will no longer constitute a majority of households, and more than half of all children will spend part of their lives in single-parent homes. By 2010 about one in three married couples with children will have a stepchild or an adopted child. Nontraditional family structures will become more prevalent, including unmarried heterosexual couples, homosexual couples, and friends who live together. As a consequence, businesses will have to become increasingly tactful in characterizing family life in advertising, on product packaging, and in marketing efforts.

Further Research

Statistical Abstract of the United States

www.census.gov/compendia/statab

The Statistical Abstract of the United States, published since 1878, is the authoritative and comprehensive summary of statistics on the social, political, and economic organization of the United States.

Teenage Research Unlimited

www.teenresearch.com

TRU is one of the pioneers in the field of youth research, focusing on "teens, tweens, and twenty-somethings."

—*Walter C. Farrell, Jr., Renée Sartin Kirby, and Nicole Cohen*

Distribution Channels

Distribution channels, or marketing channels as they are also known, direct the flow of goods from producers to final customers. Direct channels, in which the producer sells to the customer without the assistance of third parties, exist in both consumer and business markets. More often, however, distribution channels include market intermediaries or middlemen like wholesalers, retailers, brokers, manufacturers' agents, or industrial distributors.

Members of distribution channels perform critical tasks for the final customer. They make products available at the times and places consumers or business buyers demand them, and they permit those customers to obtain ownership of goods or to use them through rental or leasing agreements. Market intermediaries also provide important assistance to their channel partners. They gather market information, facilitate customer relationships, develop product assortments, coordinate promotional activities, establish pricing policies, aid in financing inventories, and manage the physical distribution of goods.

Because marketing intermediaries must be paid for the services they perform, their presence in the distribution channel does raise the final price of goods paid by customers. Critics have argued that this price increase, also known as the middleman's markup, is excessive, and perhaps even parasitic. Supporters, however, counter that channel members make marketing exchanges efficient by eliminating the need for every producer to interact with every customer. For example, if four consumers wish to examine four brands of cereal, a total of 16 producer–customer contacts are necessary. By placing the four cereal brands with an intermediary like a retail store, the number of interactions is reduced to eight.

Moreover, channel members perform essential services that must occur with or without intermediaries. Because middlemen often are focused on providing particular marketing functions, the channel and its final customers may benefit from the improved performance resulting from specialization and from cost reductions associated with economies of scale.

Kinds of Channels

Distribution channels are present in both the consumer and business marketplaces.

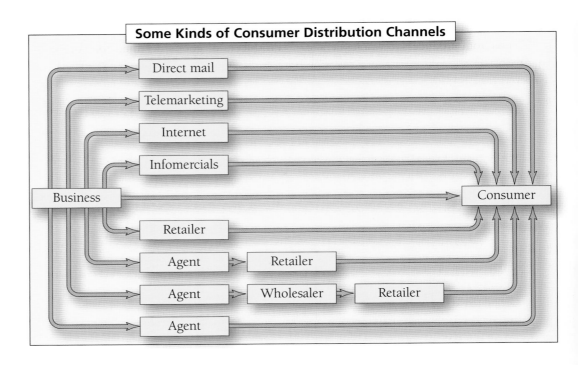

Some Kinds of Consumer Distribution Channels

Distribution Intensity		
Intensive Distribution • Many outlets • Multiple distribution channels ***Examples*** soft drinks; newspapers; cleaning supplies	**Selective Distribution** • Limited number of outlets • Outlets screened to provide appropriate services ***Examples*** major appliances; business equipment	**Exclusive Distribution** • One outlet in large geographic area • Channel members carry full product line, employ highly trained sales people; provide superior customer service • Retailer is only intermediary in distribution chain ***Examples*** expensive consumer specialty goods; major industrial equipment

The number of intermediaries in both kinds of channels depends upon the nature of the product being distributed. Another factor involved in shaping the structure of distribution channels is the firm's need to satisfy consumer demand regarding what products and services are available and at which points they are available.

Producers, who wish to reach consumers, have a number of options. Through catalogs, mailing pieces, television infomercials, telemarketing, and the Internet, they may sell directly to their customers. Alternatively, producers may sell to large retailers, who, in turn, make the product available to consumers. A third kind of channel extends from producers to wholesalers to large numbers of smaller retailers and ultimately to consumers. Finally, to achieve mass distribution of a product in a variety of outlets, the producer can use the lengthiest channel whereby the product reaches the consumer after passing through the hands of agents or brokers, wholesalers, and retailers.

Like their consumer goods counterparts, producers of products designed for business customers may consider a variety of channel arrangements. They may use a specially trained sales force, catalogs, or the Internet to sell directly to their customers. Such direct channels account for more than half of the sales of all business products. Producers of business products also use

marketing intermediaries. Those that sell goods of low or moderate value frequently sell their output to industrial distributors, who hold inventories and resell in small quantities to users. Those that require sales support for their products may use the services of manufacturers' agents, who represent the complementary products of several noncompeting firms in a given territory. Last, producers who wish to do business in a large geographic area but lack a sales force may reach their customers through a channel composed of agents and industrial distributors.

The selection of one distribution channel does not preclude the use of others. Producers of goods destined for both consumer and business customers generally employ separate channels to reach their respective markets. Producers may also target consumers or business segments with distinct distribution requirements or preferences. As a consequence, they may use a direct channel to serve some customers, but make goods available through a retail outlet, an industrial distributor, or combination of channel members to meet the needs of others. The use of multiple distribution channels, known as dual distribution, is a common practice, but the perception that one channel may be benefiting at the expense of another is a frequent cause of channel conflict.

Producers who distribute products outside the United States must often accommodate different channel structures that exist abroad. In Japan, for example, consumer goods channels generally include three wholesale levels—national or primary wholesalers, secondary or regional wholesalers, and local wholesalers—that in combination serve large numbers of extremely small retailers. When considering foreign distribution channels, businesses also need to take into account the consumer cultures and the existing technological and transportation infrastructures in the nations where they plan to do business. Such considerations are important because they may dictate the kinds of outlets in which goods need to be available or because they limit the possibilities of reaching customers through, for example, catalogs or Internet Web sites.

Distribution Intensity

Choices relating to channel structure are closely related to distribution intensity, or the degree to which a product is available to its customers. Market coverage is generally classified into three categories: intensive, selective, or exclusive. The nature of the product being handled together with the purchase behaviors of intended consumers or business buyers guide availability decisions.

Intensive distribution, which places a product in as many outlets as possible, is appropriate for convenience goods.

Consumers frequently replenish items like soft drinks, bread, and newspapers, and expect them to be readily available. Likewise, business buyers want easy access to such goods as copy paper or cleaning supplies. Given the need to maximize market coverage, producers of such products generally rely on multiple distribution channels and include those with several levels of middlemen to assure product availability not only in major outlets but also in vending machines and at small retail shops and industrial distributors.

Selective distribution places products in a limited number of outlets that are chosen using criteria like ability to provide sales support, warranty service, or an appropriate selling atmosphere. Selective distribution is common for most shopping goods and some specialty goods, including major appliances or business accessory equipment. Consumers and business customers give thought and effort when purchasing these higher-priced goods, and they will forgo the convenience of easy availability to obtain better product information or other services at the point of sale. Channels for selectively distributed products tend to have fewer levels of intermediaries than do channels for convenience goods.

Exclusive distribution allows only one outlet in a relatively large geographic area to distribute a product. Expensive consumer specialty goods and major industrial equipment are typical of the kinds of products with highly restricted availability. In return for exclusive rights, channel members generally carry a full product line, employ highly trained salespeople, and provide superior customer service. Retailers and distributors with exclusive rights are commonly the only intermediaries in the distribution channel.

Channel Cooperation

Distribution channels are composed of independent firms that must depend upon one another to achieve the common goal of making goods available to the customer. This goal necessitates a high level of cooperation in a distribution channel, and, at

Conventional Marketing Channel vs. Vertical Marketing System

Conventional Marketing Channel	Vertical Marketing System
Manufacturer	Manufacturer Wholesaler Retailer
Wholesaler	
Retailer	
Consumer	Consumer

The vertical marketing system can be more efficient than a conventional marketing channel because the vertical channel imposes uniform processes.

The enormous success of Wal-Mart is partly attributable to the company's firm and efficient control of its vertical marketing system.

the same time, suggests the possibility for conflict among channel members. Clear and timely communication among the members of the distribution channel, which has been facilitated by the Internet, is the best means of avoiding frustration and facilitating the smooth operation of partner relationships.

Some channels rely upon a channel captain to provide leadership and to organize member responsibilities. The captain may come from any level of the distribution channel but must have the authority to influence the performance of the other channel partners. Examples of captains of their respective channels include the major automobile manufacturers; the retail giant, Wal-Mart; and the grocery wholesaler, the Independent Grocers' Alliance.

One structure for distribution channels is the vertical marketing system (VMS), in which all aspects of the chain from producer to final seller are unified. A VMS offers an important means of assuring that channel activities are appropriately performed. The contractual VMS is the most common type of vertical marketing system.

In a contractual VMS, legal agreements, enforceable in court, identify the rights and responsibilities of respective channel members. Franchises are contractual VMSs.

In an administered VMS, channel members remain independent, but informal coordination is facilitated by the adoption of common inventory systems, accounting procedures, or other uniform processes. A channel captain generally plays a leadership role in an administered system.

The corporate VMS makes possible the highest level of channel control. In such systems, all channel members have a common corporate owner.

Further Research

The Stanford Global Supply Chain Management Forum
www.gsb.stanford.edu/scforum
The home page of a prominent research institute focusing on theory and excellence in supply chain management. The news section is a valuable source of current information.

—*Marilyn Lavin*

Economies of Scale

Economies of scale occur when a business's average cost of production declines as its output increases. Economies of scale enable a business to produce a greater amount at a lower per-unit cost. Economies of scale arise from the nature of the technology employed and the efficiencies gained by large-scale production. Large economies of scale can have a significant effect on a firm's business strategy and on market structure.

Businesses of all kinds transform resources, or factors of production, into some kind of output, either a good or a service. These factors of production include labor, capital (factories, machinery, and equipment), and raw materials or natural resources. Increasing output requires some increase in resources, so the total cost of production rises as more inputs are purchased and output rises. However, total cost need not necessarily rise in proportion to output, and this creates the possibility of economies of scale. For example, if a firm is able to double its output (a 100 percent increase) while incurring only an 80 percent increase in costs, then the average cost of production will actually decline. Imagine a firm making 1,000 units of output at a total cost of $10,000, or $10 per unit. If output rises to 2,000 units while total cost increases to $18,000, then the average cost of production falls to $9 per unit; the firm enjoys economies of scale and a higher profit.

The technology employed in the production process is fundamental in determining whether economies of scale will be achieved. An important source of economies of scale lies in a production phenomenon called increasing returns to scale. Increasing returns to scale occur when raising the use of all resources by the same percentage leads to an even larger percentage increase in output. Increasing returns to scale in production result in economies of scale in costs. For example, if increasing all resources by 80 percent leads to a 100 percent increase in production, then output goes up faster than costs, with a corresponding drop in average cost.

Why might increasing returns to scale result in higher production? The most common answer involves the ability to employ resources in highly specialized ways that can increase the productivity of these resources. A manufacturing firm, for example, may find that when it employs more workers, each worker can perform a more focused task better and productivity, or output per worker, rises. Henry Ford's use of the assembly line in the early days of automobile manufacturing took advantage of this highly productive division of labor.

Increasing returns to scale involves increasing of all resources proportionally. However, sometimes the optimal mix of resources changes at larger scales of operation, which can also result in economies of scale. For example, a manufacturing firm might find it needs only 50 percent more workers to staff a production facility that is twice as large as its old one. The new labor-to-capital ratio might reduce the average cost of production at the higher output level, resulting in economies of scale. Similarly, physical capital can sometimes be more productive at larger scales of operation, usually the result of certain physical characteristics. A pipeline for transporting liquid or gas, for example, might be more efficient in a bigger size. Doubling the

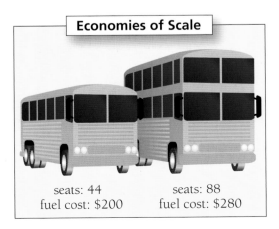

Economies of Scale

seats: 44
fuel cost: $200

seats: 88
fuel cost: $280

The double-decker bus doubles the number of seats but without doubling fuel costs.

circumference of the pipeline may double its cost to the firm, but doubling the circumference much more than doubles the volume of material that can flow through the pipeline.

A similar phenomenon occurs when the optimal production technique requires some initial input or start-up expenditure to make the process work. For example, a transmission and distribution system must be in place before electrical power can begin to be distributed in a large network. The large initial cost of the system can be spread out over more buyers as the customer base expands, thus reducing the cost per unit.

Economies of scale affect business behavior and the structure of the marketplace. In an industry in which firms can achieve significant economies of scale, small firms will typically have difficulty competing with larger firms because the small firms have a higher average cost of production. Such small firms often will either have to grow to operate at a level that takes advantage of economies of scale or settle for low profits, perhaps even being forced out of business. Industries with very large economies of scale tend to become oligopolistic: only a few firms compete with one another, typically at large scales of operation.

The automobile manufacturing industry is an example of an oligopoly with important economies of scale. At the beginning of automobile manufacture in the United States, a number of firms sprang up, but automated production techniques and division of labor quickly resulted in economies of scale. Manufacturers became large producers, consolidated their operations by merging with other manufacturers, or went out of business. For most of the twentieth century, three or four major producers dominated American automobile manufacturing. At the beginning of the twenty-first century, consolidation among manufacturers around the world continued

Economies of scale are important for electricity companies; the high cost of establishing the generation and delivery systems can be spread among many customers.

The automobile industry was profoundly shaped by economies of scale.

to be the rule, resulting in a global oligopoly in which a relatively few huge manufacturers produce the vast majority of automobiles, and smaller producers struggle to survive.

Minimum efficient scale is defined as the level of output that must be reached to exhaust economies of scale. Beyond that level of production, no further cost advantage is derived from increasing the scale of production. In some cases, economies of scale are so large that no more than one firm can reach minimum efficient scale. In these situations having multiple firms compete would likely result in inefficient, high-cost production and an unstable market structure, until one firm succeeds in capturing enough market share to drive out competitors. These cases are sometimes called natural monopolies, because it often makes economic sense to have only one firm in the industry. Historically, public utilities, such as electric power and local telephone service providers, have been considered natural monopolies.

Further Research

American Economics Association—Resources for Economists on the Internet

www.aeaweb.org/RFE

Site sponsored by the American Economics Association has links to Web-based resources.

—Randall E. Waldron

Entrepreneurship

Entrepreneurship is at the heart of the free enterprise system. At its heart, free enterprise combines different resources to provide goods and services to others. This includes traditional businesses that sell ordinary items, inventors developing new products, or not-for-profit agencies that, for example, provide disaster relief. Entrepreneurship is the engine that provides the new goods and services, job creation, and opportunity that make free enterprise so appealing.

The free market is based on two ideas. The first is that all people are free to trade as they please. Consumers and producers operate according to the laws of supply and demand and make their own decisions using their best judgment. The second premise is that of greed. Economists dating back to Adam Smith have shown that both consumers and producers make exchanges with the intention of making themselves better off.

Entrepreneurs are central to both of these ideas. Most operate in hopes of making a profit to enhance their well-being. However, because consumers are free to choose, producers must find ways to entice them to trade with them voluntarily. This combination of motives explains why entrepreneurs are the main source of innovation and creativity in an economy. Businesspeople must please their customers to be successful while making a profit. Achieving that result requires offering better products and services at lower prices.

Kinds of Entrepreneurship

Many of history's most famous entrepreneurs were inventors who created a new product. Thomas Edison is a prominent example. He became famous and wealthy by inventing dozens of new products, including the lightbulb and record player. Henry Ford took the example of Edison one step further. He did not invent the car, but he developed and refined a method to mass-produce cars through an assembly line. His Model A and Model T cars were built in large numbers, lowering their cost and leading to the adoption of the automobile for personal transportation.

Another path to success is finding methods to make existing products better or easier to use. Bill Gates became famous and wealthy through innovating in the computer industry. He and his partner, Paul Allen, collaborated to create software that offered a standard, reasonably easy-to-use operating system for personal computers.

Other entrepreneurs become successful by finding new ways to sell. Sam Walton, the founder of Wal-Mart, focused on improving management of department stores. His strategies included building large numbers of identical stores, computerizing inventory systems, and ordering goods in large quantities from manufacturers at discounted rates. These innovations worked so well that Wal-Mart became the largest consumer retail company in the world because it could offer very low prices.

Silicon Valley

Several factors contribute to Silicon Valley being a perfect incubator for entrepreneurs. First is its proximity to institutions of higher learning, including Stanford University and University of California at Berkeley, both leading schools in computer science, business, and engineering. Professors and students frequently start new businesses as the product of research or course work.

The most famous example of a company emerging from academia is Hewlett-Packard. Its founders were trained at Stanford and received valuable guidance in the development of the company and its products from a former professor. The company went from a garage start-up to the world's largest producer of personal computers and began the technological boom in Silicon Valley.

Universities also attract young, talented individuals with bold new ideas. This was a perfect match for the young computer industry. The field was wide open, with abundant opportunities for innovation that provided a natural outlet for entrepreneurial energy. Another advantage of the area was the relaxed culture. Internet start-up firms became famous for casual clothing, in-house chefs, and other luxuries unheard of in most businesses. This helped companies attract and retain talented programmers in an environment where ideas were critical to success.

Despite all of these advantages, even Silicon Valley is not immune to the ups and downs of business. After three decades of rapid expansion, the computer industry experienced a speculative bubble, or period of unsustainable growth, driven by an investor mania for anything related to the Internet. The bubble burst in 2000 after investors realized that many of the new companies had no ability to make profits. Hundreds of companies developing Internet applications or other technology quickly went out of business. In their enthusiasm, investors had overlooked a fundamental piece of business wisdom: invest only in companies that have a solid business plan.

The National Foundation for Teaching Entrepreneurship gives awards for Young Entrepreneur of the Year. Winners are selected both nationally and internationally.

Job and Wealth Creation

This process of innovation and creativity leads to another reason why entrepreneurs are important. The graph on page 426 shows that more than half of all workers in the United States work for a company that employs fewer than 100 workers. An additional 25 percent work for companies with fewer than 500 employees. Taken together, almost 80 percent of workers in the United States are employed by small or moderate-sized businesses, the vast majority of which are owned by entrepreneurs. Only about 20 percent of Americans work in medium or large businesses, which tend to be corporations.

It is a common misperception that the majority of Americans work for large companies that do the majority of hiring (and firing). In fact, businesses with fewer than 500 workers created almost 65 percent of all new jobs in 2007.

Most Americans work for small businesses and these small businesses create the vast majority of new jobs. Larger companies play a different role in the economy. They became big companies by mass marketing, or selling products on a large scale, to generate sizable profit. Thus, they focus their energies on improving their current product or offering others with large profit potentials. Prescription drug companies are one example: they focus on products that many people can use but that are too expensive for smaller businesses to develop.

The strategies of large businesses explain the differences in the graph. Large firms create fewer jobs because they operate on a large scale with mature products. Rather than hire and fire many employees, large firms tend to shift production over time. Their numbers are also less dramatic because they can use mass production more efficiently and so may not need to hire as many workers.

Entrepreneurship offers a path to success for anyone willing to take the financial and personal risks. Anyone of any age, race, educational attainment, or gender can start a business. This variety of ideas and approaches serves society as a whole.

Entrepreneurship is also the main method for achieving economic success in America. The majority of millionaires in the United States have not inherited their wealth: they are successful entrepreneurs who operate mundane businesses like dry cleaning, asphalt paving, and insect extermination. Wally Amos, an African American entrepreneur from New York, is a famous example. He started Famous Amos cookies in 1975 equipped with a recipe and a strong work ethic. Amos became financially successful and famous without a college degree or formal business training.

Is Small Better?

The benefits of starting one's own business are well known. Entrepreneurs are their own bosses, make all of the decisions, and can claim the credit for their success. Small companies also have two advantages over their larger competition. First, they can focus on small markets that bigger companies ignore for lack of profit potential. Overnight delivery services and plain paper copiers are both examples of products that entrepreneurs developed for niche markets.

Second, small companies can adapt to change quickly. As most are owned by one or two people, they can alter their hours of operation, product lines, prices, and other strategies very rapidly. Larger firms recognize flexibility's value and often structure parts of their businesses to so operate.

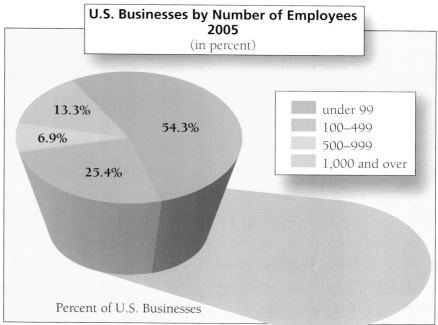

U.S. Businesses by Number of Employees 2005
(in percent)

13.3%
6.9%
54.3%
25.4%

under 99
100–499
500–999
1,000 and over

Percent of U.S. Businesses

Note: Numbers may not total 100 due to rounding.
Source: U.S. Census Bureau.

The challenges in entrepreneurship are daunting. The difficulties are reflected in one powerful statistic: 90 percent of the businesses created each year go bankrupt for one reason or another. Poor management is one reason for the low success rate of businesses in their early years. Entrepreneurs must understand their business, communicate well with customers, understand marketing, and be highly competent at a number of other areas. Very few people are strong in all of these areas and, consequently, they may make bad decisions.

Another problem for entrepreneurs is the tremendous amount of time required to start and run a business. A new business

The importance of small entrepreneurial firms is shown in the graph above—more than half of all U.S. workers are employed by small businesses.

A lot of people come to me and say "I want to be an entrepreneur." And I go "Oh that's great, what's your idea?" And they say "I don't have one yet." And I say "I think you should go get a job as a busboy or something until you find something you're really passionate about because it's a lot of work." I'm convinced that about half of what separates the successful entrepreneurs from the nonsuccessful ones is pure perseverance. It is so hard. You put so much of your life into this thing. There are such rough moments in time that I think most people give up. I don't blame them. It's really tough and it consumes your life. . . . Unless you have a lot of passion about this, you're not going to survive. You're going to give it up. So you've got to have an idea, or a problem or a wrong that you want to right that you're passionate about, otherwise you're not going to have the perseverance to stick it through. I think that's half the battle right there.

—Steve Jobs, Smithsonian Oral History interview

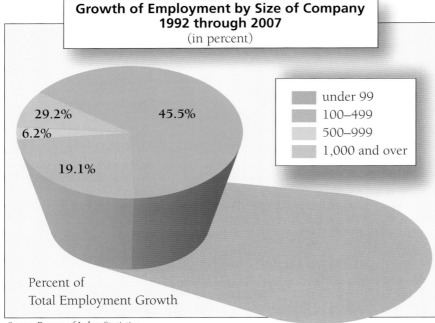

Growth of Employment by Size of Company 1992 through 2007
(in percent)

29.2%
6.2%
19.1%
45.5%

Legend:
- under 99
- 100–499
- 500–999
- 1,000 and over

Percent of
Total Employment Growth

Source: *Bureau of Labor Statistics.*

Individual entrepreneurs can take credit for their enormous contribution to overall growth in employment in the United States.

can easily take 12 or more hours each day and often results in owners becoming burned out and quitting.

The leading cause of small business failure is inadequate funding. Banks and other lending institutions are very aware that most businesses are not successful and often refuse to extend loans. Thus, most entrepreneurs must use their own savings or borrow from friends and relatives. Both sources are often very limited and run out before the business develops.

Other sources of funding for new businesses include loans from state or local government. Successful new businesses create jobs, pay taxes, and provide other benefits; thus, governments have created many lending programs to encourage the development of small businesses.

Another source of funding is called venture capital. These are loans offered by businesses that specialize in investing in new companies. In return for providing funds and advice, the venture capital companies receive a portion of ownership. Venture capital is a fundamental element in the world's leading entrepreneurial region: Silicon Valley in northern California. This region experienced two periods of explosive growth, in the 1980s with the advent of the personal computer and

in the 1990s with the expansion of the Internet and in the twenty-first century with the growth in sustainable technologies.

Starting a Business

When starting a new business, a solid business plan is imperative. This document outlines the product or service to be offered, how much it will cost to start and run the business, and so on. Business plans have two major uses: the plan requires the entrepreneur to create a strategy for success, which greatly improves prospects; the plan can be made available when applying for additional funding. If convincing, a well-conceived and thorough business plan can convince others of potential success.

Obtaining adequate funding and the process of planning can present a major barrier to creating a business. One common solution is to create a partnership. Partners may bring a variety of skills, additional funding, and a reduction in the workload to a business. The partnership business model is very common in the legal and medical professions. Partnerships come with drawbacks, however. Partners may disagree about business decisions. Many businesses fail or break up because of management discord. Other problems include limited funding and issues of legal liability.

Another solution is offered by franchises. Essentially franchises provide the opportunity to buy your own pre-made business. H&R Block, McDonald's, and Midas Mufflers are all franchises. Franchising offers advantages to both parties. The entrepreneurs purchase a business with name recognition, an established business plan, and already existing expertise in advertising. In return, the corporations receive payment for the name, a portion of all profits in the future, and the ability to easily expand. This is demonstrated by Subway Subs and McDonald's—each has more than 10,000 locations worldwide.

Entrepreneurship and Government

The opportunities for business and the business climate play a central role in the suc-

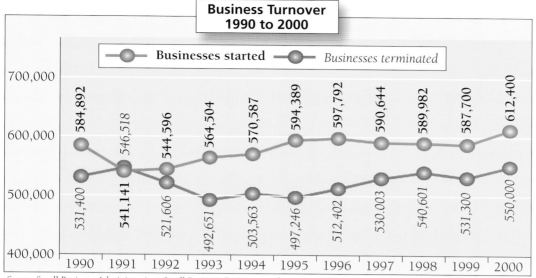

Business Turnover 1990 to 2000

Businesses started — Businesses terminated

Year	Businesses started	Businesses terminated
1990	584,892	531,400
1991	546,518	541,141
1992	544,596	521,606
1993	564,504	492,651
1994	570,587	503,563
1995	594,389	497,246
1996	597,792	512,402
1997	590,644	530,003
1998	589,982	540,601
1999	587,700	531,300
2000	612,400	550,000

Source: Small Business Administration, Small Business Economic Indicators, 2000, Washington, D.C., Government Printing Office, 2000, http://www.sba.gov/advo/stats/sbei00.pdf (January 13, 2003).

The failure rate for new businesses is high; each year nearly as many businesses end as are started.

cess and vitality of a country. The world's wealthiest nations share a strong private sector featuring hard working, talented risk takers.

The United States and Hong Kong consistently lead the world in living standards. Both countries encourage entrepreneurship through relatively low taxes, limited government intervention, and strong protections for property rights. The last are especially important because they ensure that citizens can keep any wealth they accrue.

In general, economists have found that as property rights erode and taxes increase, the economic growth and living standards of nations decline. The most prominent example is North Korea, which drastically limits entrepreneurship and property rights. North Korea consistently experiences famine and other economic problems, in part because citizens lack incentives to become economically productive.

Entrepreneurship is an expression of optimism and self-confidence. While most businesses fail, those that succeed offer new goods and services and create the majority of new jobs each year. This process of competition and innovation is the central engine of economic progress.

Further Research
Consortium for Entrepreneurship Education
www.entre-ed.org/index.htm

The Consortium developed 15 standards for entrepreneurial education based on the idea that entrepreneurship education is a lifelong process.

Ewing Marion Kauffman Foundation
www.kauffman.org/

The Ewing Marion Kauffman Foundation works with partners to encourage entrepreneurship and entrepreneurship education and training efforts, to promote entrepreneurship-friendly policies, and to assist entrepreneurs and others in commercializing new technologies.

—*David Long*

Web Resources on Entrepreneurship

www.sba.gov is the home page of the federally run Small Business Administration, which offers a wide range of helpful materials.

www.canadabusiness.ca provides a variety of resources for entrepreneurs, including an interactive business planner and links to information on starting a small business in Canada.

www.ecorner.stanford.edu is a free online archive of entrepreneurship resources for teaching and learning, including podcasts and videos, many developed by the Stanford Technology Ventures Program.

www.eonetwork.org is the home page of the Entrepreneurs Organization, a global-network for entrepreneurs, with members in more than 38 countries.

www.entrepreneurship.org provides a variety of resources for entrepreneurs.

www.aeeg.org is the home page of the American Entrepreneurs for Economic Growth, a group focused on supporting government legislation that benefits the entrepreneurial communities and promotes economic growth.

Exchange Rates

Different countries use different forms of money, thus the purchase of foreign goods requires that funds be converted from one currency to another. Exchange rates are the price of one currency in terms of another. The majority of countries allow the value of their currencies to float, or regularly change, just like prices on goods in a store vary regularly. Thus, exchange rates are subject to constant change.

The price of money is determined in the same way as other prices—by supply and demand. If the demand for a currency suddenly drops, it will become cheaper in relation to other currencies; if the supply of a currency suddenly rises, it will also decline in value.

Several factors can affect the supply of and demand for a currency. One is the nation's balance of trade, or the difference in monetary value between its imports and exports. As a nation exports more goods, demand for its currency tends to rise, increasing the value. The reverse is also true.

A nation's monetary or fiscal policy can also affect its exchange rate. Nations often deliberately increase their money supply, either through printing more money or increasing government spending to stimulate economic growth. One consequence of this increase is downward pressure on the exchange rate for its currency. Expectations also play a very important role in the value of a nation's currency. For example, if a country has a poor record of managing its money supply, or is often beset by economic problems, the demand for its currency will be relatively low.

These factors work both in favor and against a strong valuation for the U.S. dollar. The United States routinely runs a trade

Typical Exchange Rate Table

Exchange Rates as of December 31, 2008

Code	Country (Currency)	Units/USD	USD/Unit	Code	Country (Currency)	Units/USD	USD/Unit
ARP	Argentina (Peso)	3.5352	0.2829	MAD	Morocco (Dirham)	8.0832	0.1237
AUD	Australia (Dollar)	1.4323	0.6982	NZD	New Zealand (Dollar)	1.7202	0.5813
BSD	Bahamas (Dollar)	1.0000	1.0000	NOK	Norway (Krone)	6.9778	0.1433
BRL	Brazil (Real)	2.3145	0.4321	PKR	Pakistan (Rupee)	78.905	0.01267
CAD	Canada (Dollar)	1.2246	0.8166	PAB	Panama (Balboa)	1.0000	1.0000
CLP	Chile (Peso)	0.6385	1.5662	PEN	Peru (New Sol)	3.1384	0.3186
CNY	China (Renminbi)	6.8223	0.1466	PHP	Philippines (Peso)	47.465	0.02107
COP	Colombia (Peso)	2.2470	0.4450	RUR	Russia (Ruble)	30.539	0.03275
DKK	Denmark (Krone)	5.3499	0.1869	SGD	Singapore (Dollar)	1.4380	0.6954
EUR	Europe (Euro)	0.7184	1.3920	ZAR	South Africa (Rand)	9.3410	0.1071
FJD	Fiji Islands (Dollar)	1.7572	0.5691	KRW	South Korea (1000 Won)	1.2625	0.7921
GHC	Ghana (Cedi)	1.2727	0.7857	XDR	Special Drawing Rights	0.6505	1.5374
GBP	Great Britain (Pound)	0.6843	1.4614	LKR	Sri Lanka (Rupee)	112.970	0.00885
HNL	Honduras (Lempira)	18.895	0.05292	SEK	Sweden (Krona)	7.8803	0.1269
HKD	Hong Kong (Dollar)	7.7502	0.1290	CHF	Switzerland (Franc)	1.0675	0.9368
ISK	Iceland (Krona)	121.488	0.00823	TWD	Taiwan (Dollar)	32.778	0.03051
INR	India (Rupee)	48.615	0.02057	THB	Thailand (Baht)	34.750	0.02878
IDR	Indonesia (Rupiah)	10.9339	0.0915	TTD	Trinidad/Tobago (Dollar)	6.2897	0.1590
ILS	Israel (Shekel)	3.7796	0.2646	TND	Tunisia (Dinar)	1.3144	0.7608
JPY	Japan (Yen)	90.778	0.01102	TRL	Turkey (1 million Lira)	1.5394	0.6496
MYR	Malaysia (Ringgit)	3.4525	0.2896	USD	United States (Dollar)	1.0000	1.0000
MXP	Mexico (New Peso)	13.833	0.07229	VEB	Venezuela (Bolivar)	2.1473	0.4657

Note: Units/USD provides the quantity of foreign currency that is purchased with one U.S. dollar; USD/Unit provides the price of one foreign currency unit in terms of U.S. dollars. For the currencies of Austria, Belgium, Finland, France, Germany, Greece, Italy, Ireland, Luxembourg, Netherlands, Portugal, and Spain: refer to the euro.
Source: Courtesy Bank of Canada.

deficit, importing tens of billions of dollars worth of goods above the amount it exports, exerting downward pressure on the currency. However, America's strong record of low inflation and economic growth over the last 20 years has more than compensated for its trade imbalance, resulting in the dollar being relatively valuable.

Buying or selling currency has become a major business with the growth of international trade and travel. Most of the large stock exchanges in the world also include currency exchanges, where billions of dollars, euros, and other currencies are traded daily by licensed traders working for banks, stock brokerages, and other institutions that profit by charging a small fee for executing trades.

Some of this currency trading is done to accommodate the exchange of goods and services. Companies with international receipts often convert that money into their native currency to pay employees, pay stock dividends, or make other purchases. Such companies may also need to buy foreign money to pay for raw materials or activities abroad.

However, the majority of money trading is speculative. International currency traders constantly bet on the value of different currencies. For example, they may buy large amounts of dollars, hoping that their value will increase over time. These trades can result in significant changes in the value of

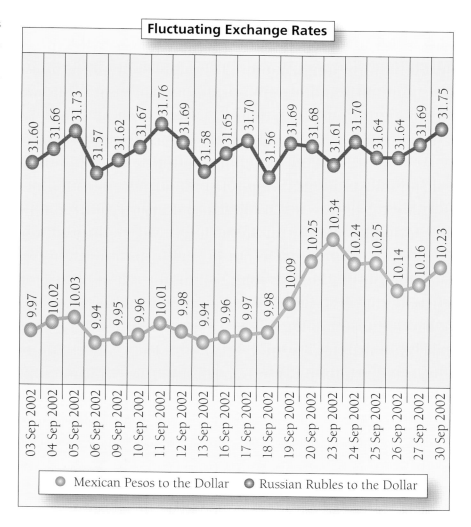

Fluctuating Exchange Rates

Date	Russian Rubles to the Dollar	Mexican Pesos to the Dollar
03 Sep 2002	31.60	9.97
04 Sep 2002	31.66	10.02
05 Sep 2002	31.73	10.03
06 Sep 2002	31.57	9.94
09 Sep 2002	31.62	9.95
10 Sep 2002	31.67	9.96
11 Sep 2002	31.76	10.01
12 Sep 2002	31.69	9.98
13 Sep 2002	31.58	9.94
16 Sep 2002	31.65	9.96
17 Sep 2002	31.70	9.97
18 Sep 2002	31.56	9.98
19 Sep 2002	31.69	10.09
20 Sep 2002	31.68	10.25
23 Sep 2002	31.61	10.34
24 Sep 2002	31.70	10.24
25 Sep 2002	31.64	10.25
26 Sep 2002	31.64	10.14
27 Sep 2002	31.69	10.16
30 Sep 2002	31.75	10.23

○ Mexican Pesos to the Dollar   ● Russian Rubles to the Dollar

money because the traders often leverage, or borrow, enormous amounts in an attempt to increase their profits.

Currency speculation can be damaging, especially to smaller nations, because large fluctuations in exchange rates can hurt countries' abilities to borrow money or sell goods abroad. Accordingly, nations have tried various methods to stabilize their exchange rates. For example, central banks often coordinate the purchase and sale of currencies to limit these swings.

Further Research
FX Converter
www.oanda.com/convert/classic
This site offers conversions of 164 currencies as well as three metals.
Financial Management Service
www.fms.treas.gov/intn.html
Rates provided by the U.S. government.

—*David Long*

Exchanging U.S. dollars for rupiah notes in Jakarta, Indonesia.

Finance, Personal

People can use their money in four ways: spend it, save it, invest it, or give it away. Individuals' money-use decisions should be based on their income, priorities, and goals. Unfortunately, many people base their spending on the desire of the moment, the latest advertising, or the limit on their credit cards. To avoid these pitfalls, a well-thought out financial plan should be made for all income. A financial plan takes into account basic necessities, desires, charitable giving, and long-term savings and investing goals.

Setting Priorities

People's priorities are determined by their values. Do they think that possessions are a privilege or a right? Is debt a negative to be avoided or a necessary evil? Do they continue to purchase products that consume their time and money beyond those products' ability to increase quality of life, or do they scale back or cut such products out completely? Is appearing to have attained a certain level of affluence more important than staying within one's income? These are the kinds of questions that help determine priorities.

In the United States, most people's basic necessities can be met either through personal income or government assistance. The United States has neither mass homelessness nor mass starvation. Once the basics are met, the rest of spending relates to desires. The trickiest part for most people is determining the difference between a need and a desire. Most people have a set idea of the standard of living they would like. Desire for a particular standard of living may be influenced by advertising, the media, a social circle, or business associates.

In order to manage money well, it is important to create a solid financial plan.

When the cost of maintaining a desired living standard exceeds income, people have a choice to make. They can go into debt or choose to live within their means.

Managing Debt

The two basic kinds of debt are consumer debt and investment debt. Consumer debt is characterized by the purchase of consumable goods that have little or no lasting value once purchased, for example, food, clothing, vehicles, or household goods. Investment debt is typically longer term, for example, a home mortgage.

Almost three-quarters of personal debt is attributable to mortgages and home-equity loans, which are secured by the real estate itself. Home owners make regular payments to the institution holding the mortgage. A portion of each payment is used to reduce the amount of the principal (the actual cost of the home) and the rest of the payment is used to pay the interest on the loan. Interest payments on home mortgages are tax deductible. In this way, the U.S. government encourages people to become home owners. Real estate is generally considered to be a good investment and well worth taking on debt.

Consumer debt, on the other hand, decreases a person's net worth, whereas investment debt should increase a person's net worth over time. When considering a purchase through debt, take into account (1) whether the item has the potential to appreciate in value or increase income, and (2) whether the value of the item equals or exceeds the amount borrowed. If the purchase does not meet these criteria, it

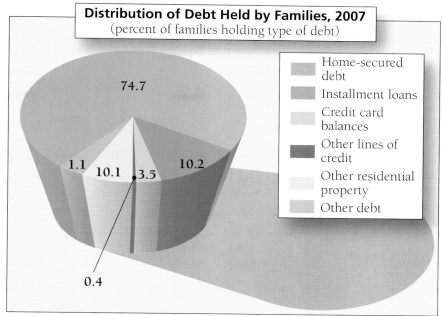

Distribution of Debt Held by Families, 2007
(percent of families holding type of debt)

74.7

1.1 10.1 3.5 10.2

0.4

- Home-secured debt
- Installment loans
- Credit card balances
- Other lines of credit
- Other residential property
- Other debt

Note: Home-secured debt includes first and second mortgages, home-equity loans, and lines of credit secured by the primary residence.
Source: Federal Reserve.

should be closely evaluated against the household budget, priorities, and goals.

The use of credit instead of savings to make purchases erodes a household's financial foundation. One problem with purchasing consumable items on credit is that the high interest rates can easily double or triple the original cost of the item if payments are always made at the minimum amount. If debt has become a problem, then goals need to be set for getting out of debt. The logical solution might seem to pay off everything as quickly as possible. However, if during this process the need arises for emergency cash, more debt will likely be incurred. The best approach is to begin saving while accelerating debt repayment. A typical approach is to pay off the smallest debts first. Each time a debt is paid off, it increases cash available to pay off more debt. Paying off the debts with highest interest rates first is preferable because the most money is saved.

Setting Goals

Financial planning requires setting goals to satisfy long-term and short-term needs and desires. Percentage guidelines are available to help in this process. For example, housing costs should be approximately one-third of

The Real Cost of Credit Card Debt

CREDIT CARD

Amount on Credit Card:	$3,000
Interest Rate:	19%
Minimum Monthly Payment:	$50
Time to Pay Off Loan:	8 ⅓ years
Total Finance Charges:	$2,990
Total Cost:	**$5,900**

When consumers make purchases with credit cards, they sometimes forget that they will later be paying interest. In this example, interest payments nearly exceed the amount originally spent.

household income. Debt should not exceed more than 10 percent of income, and none of it should be consumer debt unless all other areas are taken care of. Insurance can take anywhere from 4 to 7 percent. Starting with percentages like these helps put the big picture in perspective. Desires can then be tailored to fit within the percentages.

When desires surpass income available to satisfy them, then one financial goal should be to increase income. This may require more schooling or training, which will need to be factored into a budget. If schooling is required and student loans are used, their repayment must be factored into the future budget. However, a student loan can be considered an investment debt because it provides the potential to increase income.

Another long-term goal is a retirement fund. The purpose of saving for retirement is to create a money machine that will continue to generate a suitable income after retirement. The government helps people plan for retirement by setting up retirement plans. In the past, those were called pensions; then came other plans like 401(k) plans and IRAs. The longer money is put into and stays in a retirement account, the better chance it will be a money-generating machine for retirement. To help individuals save the maximum possible, some companies match employee contributions in part or in full.

Some other long-term goals might be a college education or saving for a down payment on a house. When saving for the long term, it is wise to move small accumulations to higher yielding but still liquid investments like certificates of deposit (CDs) or mutual funds.

Short-term financial goals might include the purchase of furniture, appliances, a car, or a vacation. Putting aside money each month makes these items affordable without going into debt. For example, if the cost of next year's vacation is $1,000, then divide that by 12 and begin putting aside $83.33 a month. When vacation time rolls around, the funds are available and no debt need be incurred. Europeans habitually purchase their vacations a year in advance and pay on them all year, so when it is time to go, the vacation is paid for.

Creating a Budget

Household finances should be handled like a small business—both function the same way, with money coming in, money going out, assets, liabilities, and so on. Many software packages are available that contain the elements needed for creating a spending plan and tracking income, debt, savings, and investments. Once priorities are identified, goals are set, and percentages are agreed on, the last step is to allocate the money coming in: basic living expenses, transportation, taxes, savings, debt

Tracking personal expenses is key to creating and sticking to a budget.

Net Worth Statement				
Assets		**Liabilities**		
Cash	$3,000	Mortgage	$450,000	
Stocks, bonds, mutual funds	$210,000	Installment loans	$25,000	
Cash value of life insurance	$7,000	Credit card debt	$100,000	
Money owed you by others	$3,000	Unpaid bills	$25,000	
Annuities, retirement plans	$250,000	Money owed others	0	
Home	$500,000	Other liabilities	0	
Automobiles	$30,000			
Household furnishings	$50,000			
Personal property (jewelry, books, etc.)	$10,000			
Total assets	**$1,063,000**	**Total liabilities**	$600,000	
		Net worth	$463,000	

Liabilities are deducted from assets in order to calculate net worth.

repayment, and charitable donations. Creating a budget is a trial-and-error process that takes about a year to fine-tune.

Money should be allocated in a budget in the order of savings, necessities, then desires. Most people spend their money in this order: necessities, creditors, and desires, with little or nothing put aside for savings. Sometimes, when desires have consumed future income through debt, the list is narrowed to necessities, then creditors.

If living expenses are not met with current income, then one of two things must happen to avoid going into debt. Income must increase or lifestyle must change. Sometimes this change may be only for a short time, where sacrifices are made in the short term for longer-term goals. At other times, change may be for a lifetime.

Most categories of spending beyond living expenses are considered discretionary: personal preference decides how the money is spent. For the outdoors person, it might pay for camping and hunting supplies. For the creative person, it might buy art supplies, photography equipment, or decorative items for the home. This is the category of spending where desire can overtake income. Living by a spending plan helps avoid getting into debt without first planning for it.

Giving is a good discipline to add to the budgeting process. First, it provides a tax break because charitable giving is deductible from income. The value of anything given away within IRS guidelines is subtracted from the amount of income, lowering the total amount of taxes due. Giving also puts personal finances in perspective, especially when giving to others less fortunate.

When first creating a financial plan, reality usually intrudes: you cannot have it all. Spending drives the economy, so the advertising industry creates desires for products to keep people spending. Businesses and credit card companies make achieving these desires possible with no down payment and easy terms. The reality is that spending more than what comes in equals debt. Another reality check is that managing money takes discipline, time, and energy. However, the best and most surprising reality check is that the discipline of a financial plan provides freedom from constantly worrying about money.

Further Research
Budget worksheet
http://financialplan.about.com/cs/budgeting/l/blbudget.htm
A useful template for setting up a personal budget.
CNNMoney.com
money.cnn.com/pf/
News and advice on personal finance and investing from CNN and *Money* and *Fortune* magazines.
Understanding and Controlling your Finances
www.bygpub.com/finance/finance0.htm
Excerpted from *The Teenager's Guide to the Real World* by Marshall Brain.

—*Stephanie Buckwalter*

Franchise

Franchising is a method of distributing products or services. Two people or organizations are involved in a franchise: the franchiser, who lends the trademark or trade name and business system, and the franchisee, who pays a royalty and often an initial fee, for the right to do business under the franchiser's name and system. The contract that binds the two parties is called the franchise, but the word *franchise* is also used to refer to the actual business that the franchisee operates.

Franchising History

The word *franchise* comes from an Old French word meaning "privilege" or "right." In the Middle Ages, franchising might involve the permission to hold a fair or operate a ferry, granted by a king or local lord. Kings would also grant franchises for commercial activities like collecting taxes, building roads, and brewing ale. The original franchise was simply the right to a monopoly for a certain kind of commercial activity.

A more familiar form of franchising developed in Germany in the 1840s, when ale breweries began giving specific taverns

An advertisement for one of the earliest franchises, Singer sewing machines.

exclusive right to sell their ale. In 1851 the Singer Sewing Machine Company began granting distribution franchises for its sewing machines, giving certain salespeople the exclusive right to sell Singer machines within a specific area. Later, oil refineries and automobile manufacturers granted similar distribution franchises.

Until the end of World War II, almost all franchises were simply granting the right to distribute and sell a manufacturer's product. When the war ended, businesses needed to expand rapidly to keep pace with the fast-growing economy. To open new outlets without having to raise large amounts of capital, business-format franchising was developed. This kind of franchise was responsible for rapidly covering the United States (and much of the rest of the world) with fast-food restaurants, one-hour photo shops, and budget motels.

Business-Format Franchising

In business-format franchising, the franchiser provides the franchisee with a complete plan, or format, for managing and operating the business. The business plan is usually very detailed. It may give step-by-step procedures for all aspects of the business and a complete system for making management decisions. The franchiser may also provide advertising and product distribution as well as training for the franchisee. Some franchises operate training "colleges," where new franchisees are taught all they need to know about the business.

In exchange for the business plan and the right to use the franchiser's trademark, the franchisee pays a one-time fee, along with a percentage of the yearly profits. The franchisee must also assume the cost of setting up the business—building and construction costs, hiring the staff, purchasing products, and so on. Some franchisers also operate their own loan companies, lending the franchisee the seed money to establish the franchise.

The major advantage of business-format franchises is that the product and business system have already been developed and tested. Franchises are consistent, which appeals to customers who like to know what to expect. Many people want to know that they can order exactly the same hamburger or receive exactly the same quality of service in Sioux Falls, South Dakota, as in Detroit. Thus, most stores in each franchise are identical, so the customer will have no trouble recognizing a particular brand.

This strategy works—franchises are popular places to shop. In 2000 analysts estimated that franchises accounted for $1 trillion in annual U.S. sales and more than 40 percent of all U.S. retail sales. Industry analysts estimate that franchising employs more than eight million people, a new franchise outlet opens somewhere in the United States every eight minutes, and approximately one of every 12 retail businesses is a franchise.

Franchising was unregulated until 1978, when the Federal Trade Commission began requiring that all franchisers submit a document called the Uniform Offering Circular (UFOC) to all potential franchisees before receiving money. The UFOC provides very detailed information on the franchise company and has helped reduce sale of fraudulent franchises.

The Franchise Trend

Although the stereotypical franchises are fast-food restaurants, convenience stores, and motel chains, many kinds of businesses operate franchises. These include dating agencies, tax preparation, check cashing,

Subway founder Fred DeLuca (left) helps out during his visit to a Subway franchise in Anaheim, California.

financial services, home inspection for radon leaks, dry cleaning, and computer services.

The proliferation of franchises has caused many people to become concerned about the very uniformity that makes franchises so appealing. Because every store in each franchise looks the same, concern has been voiced that cities are losing their individual character. Franchise chains drive out local businesses, and some argue that the sense of community is destroyed thereby. Concern has also grown about the way franchise chains appeal to poorer people who may spend money they cannot afford on a burger or product they do not need simply for the cachet of buying from a store with a particular image.

Further Research
Franchise Update Network
www.franchising.com
This portal offers news, articles, and information on franchising and franchise opportunities.
International Franchise Association
www.franchise.org
The IFA is a membership organization of franchisors, franchisees, and suppliers. Its comprehensive Web site provides information on legal and regulatory issues as well as a state-by-state assessment of franchise markets.

—Lisa Magloff

U.S. Economic Impact of Franchises 2005	
Franchised businesses	
Jobs	11,029,206
Payroll	$279 billion
Establishments	909,253
All businesses	
Jobs	136,709,071
Payroll	$5,268 billion
Establishments	27,891,770

Source: International Franchise Association.

Inflation

In economics, inflation is defined as a steady and persistent rise in the cost of goods and services. In an inflationary situation, a rise in prices causes a fall in the value of money. Distinction must be made between inflation and a rise in relative prices; a rise in prices of certain limited items (a weather-related rise in coffee prices, for example) is not necessarily inflationary, while a rise in the price of a vital product (oil, for example) can be.

In the United States, inflation is generally measured by the Consumer Price Index (CPI), which is calculated monthly by the U.S. Bureau of Labor Statistics. The CPI is a measure of the average change over time in the prices paid by urban consumers for a market basket of consumer goods and services, and the inflation rate is the percentage of change in the CPI. Economists recognize that the CPI is not a perfect indicator of inflation: The items included in the index do not necessarily reflect what all consumers buy; different families have different needs; a national CPI does not account for regional differences; and new products may be slow to be included.

Throughout history, inflation has often accompanied wars, but inflation was rare until the twentieth century. In the United States, for example, the price level of a good in 1900 was about the same as it was in 1770. One often cited historical example of inflation was the "price revolution" that occurred in Europe between 1500 and 1650, which economists usually attribute to a combination of an influx of gold from the New World, increased silver production in Europe, and a rapidly rising population. At a rate of 1 percent a year, however, the episode rates as only mildly inflationary by contemporary standards.

The twentieth century witnessed some spectacular examples of runaway inflation, or hyperinflation. In Hungary from 1945 to 1946, for example, inflation reached almost 20,000 percent a month. A more famous example is the hyperinflation in Germany in 1923; at one point the conversion rate for deutsche marks was four trillion to the dollar. In the United States prices began to rise steadily after World War II. Although the inflation rate reached 14.5 percent in 1947, inflation remained low in the 1950s and did not become worrisome again until the late 1960s. Overall inflation for the decade of the 1970s was 103 percent, with the annual inflation rate peaking at 13.5 percent in 1980. Recessions in the early 1980s and the early 1990s served to slow inflation, and the inflation rate remained low in the late 1990s despite heady economic growth.

In modern economies an inflation rate of less than 2 or 3 percent is considered normal and acceptable. Inflation is harmful,

In the 1920s in Germany, inflation was so bad that deutsche marks were essentially useless except for lighting stoves.

however, when it increases economic uncertainty, thus discouraging investment and saving. If one nation experiences excessive inflation while most others do not, its exports become more expensive and its imports cheaper, thus leading to a trade deficit. Although inflation can cause wages to rise, prices normally rise faster than compensation, resulting in a lowering of real wages. Inflation also hurts people on fixed incomes, for example, people receiving pensions. Their incomes decline as inflation rises (an inflation rate of 6 percent a year causes prices to double every 12 years). Inflation is beneficial to borrowers, however, as they pay their debts in money that has less value than when they borrowed it.

Causes of Inflation

Economists disagree on inflation's causes. Broadly speaking, inflation analysts are often divided into two camps—advocates of the "demand pull" view (also known as monetarists) and advocates of the "cost push" theory (also known as institutionalists).

Monetarists consider the money supply to be the most significant factor in determining the level of spending. Demand pull inflation is seen as a matter of supply and demand—it occurs when there is a constant demand for a particular good or service but the supply of that good or service decreases or, alternatively, occurs when the demand rises and the supply does not keep pace. Demand pull inflation can also be explained as a relationship between the economy's output (supply) at full capacity and the level of overall spending (demand). Monetarists generally argue that hikes in the cost of goods and services will not normally cause inflation unless the government increases the money supply.

Inflation can hit people on fixed incomes very hard, if prices go up but their income does not.

The key is whether the economy is operating at full capacity. If it is not, demand pull theory states that increasing the money supply will raise real income and will not cause inflation. If, however, productive capacity is at maximum, an increase in the money supply will serve only to raise prices—the classic inflationary scenario.

The demand pull theory includes what is known as the Phillips Curve. Developed by the American economist A. W. Phillips in the late 1950s, the Phillips Curve establishes a relationship between unemployment and inflation—low unemployment is associated with rising prices—an uncomfortable thought, as it leads to the conclusion that inflation can be held in check only if unemployment is relatively high (or, conversely, a certain level of inflation must be accepted to minimize unemployment). Thus, price stability depends on the level of unemployment; the point at which this is possible is known as the Non-Acceleration Interest Rate of Unemployment (NAIRU). The legitimacy of the Phillips Curve seemed certain in the 1960s but was called into question in the 1970s, when many industrialized countries entered a period of "stagflation," which combined high unemployment with high inflation. In response, the monetarists, led by Milton Friedman, adopted the theory of "the natural rate of unemployment," which, they argued, is consistent with a stable rate of inflation. The economy, in this view, should find its own natural rate of employment.

Economists who support the cost push view of inflation argue that economic and social conditions in developed countries are not sufficiently appreciated by the demand pull theorists. In the institutionalists' view, inflation is caused by strong economic forces—increased taxes, for example, or the actions of corporations and the labor market (in the form of trade unions). Corporations can cause a rise in prices by eliminating competition and establishing near-monopoly conditions. Collusion and price fixing are possibilities, but price stability or price rises are more likely if a particular area of production is dominated by a small number of firms: none will attempt to undercut the others' prices because the interests of all are served by keeping prices high.

On the other hand, the upward pressure on prices may be the result of wage gains by workers. When workers win increased wages, their employers seek to cover those costs through price increases, resulting in inflation. Some institutionalists, however, see this model as somewhat old-fashioned, harking back to an era when the economic landscape was more commonly viewed as a struggle between capitalism and organized labor. Given the decline in the importance of labor unions in developed economies, this view has credibility. However, certain groups of workers are still able to win inflationary wage increases.

Coping with Inflation

Just as theories about the causes of inflation differ, so do theories about its cure. Speaking for the monetarists, Friedman dramatically demonstrated their viewpoint in his 1970s television series on economics, *Free to Choose*. Standing in front of a Treasury Department printing press spewing out $20 bills, he announced, "This is how you stop inflation," and turned off the machine. Inflation is caused by too rapid growth in the money supply, thus slowing that growth will slow inflation. One way to reduce the money supply is to raise interest rates—a step often taken by the Federal Reserve Board, the nation's central bank (which also tends to lower interest rates in periods of slow growth). As reducing the money supply will also slow the economy, the monetarist cure is painful because it leads to a period, which might last several years, of lower economic output and higher unemployment.

Institutionalists are more willing to turn to direct government control as a cure for inflation. One side of this equation would be government-imposed wage–price controls, which were attempted in the United States in the early 1970s and proved difficult to implement, politically unpopular, and distorted the normal operation of

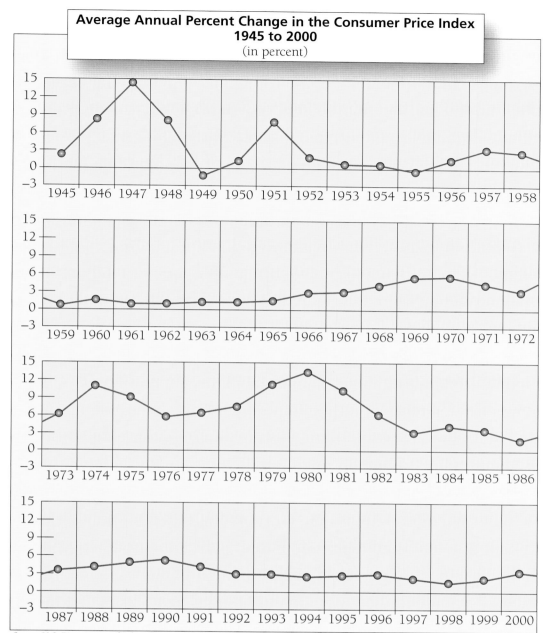

**Average Annual Percent Change in the Consumer Price Index
1945 to 2000**
(in percent)

Source: U.S. Department of Labor, Bureau of Labor Statistics.

the economy. The equation's other side would be encouraging lower prices by promoting greater competition among corporations, which can be done by enforcing antitrust legislation (restraining monopolies) and by dismantling government regulations that depress competition (a move that monetarists would also applaud).

A third approach has been called the "living with inflation" theory, which advocates protecting those most hurt by inflation by linking Social Security payments to a cost-of-living index. Although such a policy can indeed mitigate inflation's harsher effects, it does not address the real causes of inflation and can prove inflationary itself.

Further Research
Bureau of Labor Statistics
www.bls.gov/CPI/
The CPI is compiled in the United States by the Bureau of Labor Statistics.
Statistics Canada
www.statcan.gc.ca/subjects-sujets/cpi-ipc/cpi-ipc-eng.htm
The source for Canadian inflation reports.

—Joseph Gustaitis

Innovation

Innovation and invention both are concerned with making something new, but economists and businesspeople make a distinction between the two concepts. An invention is a new idea or a new product, but an innovation is made only when an invention is put to practical use. Innovation in this sense fosters business success and economic growth.

Several trends in the contemporary business world underscore the importance of innovation. Globalization is forcing companies to develop products and services for diverse populations. Fast-paced change in information technology and other industries forces businesses to modify their outputs and the means of providing those outputs. Intense competition forces businesses to search continually for new and better ways to serve their customers.

Failure to innovate often explains why companies lose their leading position in an industry. Examples include Sears being outpaced by Wal-Mart in the retail industry and U.S. Steel giving way to Nucor in the steel industry. In the 1980s IBM failed to dominate emerging sectors of the computer industry, losing out to smaller firms like Microsoft and Apple, even though IBM had a formidable head start in the sector.

Many attributes of an organization affect its ability to innovate, including its structure, culture, people, strategy, and surroundings. Economist Joseph A. Schumpeter first proposed that small, entrepreneurial firms are the most likely to innovate because small firms can implement new ideas quickly as they lack bureaucratic layers; small firms can react nimbly to their business environment; and the top manager in a small firm has the power to push for implementation of an innovation.

Later, however, Schumpeter argued that large firms with some degree of monopoly power are most likely to innovate. Large firms have the resources needed to adjust to the economic uncertainty that comes with innovating, and they can afford to support the expertise that fosters innovation. Monopoly power also gives firms a greater probability of success in commercializing an innovation. Schumpeter seems to have been right in both cases: Size does not matter; small and large firms have shown themselves capable of innovating for all the above reasons.

Innovations can take many forms. Product innovation occurs when a new product is introduced or new attributes are added to existing products. Market innovation occurs when existing products are targeted to new geographic markets or to new market segments within existing geographic markets. Process innovation occurs through alterations in the technology used to manufacture a product or provide a service. Administrative innovation occurs when organizational structure or administrative systems are changed to improve operations. Innovations can also be categorized as incremental or radical. An innovation is incremental if it leaves existing products or processes competitive; it is radical if it renders existing products or processes noncompetitive or obsolete.

Companies use various strategies to prevent others from profiting from their innovations. The block strategy is one. Blocking efforts may succeed if the innovative technology is closely held or if the innovative firm can somehow intimidate competitors. Wal-Mart uses a blocking strategy when it

---

Forms of Innovation

Product Innovation:
New product.

•

Market Innovation:
New geographic market or new market segment.

•

Process Innovation:
New technology to manufacture product or provide service.

•

Administrative Innovation:
Organizational structure changed to improve operations.

A worker cutting steel at the Nucor Steel Corporation in Utah. Nucor was able to displace U.S. Steel as the top steel producer in great part because of its ability to innovate.

expands. It first moves into a location that competitors have ignored and then blocks the competition by saturating the surrounding area with its stores. Furthermore, through its bargaining power and efficient operations, Wal-Mart may intimidate the competition (and attract customers) by offering products at very low prices.

Another method is the run strategy: an organization seeks always to stay a step ahead of the competition. Such strategy works for companies that are never satisfied with existing products or processes. Intel has used the run strategy to stay ahead in the semiconductor industry by continually introducing new generations of microprocessors, making its older microprocessors obsolete. A third is the team-up strategy, which comes into play when organizations join forces through a strategic alliance or joint venture to implement an innovation. Strategic alliances are common in the information technology industry. Sun Microsystems used a team-up strategy to establish a market for its workstations built with its new SPARC technology. Sun announced that it would license this technology to anyone who wanted it, in hopes that SPARC technology would become the industry standard.

Increased competition, the globalization of markets, and technological change are trends that will continue to require innovation in business. In such a business environment, organizations adept at fostering and managing innovation will be likely to succeed; others will be likely to struggle and fall behind.

Further Research

Information Technology and Innovation Foundation

www.innovationeconomics.org

The Web site of this foundation dedicated to innovation economics has a useful resources page.

Business Week

www.businessweek.com/innovate

The magazine's Web site has a section devoted to innovation in business.

—*Will Drago*

Interest

Many individuals and corporations have excess money and no good projects in which to invest; many other individuals and corporations have great ideas and projects but no money to spend. Those with excess money sometimes lend to those without money. What is not readily apparent, however, is who has excess and who is in need of funds. Therefore, commercial banks act as financial intermediaries that lend to and borrow from individuals and corporations. Interest is the payment made for the use of someone else's money.

Interest is calculated based on a principal amount (the dollar amount lent or borrowed), the length of the loan, and the interest rate (usually expressed in percentage terms for the length of one year). Interest has an effect on the overall health of an economy. Interest rates affect consumers' willingness to spend and save, as well as investment decisions by business. High interest rates, for example, may cause a corporation to postpone building a new plant, which would have provided more jobs in a particular town.

Calculation of Interest

The two methods of calculating interest are simple and compounded. Simple interest is calculated by multiplying the annual interest rate by the principal amount to arrive at the annualized payment. The annual interest payment is then multiplied by the fraction of the year of the loan to arrive at the actual dollar amount of interest owed. For example, if a company borrowed $10,000 from a bank for six months at an annual simple interest rate of 5 percent, the interest would be calculated as: $10,000 x .05 x (6 months / 12 months) = $250. On the first day of the loan, the bank would give the company $10,000; six months later, the company would pay the bank $10,250 ($10,000 principal + $250 interest) and the loan would be complete.

The other method of calculating interest is compounded. In this case, one needs the same information as above, as well as the number of times the interest is to be compounded. Using the above example, assume that compounding takes place quarterly (every three months). Since this loan is for six months, compounding will take place twice. To calculate the compounded interest payment, the interest in each of the compounding periods must be calculated separately and in order. The interest rate to be applied to each compounding period must be the annual rate divided by the number of compounding periods per year. Once the interest is calculated for the first compounding period, the principal plus cumulative interest is used to find the next payment, and so on. The steps below show the compounded interest calculation:

1. Period 1 interest: $10,000 × (.05 / 4 compounding periods) = $125
2. End of period 1 new principal: $10,000 + $125 = $10,125
3. Period 2 interest: $10,125 × (.05 / 4 compounding periods) = $126.5625
4. End of period 2 new principal: $10,125 + $126.5625 = $10,251.5625
5. Total interest = $251.5625

In this case, on the first day of the loan, the bank lends the company $10,000. Then, six months later, the company repays the bank $10,251.56 ($10,000 + $125 + $126.5625), and the loan will be complete. Note that compounding always yields higher interest than simple interest because compounding incurs interest on interest earned, while simple does not.

One final concept, the day-count convention, is needed to accurately calculate interest payments. The previous examples assumed that the six-month loan was for exactly one-half year. This day-count convention is called 30/360 (an assumption that each month has 30 days, and a year has 360 days). In reality, months and years differ in their number of days. The other conventions are actual/360, actual/365, and actual/actual. If an actual/actual convention were used in the above example, when the six months of the loan covered 182 days and the year had 365 days, the tenor of the loan would be expressed as 182/365 (or .4986), not 6/12 (or .5). When loan amounts are large, the differences can be very significant. The borrower and lender must agree upon the interest calculation beforehand to avoid any disagreements upon the final loan payment.

Interest Rate Fundamentals

Each bank sets the interest rate it will charge based on: the supply and demand for money, opportunity cost, the length of the loan, the riskiness of the loan, and the Federal Reserve (the Fed).

The supply of and demand for money is the most straightforward driver of interest rates. If every individual and company in the world wanted to borrow money and no one wanted to lend, the banks would have to raise interest rates to discourage borrowers and encourage lenders. If everyone wanted to lend money and nobody wanted to borrow, the banks would lower interest rates. Banks raise and lower interest rates frequently to assure an even balance between borrowers and lenders.

Opportunity cost is another driver of interest rates. Consider a lender who has excess money to invest. The lender can invest this money in any number of assets, each with a specific return. If the lender chooses to lend the money, the interest rate of the loan should be just as good or better than other investments (given a certain level of risk). Therefore, if returns on other investments increase, interest rates should increase, and vice versa. Typically, economists study inflation rates to understand opportunity costs. Inflation rates drive most investment opportunities in developed countries like the United States.

The length of the loan also affects interest rates, but not always consistently. To understand the relationship between interest rates and length of loans, economists like to use the yield curve (a graph that shows time on the X axis, and interest rates, or yields, on the Y axis). In theory, interest rates should be higher for longer-term loans because as more time goes by, the lender's opportunity cost increases. Economists would say that the yield curve is upward sloping. Although this is usually true, it is not always the case. Sometimes supply and demand drive rates up or down at only those points. For example, assume people thought the economy (and inflation) would increase for five years but

Interest rates paid to lenders are higher for longer loans because the cost to the lenders increases over time.

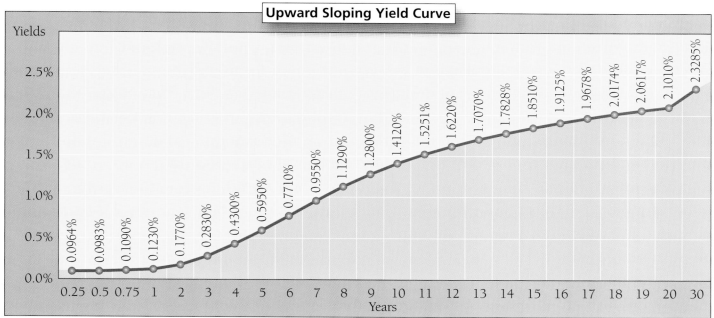

Source: Federal Reserve Board, "Economic Research and Data," http://www.federalreserve.gov/rnd.htm (March 27, 2003).

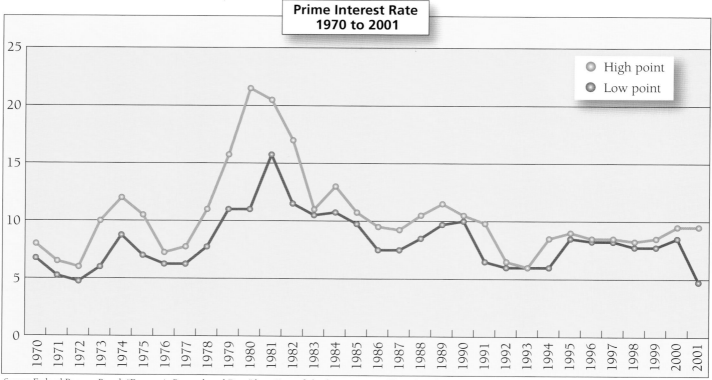

Prime Interest Rate 1970 to 2001

Source: Federal Reserve Board, "Economic Research and Data," http://www.federalreserve.gov/rnd.htm (March 27, 2003).

decline after that. In this case, the yield curve could be downward sloping and the interest rate on a longer-term loan will be lower than that for a shorter-term loan. Although a downward sloping yield curve is possible, the United States has mostly seen upward sloping yield curves throughout its history.

Holding all other variables constant, the more risky the loan, the higher the interest rate, and vice versa. The lender must be compensated for the increased chance that he will not be paid back. Typically, this is referred to as credit risk, and different companies and individuals have different credit risks. When considering credit risk, banks take the interest rate of a loan to a company or individual and subtract the interest rate of a risk-free loan (for example, a loan to the U.S. government). The difference is called the credit spread.

The Fed is responsible for monitoring and correcting economic performance. One of the Fed's tools to carry out this function is the ability to set the interest rates for banks to borrow from the Fed and to borrow from each other. If the Fed raises these

rates, the banks must raise interest rates on loans to corporations and individuals.

Interest rates are considered by many economists as the leading indicator for predicting whether the economy is headed for a boom or a recession. Thus understanding why interest rates change and how these fluctuations affect individual or company finances is crucial. More important, every household and business pays and receives interest in some form, so understanding how those interest rates are set and the interest payments are calculated is essential for good money management.

Further Research
Federal Reserve Board
www.federalreserve.gov
The Federal Reserve, which sets U.S. interest rates, provides both current and historical data on its comprehensive Web site. It also offers a live feed function with rapid updates on interest rate changes.
Interest calculators
www.webmath.com/simpinterest.html
www.webmath.com/compinterest.html
The educational site Webmath offers calculators for both simple interest and compound interest.

—*David Korb and Andréa Korb*

Inventory

Inventory is a term for goods that are held by a business for sale or for use in production. The goods can be raw materials or parts used by manufacturers to produce finished goods. They can also be the finished goods themselves, which are held by manufacturers until they are sold to wholesalers, then held by wholesalers until they are sold to retailers, then held by retailers until they are sold to the public.

Although inventory is a simple idea, managing inventory can be very complicated. Stores often stock hundreds or thousands of different items, all of which need to be tracked and accounted for. A manufacturer might have inventories of hundreds of parts and dozens of different finished products.

Having too much or too little inventory can cause problems for a company. Too much inventory is quite expensive; the inventory must be stored, so space must be bought or rented and outfitted with security staff, light, and, depending upon the kind of inventory, refrigeration or other climate control. The longer inventory sits, the higher the risk that it will be damaged, stolen, become obsolete, or otherwise become worthless.

In addition, too much of inventory can represent a serious opportunity cost, which is the price of making one choice as opposed to another. For example, if a furniture wholesaler buys $10,000 worth of chairs, that $10,000 is lost to the wholesaler until the chairs are sold. If the chairs do not sell, the wholesaler's money remains tied up in inventory and cannot be used for anything else. Having too little inventory, however, is also a problem. If a manufacturer cannot produce a product in a timely fashion because she keeps running out of the necessary parts, her clients will buy the product from someone else.

Too little inventory also creates missed opportunities. In November 2006, for example, the Nintendo Wii game console was launched in the United States. The Wii sold out on its launch day, with retailers quickly running out of consoles as well as nunchuks and controllers. While some disappointed gamers (or their parents) probably bought the product later, others probably did not, limiting the profits of retailers, creators, and manufacturers.

The first step in properly managing inventory is to determine how much a company has on hand. One method is to look at how many goods a company had, for instance, at the beginning of the year, determine how many new goods were ordered during the year, and then see how many were sold or used during the year. This method assumes that those numbers are accurate and that nothing else happened to the inventory—no theft, no breakage, no loss.

Stacks of lumber in a hardware store. Stores must carry inventory so products are available when customers want to buy them.

Companies generally want a more accurate inventory count. Before the widespread use of computers, most companies periodically "took inventory," often closing operations to count the number of units of the various goods held in inventory. This method lets a company know how much of a particular good is left; however, it is time-consuming and disrupts operations. Companies usually took inventory once or twice a year; for the rest of the year, exact inventory levels were unknown.

Computers have made so-called perpetual inventory—once reserved for companies that sold only a few very expensive goods—accessible to most businesses. By using bar codes and scanners, a grocery store can determine at any time how much of which products are being sold. This means that if a new cereal is wildly popular, the store's management knows immediately and is able to order more. The managers can even put up a special display of the cereal and find out whether that leads to more sales. Even with perpetual inventory, however, most stores find that occasionally taking inventory the old-fashioned way is useful to determine theft and breakage.

Computerized inventory systems can be networked to each other, which helped give rise to just-in-time inventory systems in the 1990s, an idea originally developed in Japan. Just-in-time inventory especially influenced manufacturers of complex machinery requiring lots of parts and supplies. In a perfect just-in-time inventory system, inventory all but disappears because networked inventory systems enable the supplier to provide the manufacturer with what she needs just when she needs it. In the real world, just-in-time systems tend to shift inventory costs from manufacturers to suppliers; however, such systems often result in less inventory overall.

This reduction appears to have benefited the U.S. economy. Usually when an economic recession or depression begins, manufacturers do not realize immediately that demand has slowed. (Manufacturers respond with layoffs or temporarily shutting plants and production lines.) During the lag time, inventories often build up just as demand has slacked, resulting in a large inventory "overhang." Because manufacturers have so much excess inventory sitting around (which costs money to store), they suddenly slow down production, selling goods out of inventory instead of manufacturing new goods. If enough manufacturers are affected, unemployment can suddenly increase, worsening the downturn.

In 2000, after many companies had adopted just-in-time inventory systems, an

Turnover Analysis

A turnover analysis helps decide if the investment in an individual inventory item is too low, too high, or just right. For example, this turnover analysis from a publishing company looks at the inventory of particular book titles.

Fall Publishing List			
Title	Number of units in stock	Number of units sold in last 30 days	Days until title is out of stock	Action
American First Ladies	2,500	357	210	None
Animals A-Z	750	250	90	Reprint title (increase inventory)
Astronomy Firsts	4,000	400	300	None
Cartoons for Everyone	10,000	35	8,571	Remainder 5,000 units (decrease inventory)
Geography of Afghanistan	1,300	856	45	Reprint title (increase inventory)

Computerized inventory systems enable companies to analyze up-to-the-minute data on the status of inventory.

economic slowdown began. Initially, the slowdown demonstrated the limits of such systems; high-tech companies like Sun Microsystems were caught unawares by the slowdown, did not decrease production in time, and had massive inventory overhangs. However, the slowdown proved to be mild, in part because manufacturers in general had little excess inventory. The shallowness of the recession was attributable to a number of other factors as well, including consumer demand falling only mildly, so inventories cleared out faster. Nonetheless, the pace with which the U.S. economy recovered in 2001 raised the possibility that advances in inventory management could result in less economic volatility in the future. However, in the fourth quarter of 2008, production overtook sales as both business and consumers reined in their spending dramatically. Retailers were caught by surprise, and many resorted to deep discounting in order to reduce inventories.

Further Research
APICS The Association for Operations Management
www.apics.org
APICs is a valuable source of information on operations management, including production, inventory, supply chain, materials management, purchasing, and logistics.
Inventory Management Today
inventorymanagementtoday.com
A collection of current articles based on real world experience.

—*Mary Sisson*

Job Search

A job search is not a once-in-a-lifetime opportunity. A worker typically is in the job market many times in his or her career. The basics of a job search—preparation, process, contact, and negotiation—are the same for the searcher just starting out or one close to retirement.

Preparation
The largest amount of time is usually put into the preparation phase. Preparation includes self-analysis for career direction, writing a resume, determining a target market or target company, and basic research on salary and benefits for the target market.

The first question to be answered is, "What do I want to do with my life?" Although it may take many years to find the answer, asking questions along those lines can help direct a job search. For example, do I like to work with people or things? Do I want a traditional job or something a little out of the ordinary? Am I willing to get additional education or

Job hunters can use interviews as an opportunity to learn more about the company and the job prospect. Curiosity and engagement are positive traits to demonstrate.

training to meet my goals? How much money do I need to be making in five years to live the way I desire without going into debt? The answers to these questions either open up areas or close them off during the job search. Fewer options are best when starting the task of creating a resume as a resume should be somewhat tailored to a specific job or industry.

A potential employer's first impression is typically taken from a resume. A resume should give the reviewer a fair idea of the person's experience and career goals or employment objective. When just starting out, a resume should be kept to one page. The key to a just-getting-started resume is to quantify everything possible. Quantifying experience adds value beyond the job description. For example, the job description for a food service job should go beyond flipping burgers and bussing tables. It should also say something like "learned excellent communication skills through public contact." To quantify experience as a lifeguard, the resume could read, "ability to think clearly and act quickly in life-threatening situations" or "ability to remain calm in stressful situations, influencing others to stay calm." As early experience probably does not match career goals, these statements tell potential employers a tremendous amount about how the applicant interacts with others or functions in a work environment. Known as soft skills, they can be just as valuable as work experience.

Targeting a market further narrows the job search. A target helps job hunters clarify their objective in applying for particular jobs. A target also helps define how much they can expect to get paid for a job and where the career path will most likely lead in a few years.

Process

Once preparation is complete, the job search begins. A job search should be treated as a full-time job with office hours and appointment scheduling. The search can be an emotional roller coaster with highs and lows as interviews take place

and offers may or may not be made. The key to keeping the emotions level and the number of interviews high is to keep sending out resumes and making contacts in a steady stream, even when a particular job seems promising. If the job falls through, valuable time has been lost if the search has stopped, and sometimes getting the momentum going again is difficult.

The most typical places to look for jobs are newspapers and the Internet, which offers a variety of job listings and other employment forums. However, several other options are available, and although use of the Internet for job searches is increasing, traditional search methods are still very valuable. In fact, data from the Bureau of Labor Statistics suggest that people who use many different job search methods find work faster than those who use only one or two. Networking with other people often pro-

Average Number of Jobs Held from Ages 18 to 37 1978 to 2006				
Sex and educational attainment	Number of jobs held by age			
	Total[1]	18 to 22 years old	23 to 27 years old	33 to 37 years old
Men	11.0	4.6	3.5	2.3
Less than a high school diploma	12.5	4.6	3.8	2.4
High school grad., no college (2)	10.7	4.5	3.4	2.2
Some college or associate degree	11.1	4.5	3.5	2.4
Bachelor's degree and higher (3)	10.7	4.6	3.4	2.2
Total	11.0	4.6	3.5	2.3
Women	10.6	4.3	3.1	2.1
Less than a high school diploma	8.7	2.9	2.3	1.9
High school grad., no college (2)	10.2	3.9	2.7	2.2
Some college or associate degree	11.0	4.5	3.3	2.2
Bachelor's degree and higher (3)	11.5	5.3	3.7	2.0
Total	10.6	4.3	3.1	2.1
Total				
Less than a high school diploma	10.9	3.9	3.2	2.2
High school grad., no college (2)	10.5	4.2	3.1	2.2
Some college or associate degree	11.1	4.5	3.4	2.3
Bachelor's degree and higher (3)	11.1	5.0	3.6	2.1
Total	10.8	4.4	3.3	2.2

[1] Jobs held in more than one age category were counted in each category, but only once in the total.
Source: : U.S. Bureau of Labor Statistics, National Longitudinal Survey of Youth, 1979 to 2007.

Traditional Methods of Job Searching
1994 to 1999
(in percent)

Search method	1994	1995	1996	1997	1998	1999
Contacted employer directly	67.4	65.1	64.7	67.3	64.5	65.1
Public employment agency	20.4	20.1	18.9	19.1	20.4	15.9
Private employment agency	7.2	7.1	7.5	6.6	6.6	7.0
Friends or relatives	15.7	18.0	16.6	14.6	13.5	13.4
School employment center	2.3	1.9	2.3	2.7	2.3	1.6
Sent out resumes/filled out applications	40.2	46.9	48.3	46.6	48.3	47.6
Checked union/professional registers	2.7	2.4	2.5	1.7	1.5	1.9
Placed or answered ads	16.7	17.7	17.3	16.3	14.5	12.5
Other active search methods	3.5	2.9	3.9	4.6	4.4	5.7

Note: Civilian noninstitutionalized population 16 and over who are unemployed active job seekers; based on the *Current Population Survey.*
Source: U.S. Bureau of Labor Statistics, *Monthly Labor Review,* October 2000.

Many job searching strategies have remained the same over the years. When the U.S. Bureau of Labor Statistics conducted a similar survey in 2007, it found that fewer people were contacting employers directly (only 57 percent of respondents) but more people (almost 22 percent) were using help from friends or relatives. In the twenty-first century, the Internet is an essential tool, aiding in all these methods.

duces good job matches for both the employer and job hunter because the personal referral works both ways. The person doing the referring usually knows a little about the company and a little about the person; that person has, in effect, done the first round of screening for the company. Bulletin boards at colleges and universities have job listings and internships. Another method is to list companies that fit certain criteria and contact them directly.

Contact

An employer typically requires one or more interviews before making a hiring decision. A series of interviews might include an initial phone interview, then a personal interview with the hiring manager, then a team interview with peers. Each of these interviews serves a different purpose. The phone interview gives the employer basic information: How does the applicant handle himself over the phone? It also allows the employer to verify that the resume is true on a very basic level. The interview with the hiring manager gives the manager a feel for how the candidate's experience and personality will fit within the team dynamic and the corporate culture. The interview with peers serves two purposes. One is to verify hands-on experience at an in-depth level and the other is to see if the person is a fit for the company overall.

Several interviews allow the company to evaluate experience plus soft skills, thus allowing the firm to make better hiring decisions.

An interview is a good time for the job hunter to find out some details about the company, too. For example, does the company offer any specific career paths? Does it have a mentoring program and who is eligible for it? What is the management structure like? Does the company pay for training as skills become outdated or new technology is developed? Another issue is the total benefits package. Often, this information is not available until after the company makes a job offer. Benefits can include various kinds of insurance, tuition reimbursement, telecommuting opportunities, flexible hours (flex time), overtime pay, retirement plans, and stock options.

The key to a good interview is preparation and confidence. Before the interview, research the company: check its Web site, check its reputation, know a little about its major products or services, and know what the company is looking for in new hires.

Questions about age, race, marital status, sexual orientation, number of children, or medical history are illegal. However, companies can, and often do, look up credit reports, which have information about litigation settlements, amount of debt, medical payment history to hospitals or doctors, and marital status. Some companies have requirements like drug testing before employment or the signing of non-compete agreements in which an employee agrees not to take a new job with a competing firm for a set amount of time. Job hunters should know the legal restraints on employers.

Once an interview is finished, a job seeker should follow up. Asking when a hiring decision will be made is appropriate; follow up with a phone call if the deadline passes. A thank you note for time spent with various interviewers lets the company know the applicant is serious and still interested. Follow-up is professional and it makes a big impression.

Negotiation

Subtle negotiation begins the minute the conversation turns to salary, compensation, or benefits. Every job hunter should be prepared to work through the salary negotiation process. Usually the negotiations begin awkwardly, with each party trying to have the other name a starting salary first. The job hunter can prepare by researching appropriate answers and practicing them beforehand. The salary figure is key because, in general, all future raises are based on the starting salary. Most employers work within a salary range for hiring based on demand for those skills, geographic location, and their own financial situation.

Salary is just one issue for negotiation. Benefits can sometimes be negotiated. Health insurance is usually not negotiable, but flex time, telecommuting, bonuses, number of vacation days, or relocation packages often can be negotiated. Successful negotiation in these areas primarily depends on demand. If the job market is soft or the skill set of the jobseeker is readily available, then the employer has no motivation to negotiate over these items.

After negotiation, the final step is evaluating offers. As noted above, the offer is more than just a salary. It is a total compen-

Web Resources for Job Searches

www.monster.com is a comprehensive job search engine for both employers and candidates; it includes information on job openings, resumes, and interview guidelines.

www.dice.com provides employment resources for technology professionals.

www.careerbuilder.com posts employment opportunities for a variety of companies in many different fields.

www.fedworld.gov/jobs/jobsearch.html and **www.federaljobsearch.com** are Web sites listing employment opportunities with the federal government.

www.rileyguide.com is a guide to employment opportunities and job resources on the Internet.

www.provenresumes.com is a resource for helpful guides to resumes and cover letters.

www.job-hunt.org is a comprehensive list of the Web's best job search sites.

www.idealist.org is a resource for employment in the not-for-profit sector.

sation package. It must be reviewed in light of the job hunter's long-term and short-term goals. For example, if the job is simply a stepping stone to another company, salary may be most important. If the job hunter's plan is to stay in the job for a while, then family medical plans, matching funds for retirement packages, and telecommuting may weigh heavily in the decision to accept an offer. If a goal is to relocate, then paid relocation can have tremendous value.

The four phases of a job search—preparation, process, contact, and negotiation—can occur in a very condensed period, or they may take months. In many ways, a job search is a numbers game. The more potential employers that see a resume, the better the chances of getting a job. The keys to a successful job hunt are preparation and diligence in carrying out the search.

Further Research

Bolles, Richard Nelson. *What Color is Your Parachute? 2009: A Practical Manual for Job Hunters and Career Changers.* Berkeley, Calif.: Ten Speed Press, 2008.

Bolles, Richard Nelson, Carol Christen, and Jean M. Blomquist. *What Color is Your Parachute? For Teens.* Berkeley, Calif.: Ten Speed Press, 2005.

—*Stephanie Buckwalter*

Market Research

Somewhere between science and psychology lies market research. The objective of market research is to gain an understanding of customers in an attempt to sell them products or services. Although many business owners would like market research to be a science, the unpredictable human elements of preference and circumstance factor into every marketing formula ever designed. The buying public's fancy is not always predictable.

The science component of market research takes into account demographics: age, income, race, occupation, and level of education. The psychology component, called psychographics, relates to lifestyle. Market researchers look at where people live, both address and kind of residence. They track where they are in their life cycle—single, just married, newly pregnant, retired. They also study changing roles in the home, for example, who cooks and who shops. Lifestyle can also be more general in nature, including trends toward healthier living, later marriages, and fewer children. Psychographic variables make conducting completely accurate market research impossible, but companies strive to learn as much as possible about people and their lifestyles so they can make smart business decisions.

Early Market Research

The first American market researcher is generally considered to be Charles Coolidge Parlin. In 1910 he did research for the Curtis Publishing Company. His mission was to gather information that might be helpful to businesses that advertised in the company's numerous magazines. His information allowed advertisers to fine-tune their marketing plans to fit each magazine's readership and make better use of their advertising dollars.

Many companies, Coca-Cola and the Chicago Tribune among them, followed suit with their own versions of market research. By the 1920s the field of market research blossomed. It also began a subtle shift in emphasis. In the early days, market research was based on function: how to get goods to people who were geographically dispersed. As companies began to fear market saturation for their products, they changed focus from function to style. Instead of worrying about how to get products to people, they strove to figure out how to get people to buy more products. For example, General Motors responded to the fear of market saturation by changing the style of its cars every year beginning in 1927. The purpose was to create dissatisfaction in the consumer: "I have an old style of car, and I want the newer [implicitly better] style of car." GM used market research to both find and create that dissatisfaction.

The mass popularity of radio in the mid-1920s changed market research, and the television boom of the 1950s changed it further still. The idea of the mass market was born with the widespread coverage made possible by radio and television. Because companies could no longer take the people's purchasing pulse directly, they began using a relatively new technique for

Ways of Conducting Market Research	
Type of Market Research	**Methodology**
Observation	Observe consumers; read trade publications; watch competition.
Face Time	Utilize focus groups; one-on-one interviews; questionnaires; product tests and demonstrations.
Personal Research	Research government, library and trade associations; collect information from company Web site.
Information Purchase	Purchase data from information brokers.

that time, scientific polling. Companies would ask people a series of questions, then tabulate the results to get a feel for their customers.

The Census Bureau

The technology needed to compile large amounts of market research came from a somewhat unexpected place. Oddly enough, it was inspired by a decree in the Constitution—that the United States should count its citizens every 10 years. In 1880 Herman Hollerith, an employee at the Bureau of the Census, designed and built a tabulating machine that used punch cards, metal pens, and electrical contacts to compile information. This machine, which was to become the forerunner of computer punch card systems, was used to tabulate the results of the 1890 census. Hollerith started his own company and, in 1911, merged it with three others to form what would become International Business Machines, or IBM.

Around the same time, businesses began showing an interest in U.S. census data for their market research. The Census Bureau had subdivided the whole United States into census tracts (about 4,000 people) and then into census blocks (approximately 85 people in urban areas, 30 in rural areas). The bureau's purpose was to help the census takers as, at the time (and up until 1960), all data gathering was done in person. The bureau's subdivisions, coupled with Hollerith's tabulating machine, made possible the tabulating of census data in small pieces. Companies could now get a very specific look at the people they were selling to. Having a little information increased companies' desire to know more.

By 1951 the Census Bureau had begun using the world's first commercial digital computer, called the Universal Automatic Computer (UNIVAC). It too used punch cards, but the data were registered on magnetic tape that could be used to create custom reports of the census information. Although the UNIVAC arrived too late for the 1950 census, the computer was used to compile almost all of the 1960 census data. A

few years after the census, though still early in the computer revolution, companies gained access to computers that had enough speed and memory to manipulate and analyze the numbers from the census. At that point, the U.S. Census Bureau became more than a government agency that counted people. It began to sell its data to commercial concerns. In 1963 the then–Post Office began using zip codes, giving companies yet another way to coordinate and analyze data in conjunction with the census data.

For many years the Census Bureau was a major supplier of market research data. The bureau still provides helpful information, especially for small businesses, but its role in market research has diminished because of the vast array of information available from other sources. Census information forms only a small part of what market research firms collect today.

A sorting machine used by the U.S. Bureau of the Census, circa 1911. For many years the Census Bureau was the primary provider of market research data.

Kinds of Market Research

Market research is the first step in creating a marketing plan. Good research methods collect both demographic and psychographic information, which can be used to identify potential new markets, increase market share, determine pricing, and support market segmentation analysis. Research is conducted in a number of ways: observation, "face time," personal research, and information purchase.

The least costly form of research is simple observation of what is going on in the marketplace. To stay profitable, companies must be aware of trends in the marketplace and must distinguish them from fads. A trend is a sustained interest in a product that lasts at least five to 10 years whereas a fad is a short-term interest in a product, usually one to two years. Reading trade publications or simply seeing what people are buying and doing can alert researchers to trends. Another way to spot trends is to watch the competition. What subtle shifts are other companies making to adjust to the market? Are they offering new products, advertising in a new area, promoting a new color? Changes may point to a new trend.

A huge part of market research includes "face time"—time spent talking to the customer base face-to-face, for example, in focus groups, one-on-one interviews, questionnaires, or product tests and demonstrations. This kind of market research is either qualitative or quantitative. Qualitative research involves a free flow of ideas between the consumer and the researcher. This kind of interaction typically happens during a focus group or a personal interview. Questions are open-ended and the researcher encourages a certain amount of antagonism toward the product, needing the bad news as well as the good. Qualitative analysis helps the researcher identify the customer and the customer's concerns.

Some market research is conducted by telephone, with operators calling people to ask their opinions on different products, companies, or issues.

Quantitative research is more structured. Questionnaires are the best example. The questionnaire should be designed to test the validity of the conclusions drawn from the earlier qualitative analysis. The questions should lead to very specific answers, either enforcing or destroying the researcher's earlier conclusions.

Prototypes and test markets are used to get both qualitative and quantitative information. A prototype is a working model of a product. Consumers can respond in an informal way or by answering specific questions. Test markets, small geographic areas used to test new products alongside the competition, provide valuable insight into how the products measure up in the real world.

Personal research is research that a company conducts on its own, as opposed to information purchase, which is research a company buys. A variety of resources can be used for personal research, starting with a public or college library and trade associations. The government provides a wealth of research material through the Department of Commerce, Small Business Administration, chambers of commerce, and of course, the Census Bureau. If a company has a Web site, it can track each visitor's activity on the site through "cookies," bits of encrypted information deposited on a computer's hard drive.

The key to market research is gathering useful information. When beginning a research project on its own, a company must know what kind of information it is looking for and how it plans to use it. Using all these resources is time consuming, but the investment in research gives companies an edge over their competition.

Information Brokers

One popular method of conducting market research is to purchase the needed research from companies that specialize in gathering information and analyzing and combining it in any number of ways. One company, Experian, keeps a database that includes information on more than 235 million individuals and 113 households; its custom databases can include up to 1,000 data elements per record.

The first places to look for information on individuals and households are usually state, local, and national public records, including those of the Census Bureau. For example, all real estate transactions are a matter of public record, so a research company can get a lot of information from a single transaction: names, addresses, income, price paid for the home, property assessment, amount of down payment, and more. State Departments of Motor Vehicles have information on driving records, what kind of car a person drives, and its value. Those two sources alone tell a lot about people: where they live and what they drive often speak volumes about their preferred lifestyle.

Credit bureaus collect and sell information about people, including income, number of credit lines, and legal obligations related to money. They typically know marital status, number of children, and other personal information gleaned from credit applications. They also collect information from creditors

Pros and Cons of Information Brokers	
Pros	**Cons**
• Information available quickly	• Data may not address specific question
• Cost modest	• Answers may lack specificity
• Information objective	• Data may not be comparable with other sources
• May be only source of specific data	• Quality varies
• Improves focus of additional research	• Information may be dated

Source: Edward F. McQuarrie, *The Market Research Toolbox: A Concise Guide for Beginners,* Thousand Oaks, Calif., Sage Publications, 1996.

Market research data can be presented in a variety of ways, and graphic presentations are often very useful.

who can then be targeted for specific kinds of advertising and specific products. One kind of target marketing is life-cycle marketing. Companies identify people who are at a particular stage of life, then send them the appropriate advertisements and marketing materials. For example, a pregnant woman would be a target for offers involving formula, diapers, nursing pads, and so on. Singles are targets for dating services. Seniors are targets for life insurance, leisure activities, and health aids.

Is moving often a good way to escape the list companies? Only if no forwarding address is left with the United States Postal Service, which provides forwarding address services to the list companies because advertising ("junk") mail provides a large portion of its revenues. If the post office did not sell forwarding information, many consumers would be lost in the shuffle.

Many people are surprised to find just how much personal information is available to whomever wishes to pay for it. To some it may seem reminiscent of George Orwell's *1984*, in which mind police could get into people's brains to know what they were thinking—violating their privacy the way marketing research firms try to do with psychographic studies. However, many· people have such busy lives that they thrive on convenience—frozen foods, drive-through drug stores, or ordering goods over the Internet at any time of day. All this convenience and product improvement owe a great deal to the wealth of data accumulated through market research.

and landlords about payment history on a monthly basis. Credit bureaus are major sources of information for data collectors.

Smaller sources of information are also available. Catalog companies can track who their catalogs go to and which customers buy, then document that information and sell it to others. Magazine companies sell their subscription lists with whatever information they have accumulated. Rebate offers are a way of identifying the segment of the market that responds to such offers. The list of those consumers can be sold to companies that seek coupon and rebate redeemers. A general rule is that any time a customer deals with a company by filling out a form of any kind, unless that company specifically states otherwise, any information shared should be considered as available to be sold in the information market.

Businesses can purchase lists from list companies that identify potential customers,

Further Research

Marketing Research Association

www.mra-net.org

The Marketing Research Association Web site offers useful information, including a resources section with a glossary.

Rutgers University Library Market Research

www.libraries.rutgers.edu/rul/rr_gateway/research_guides/busi/markres.shtml

Compiled by the business librarian, this guide includes pointers to several important sources of statistical data on income, consumption, and demographics.

—*Stephanie Buckwalter*

Minimum Wage

The minimum wage is the lowest rate of pay for workers. A minimum wage can be set by federal legislation, unions, and associations. The federal minimum wage set by governments is most often used as a policy strategy to reduce poverty. In the United States, the Fair Labor Standards Act (FLSA) of 1938 was the first major piece of legislation adopted to set a minimum wage that applied to the entire nation. At that time, the law covered only 43 percent of all nonsupervisory wage and salary workers and was set at 25 cents per hour.

In 2009 the minimum wage was $7.25 an hour; there are also provisions for overtime payments after 40 hours a week. Workers not covered include those at small businesses that fall below the revenue threshold ($500,000 annual volume of business or less) addressed by the FLSA. More than 130 million American workers are covered by the FLSA, which is enforced by the Wage and Hour Division of the U.S. Department of Labor. The FLSA also sets rules prohibiting people under 18 years old from working in certain jobs and limits the hours and times that employees under 16 years of age may work.

Determining the proper level of the minimum wage is hotly debated among competing interests. Setting an effective minimum wage is based on a balance of two considerations. On the one hand, the higher the minimum wage rate, the higher the guaranteed income of workers, which helps reduce poverty. On the other, as the minimum wage is increased, employers have a harder time paying salaries and maintaining a profit and thus may be forced to stop hiring or even lay off existing workers because they are too costly.

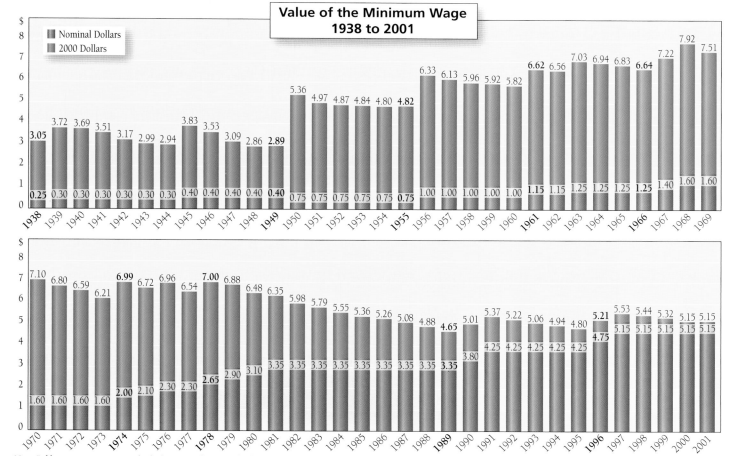

Value of the Minimum Wage 1938 to 2001

Note: **Bold** represents years in which the Fair Labor Standards Act was amended to raise the minimum wage.
Source: Bureau of Labor Statistics.

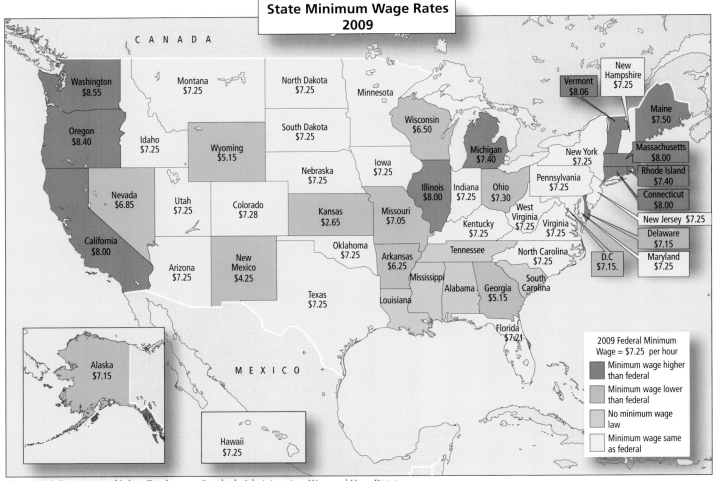

State Minimum Wage Rates 2009

Washington $8.55
Montana $7.25
North Dakota $7.25
Minnesota
New Hampshire $7.25
Vermont $8.06
Maine $7.50
Oregon $8.40
Idaho $7.25
Wyoming $5.15
South Dakota $7.25
Wisconsin $6.50
Michigan $7.40
New York $7.25
Massachusetts $8.00
Rhode Island $7.40
Connecticut $8.00
Nevada $6.85
Utah $7.25
Colorado $7.28
Nebraska $7.25
Iowa $7.25
Illinois $8.00
Indiana $7.25
Ohio $7.30
Pennsylvania $7.25
West Virginia $7.25
New Jersey $7.25
Delaware $7.15
California $8.00
Arizona $7.25
New Mexico $4.25
Kansas $2.65
Missouri $7.05
Kentucky $7.25
Virginia $7.25
D.C $7.15.
Maryland $7.25
Oklahoma $7.25
Arkansas $6.25
Tennessee
North Carolina $7.25
Mississippi
Texas $7.25
Louisiana
Alabama
Georgia $5.15
South Carolina
Florida $7.21
Alaska $7.15
Hawaii $7.25

CANADA
MEXICO

2009 Federal Minimum Wage = $7.25 per hour
- Minimum wage higher than federal
- Minimum wage lower than federal
- No minimum wage law
- Minimum wage same as federal

Source: U.S. Department of Labor, Employment Standards Administration, Wage and Hour Division.

Many states have enacted legislation to set their own minimum wage higher than the national minimum wage.

Origins

The first national minimum wage law applying to all workers was enacted in New Zealand in 1894. In the United States, Massachusetts enacted the first minimum wage law in 1912. In the same year, eight other states also passed such laws. At that time, minimum wage legislation applied only to women and children. American labor unions opposed applying the minimum wage to men. Because unions helped their members bargain for higher wages with employers, the unions thought that the federal minimum wage would undermine the benefits they could provide to their members as the federal rate could supersede union-negotiated rates.

By 1923 minimum wage laws for women and minors were in place in 15 states, Puerto Rico, and the District of Columbia. However, that year a decision of the U.S. Supreme Court eliminated all minimum wage laws on the basis that they were an unconstitutional government interference on private affairs.

In 1933, in response to the widespread economic hardships of the Great Depression, the Congress passed the National Industrial Recovery Act, which set minimum wage rates for both men and women. Two years later, however, the Supreme Court also declared this act unconstitutional.

The economic suffering of workers was a major campaign issue in the 1936 presidential race. The Democratic platform proposed to improve labor standards. Franklin D. Roosevelt campaigned on his New Deal vision, which promised to develop worker protection policies that could not be overturned by the Supreme Court. Roosevelt won the 1936 election by 523 electoral votes to 8 and interpreted his landslide victory as support for the New Deal.

On May 24, 1937, President Roosevelt sent a bill to Congress saying that America should be able to give "all our able-bodied working men and women a fair day's pay for a fair day's work." The initial proposal provided for a 40-cent-an-hour minimum wage, a 40-hour maximum workweek, and a minimum working age of 16 except in certain industries. The bill also proposed a five-member labor standards board, which could authorize still higher wages and shorter hours. Opponents of the bill said that it would lead the country to a "tyrannical industrial dictatorship." They saw the New Deal as a smoke screen disguising socialist planning.

Initially, unions opposed the bill because they feared that what was intended as a minimum wage might in the end become a maximum wage, and that wage boards would intervene in areas that unions wanted reserved for labor–management negotiations. Unions were satisfied when the bill was amended to exclude work covered by union negotiations.

On June 25, 1938, the president signed the FLSA to become effective on October 24, 1938. In the end, the minimum wage was set at 25 cents an hour.

Expansion of Coverage

When the national minimum wage was first established in the United States by the FLSA, it applied to only 43.4 percent of nonsupervisory employees and to those primarily employed in larger firms engaged in interstate commerce like manufacturing, mining, and construction companies.

In 1949 FLSA was expanded to include workers in the air transport industry. In 1961 amendments expanded the FLSA's scope in the retail trade sector for businesses with sales over $1 million, which

A demonstration in Washington, D.C. in 2005, calling for improved enforcement of the minimum wage law.

extended coverage from 250,000 workers to 2.2 million. In 1966 coverage was further expanded to include retail businesses with sales of at least $500,000, starting in February 1967, and sales of at least $250,000 starting in February 1969. Also in 1966 changes were made to extend coverage to employees of public schools, nursing homes, laundries, and the entire construction industry. Farms were also subject to coverage for the first time.

In 1974 Congress made changes to include all nonsupervisory employees of federal, state, and local governments and many domestic workers. In 1981 the $250,000 threshold for retail trade and service enterprises was increased in stages to $362,500 to adjust for inflation.

Currently, an employee can be covered by the law in two ways: "enterprise coverage" and "individual coverage." Employees are covered if they work in enterprises that earn at least $500,000 a year in business or are hospitals, businesses providing medical or nursing care for residents, schools and preschools, and government agencies. Employees are also protected by the FLSA if their work regularly involves them in commerce between states.

Economics and Politics

The debates over whether to have a minimum wage or how much to increase the minimum wage focus on the base salary needed to make a living versus whether people will lose their jobs as a result of a higher minimum wage. Advocates on both sides of the argument—politicians, special interest groups, and activists—can find support from economists.

As employers are forced to pay their workers higher wages, their costs increase and profits shrink. At some point, if the minimum wage continues to increase, employers could be forced to avoid hiring new workers or even lay off workers to pay the higher wages. Some economists argue that workers themselves should determine the lowest wage that they are willing to work for, not the government. This reasoning is based on the idea that a worker will not accept a job unless it pays enough to support him. Setting a rate higher than this by imposing a minimum wage, they argue,

In a 1996 ceremony on the White House lawn, President Bill Clinton signed a bill raising the minimum wage. He is joined by Vice President Al Gore and the children of those earning minimum wage.

is artificial interference in the market, which prevents those who are willing to work for less from accepting certain jobs.

Other economists argue that if a minimum wage is not set, employers will exploit the poor by paying them less than they can live on, even though the employers would be able to pay more. They also argue that basic fairness requires that people who work full-time should earn enough to support themselves and their families.

Another important consideration is inflation, which erodes the purchasing power of the minimum wage. As the cost of goods rises, a person earning the minimum wage is able to buy less. Thus, advocates for increasing the minimum wage often point out that the value of the minimum wage is effectively lower than it used to be, because it is able to buy fewer goods. Thus, to maintain the basic living standards of minimum-wage earners, the rate must be increased.

Experts agree that there is always some level of the minimum wage that will be too high, such that some workers will lose their jobs. Disagreements arise around defining that figure. Most studies indicate that the recent small increases in the minimum wage cause no or minimal job loss. Some economists think that increasing the minimum wage could increase employment because, by paying more for their time, such increase would provide a stronger reason for those who are not working at all to get a job.

Employers in industries that rely heavily on low-wage workers, including small-business owners, retail stores, and restaurants, typically are the most vocal opponents of increasing the minimum wage. Meanwhile, unions are typically the most vocal supporters of minimum wage increases.

The minimum wage is usually seen as one part of a multifaceted approach to alleviating poverty. The most significant parallel policy is the Earned Income Tax Credit (EITC), which provides tax credits to working people in an effort to increase their income. As a result of the combined effects of the minimum wage and the EITC, a family with a single full-time minimum-wage worker and one or two children can now earn enough money to avoid poverty.

Raising the Minimum Wage

The first minimum wage was less than half (40 percent) of the average wage for manufacturing workers. This does not reflect the purchasing power of the minimum wage in

Hourly Workers with Earnings at or Below the Federal Minimum Wage 2008

	Number (in thousands)	Percent*
Sex and Age		
16-24	1.122	7.2
25+	1,104	1.9
Total	2,226	3.0
Men		
16-24	384	4.8
25+	345	1.2
Total	728	2.0
Women		
16-24	738	9.6
25+	759	2.5
Total	1,497	3.9
Race and Hispanic Origin by Sex		
White		
Men	560	1.8
Women	1,223	4.1
Total	1,783	2.9
Black		
Men	123	2.8
Women	186	3.4
Total	308	3.1
Hispanic Origin		
Men	132	1.7
Women	191	3.6
Total	324	2.5
Full- and Part-time		
Full-time		
Men	341	1.1
Women	532	2.1
Total	873	1.5
Part-time		
Men	388	6.6
Women	965	7.8
Total	1,353	7.4

*Percent of total number of hourly workers within category by age, sex, race, and so forth.
Source: Bureau of Labor Statistics.

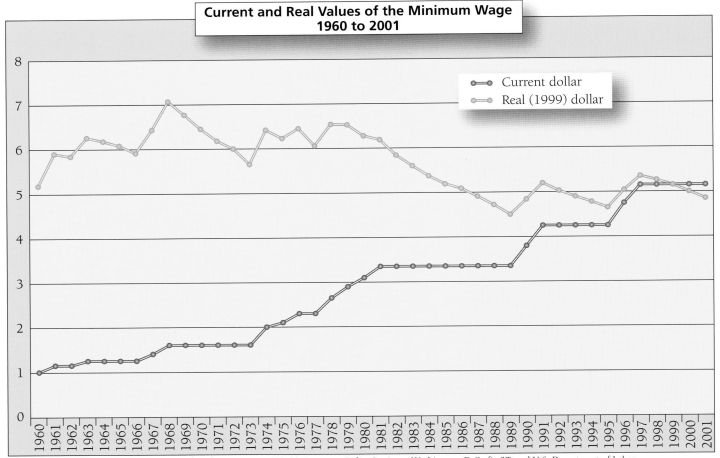

Current and Real Values of the Minimum Wage 1960 to 2001

Source: Economic Policy Institute, *The State of Working America, 2000–01*, Economic Policy Institute, Washington, D.C., fig 2T, and U.S. Department of Labor, *Value of the Federal Minimum Wage, 1954–1996*.

current dollars, because over the years inflation erodes the real value. The original rate is called the nominal rate, and the rate adjusting for inflation is called the real rate. If one were to recalculate 25 cents in current purchasing power by adjusting for inflation, in 2000 this rate would have been equivalent to $3.05.

The minimum wage rate does not increase automatically. Unlike many industrialized nations, the United States has no technical formula to determine periodic, automatic cost-of-living increases in the minimum wage. Rather, Congress must pass a bill that the president signs into law for the minimum wage to be increased.

By 2009 the minimum wage had been increased numerous times by legislation. When the minimum wage was raised to $7.25 in 2009, around 13 million workers benefited from higher wages, more than half of whom were full-time workers. The purchasing power of the minimum wage

reached a peak in 1970, when it was set at $2.65, equivalent to $7.00 in 2000 dollars. It was at its lowest point in more than 50 years in 2006; at that time, the minimum wage was set at $5.15, amounting to an annual salary of $10,712, nearly $6,000 below the poverty line for a family of three.

Further Research

Economic Policy Institute

www.epi.org/publications/entry/issue_guide_on_ minimum_wage

This issue guide on the minimum wage includes extensive data.

United States Department of Labor, Wage and Hour Division

www.dol.gov/esa/whd/flsa

An overview of the Fair Labor Standards Act, which establishes minimum wage, overtime pay, recordkeeping, and youth employment standards affecting employees in the private sector and in Federal, State, and local governments.

—Carl Haacke

Money

According to the lyrics of a song from a popular musical, "money makes the world go around." Why is money so important? The answer involves trade. In early civilizations and throughout history, people have found engaging in trade—exchanging something of value for something else—beneficial and have searched for ways to engage in trade efficiently and easily. Trading partners discovered that they could ease the task of trading by using certain instruments that would be commonly accepted as payment for goods and services. In other words, they developed money.

The advantages of money transactions can be gauged by a comparison with barter—exchanging goods and services directly for other goods and services. In most circumstances, bartering is inefficient, and in any barter economy, individuals find it difficult to specialize in those tasks at which they are most proficient. If the world's best mousetrap builder had a taste for tomatoes, she would have to search long and hard, in a barter economy, to identify a tomato grower wanting to purchase mousetraps. Rather than persisting in searches of that sort, the mousetrap producer would soon abandon her specialized craft to grow the tomatoes and other foods necessary for her survival. Thus, resources that are best used in producing mousetraps are inefficiently allocated to producing tomatoes.

Where money transactions are the norm, however, such inefficiencies are less likely to arise: the mousetrap builder uses the money she earns from selling mousetraps to purchase tomatoes in the marketplace. This allows her to do what she does best—to specialize. As a result, she benefits; society also benefits because money transactions of this sort encourage efficient use of scarce resources.

Money is commonly defined as an asset that is accepted as payment for goods and services or in settling debts. We know it mainly as bills, coins, and checks, but in other times and places money has taken many forms. Some ancient societies used cattle as money. Some Native Americans used wampum (beads of polished shells strung in strands). Prisoners of war used cigarettes as money during World War II. The last example shows that an asset need not be issued by a government authority to serve as money. With or without government sponsorship, monetary exchanges evolve from the desire to trade efficiently.

For an asset to serve as money, it must function as a medium of exchange. An exchange medium is directly convertible

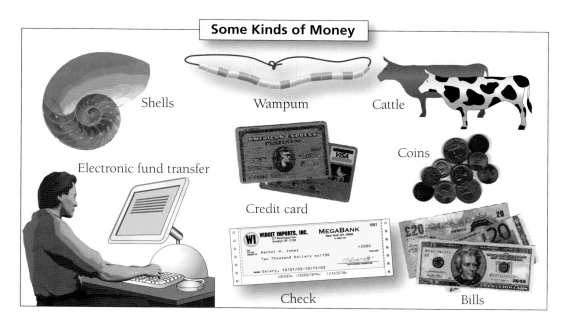

Some Kinds of Money

Shells

Wampum

Cattle

Electronic fund transfer

Credit card

Coins

Check

Bills

A worker at the Denver Mint.

dollar price of the TV (about $200) to the dollar price of the loaf of bread (about $1). Note that this comparison is possible only because the market value of each item is expressed in a common unit, dollars.

Imagine living in a world in which a common unit did not exist. A shopper might enter a supermarket to find the price of a gallon of milk listed as 10 pencils. Another store might price milk at four cans of tuna fish. A third store might charge three loaves of bread for a gallon of milk. Which is the best deal? Impossible to determine unless exchange ratios for pencils and milk, milk and tuna, and bread and milk can be calculated. Even if such ratios could be established, using them would be difficult in a modern economy in which an enormous quantity and variety of goods and services are available.

Money must also serve as a store of value (or store of wealth). Between the time people receive money and the time they use it, people usually hold money. Money must retain its purchasing power, for the most part, during this holding period. If it did not, people would be reluctant to accept money in payment for goods and services and it would fall out of favor as an exchange medium. Money is not unique as a store of value, however. Many other assets, including stocks and bonds, real estate and jewelry, are also used to store wealth.

History provides many examples of times when rapid price increases caused money's function as a store of value to break down. In Germany after World War I, hyperinflation ran rampant, driving prices upward at rates as high as 10 percent per hour. German government printing presses had to print money in ever-larger denominations to keep up with these increases (up to one-million-mark notes), and currency in smaller denominations, such as one-mark notes, became worthless. In fact, parents gave small notes to children as play money. This led to a complete economic breakdown in Germany and provided an ambitious political upstart named Adolf Hitler with an issue to exploit in his campaign for power.

into goods and services. Money also serves as a unit of account (or standard of value)—money is the common unit in which market values are expressed in modern economies. Which is more valuable: a loaf of white bread or a new television set? Certainly the TV. The market value of the TV may be about 200 times that of the loaf of bread. How is this computed? By comparing the

Major Functions of Money

- Medium of exchange: directly convertible into goods and services
- Store of value: retains purchasing power
- Unit of account: unit in which values are stated, recorded, and settled
- Standard of deferred payment: unit in which debt contracts are stated

In the United States, the payments system has evolved over time. Commodity money (coins minted from gold or silver) was common in the eighteenth and nineteenth centuries. Next came paper currency backed by precious commodities, then modern currency that is not convertible into precious metals, then checks, and most recently electronic funds transfers. Each means of payment has advantages and disadvantages. Commodity monies are bulky and awkward. Paper currency is easy to carry, but it provides purchasing power to anybody who holds it; therefore, thieves like to lift wallets. Checks need to be signed by the account holder before they can be used as payment, but it is quite costly (looking at the country as a whole) to process checks. Finally, payment by electronic transfer can be cost effective, but many people remain concerned about its security.

The future of money may be digital. Computers and personal digital assistants have become smaller, cheaper, and increasingly widespread, leading some analysts to predict that money as we now know it will disappear and will be replaced by "smart cards" or some other kind of digital cash. Companies like the Palo Alto–based PayPal have sprung up to provide a safe alternative to using credit cards online; the PayPal service allows anyone with an e-mail address to send and receive secure online payments. Whatever form future money takes, money itself will continue to foster human interaction through trade; for this reason, money is one of the most important inventions in human history.

Further Research

History of Money

projects.exeter.ac.uk/RDavies/arian/llyfr.html

Essays from a comprehensive book on the history of money from ancient times to the present day include a comparative chronology and an article on the origins of money names.

United State Mint

www.usmint.gov

The home page of the U.S. Mint has information for coin collectors as well as a growing history archive.

—*Rich MacDonald*

PayPal Chief Executive Officer Peter Thiel, left, and founder Elon Musk, right, pose with the PayPal logo at the company's headquarters in Palo Alto, California.

Mortgage

A mortgage is an interest-accruing loan granted to an individual or business for a pre-determined period of time for the purpose of buying a home, building, land, or other real estate. This loan is typically given by banks and mortgage companies and is approved only after the lender has determined that the borrower is able and willing to repay the loan. The real estate itself is used as collateral for the loan, and if, at any point, the borrower fails to make payment, the lender can force the sale of the property and return of its money. Such action is called foreclosure.

Before the 1950s personal debt was very rare. Most people paid for everything in cash, including homes. While businesses and farmers did borrow frequently, the average person did not. After World War II, when soldiers returned from war, housing was in short supply and prices for homes rose drastically. Very few people had the money to buy a home, and banks (subsidized through various government-assistance programs) began to lend money for the purpose of buying a home. As prices for homes remained high, mortgages became more common. Today, almost every home is purchased using a mortgage.

Obtaining a Mortgage

When individuals or businesses approach a financial institution for a mortgage, they most often find a specific property they would like to buy and are ready to do so. In some cases, the buyer will approach a lender before finding a property to buy to get a preapproval for a mortgage. Most lenders, before agreeing to a loan, require that the borrower have a certain amount of savings of his or her own, which will be used as the down payment for the purchase—the ideal amount for the down payment is usually 20 percent of the purchase price, but mortgages can be obtained with as little as 5 percent down payment and, in some special circumstances, even less. For example, if the buyer posts a portion of a personal portfolio (stocks and bonds) as collateral, the lender may allow the buyer to borrow the entire purchase price of the house.

A wide variety of mortgage providers are available to borrowers, but most mortgage lending is done by two kinds of lenders. Mortgage originators are companies that open a mortgage with a borrower and then, as soon as the mortgage is completed, sell it to a large bank that manages portfolios of mortgages. Mortgage originators earn a small percentage (typically around 0.15 to 0.25 percent) of the mortgage as a fee for generating the business for the large bank. Large banks also open mortgages themselves. The benefit to the large bank is that it does not have to pay a mortgage originator a fee for initiating the mortgage.

Borrowers are asked to provide documentation about employment, income, credit history, and other loans or debts. If all criteria are met, an appraisal of the real estate will be performed to confirm the value of the property, thus assuring the lender about recouping the loan in case of foreclosure.

Once the lender determines the investment is a sound one, a mortgage is granted. As a contractual agreement, a mortgage is very specific, listing in detail the amount of the loan, the interest rate charged, the repayment terms, and the length of the loan. (Mortgages are usually given for 15, 20, or 30 years.) The borrower and lender, upon agreeing to all terms of the mortgage, will have a meeting called a closing, where all documents will be signed by both parties and the actual exchange of funds takes place.

Making Mortgage Payments

The amount of each monthly payment is outlined in the mortgage agreement, including where to send the payment and when payment is due. Most agreements

Mortgage Schedule				
Month	Principal	Interest	Payment	Decrease in principal
1	$200,000.00	$1,166.67	$1,550	$383.33
2	$199,616.67	$1,164.43	$1,550	$385.57
198	$52,000.00	$303.33	$1,550	$1,246.67

include a late fee for payments that are made after a certain date of the month (for example, after the tenth day of the month). This payment consists of two figures: the principal and the interest. The principal is the amount of the actual loan. For example, a family buying a home for $250,000, with a 20 percent down payment, takes out a mortgage for $200,000 at 7 percent interest for 20 years. The principal is the amount borrowed, in this case $200,000.

Interest is the fee the lender charges for the use of its money. In this example, the interest rate is 7 percent. The interest is calculated based on the principal amount outstanding at the beginning of the month. In the early stages of the mortgage, the interest portion of the monthly payments is relatively high compared with the interest portion of the mortgage in the later months. For example, assume each monthly payment is $1,550. A portion of this repayment to the lender is interest and a portion is principal. The portion attributed to interest is calculated as follows:

Principal (start of the month) × Interest Rate × Portion of the year

In this case, the interest portion of the payment in the first month is $1,166.67 ($200,000 × .07 × [1/12 of one year]). Therefore, $383.33 ($1,550 − $1,166.67) of the payment is the principal portion. The next month, the calculation is similar. First, one must calculate the new principal outstanding: $199,616.67 ($200,000 − $383.33), then apply the same formula used in the prior month.

The interest portion of the payment in the second month is $1,164.43 ($199,616.67 × .07 × [1/12 of one year]). Therefore, $385.57 ($1,550 − $1,164.43) of the payment is the principal portion. Notice that the interest portion in the second month is slightly smaller than the first month because the mortgage balance, or principal, has decreased slightly.

Finally, assume that it is the 198th month and the principal amount is now $52,000. The next month's interest portion of the $1,550 payment is $303.33 ($52,000 × .07 × [1/12 of one year]), and the principal portion is $1,246.67 ($1,550 − $303.33). Note that the interest portion is dramatically smaller at this time because the mortgage amount has decreased significantly. Banks typically provide the borrower with tables that contain the details of each payment for the entire mortgage.

Selecting a Mortgage Type

Although several different kinds of mortgages are available, the most common are fixed-rate and adjustable-rate mortgages. Each bank decides the rate of interest it will charge for the use of its money. With a fixed-rate mortgage, the interest rate is set and remains constant throughout the life of the loan. It will not and cannot be changed, regardless of what changes the market may see or what rates were in the past or will be in the future. This kind of mortgage appeals to many people, because they feel safe knowing how much their mortgage payments will be each month for the next 15, 20, or 30 years. People also are comforted knowing that if interest rates

Some Kinds of Mortgages	
Fixed rate	Interest rate never changes; monthly payment remains the same over life of the loan.
	Mortgages are usually for 15 or 30 years.
Adjustable-rate mortgage (ARM)	Interest rate changes to reflect changes in the credit market.
	"Cap" sets upper limit above which the interest rate cannot go.
	Amount interest rate can rise annually is limited.
Balloon loan	Money is borrowed for a time (e.g., 3, 5 or 7 years) and the loan amortized as if it were a 30-year loan.
	After the end of the period, the borrower owes the bank the remaining principal.
Hybrid loan	Interest is fixed for a specific period and then the loan converts to an ARM.
COFI (cost of funds index) loan	Interest rate is tied to the rate that banks pay their depositors. Interest rate changes monthly.

The traditional method of applying for a mortgage is in person; more and more, people are applying for mortgages via the Internet.

increase, which is likely, they will keep their lower rate. If rates decrease, however, home owners can refinance, or take out a new mortgage at the new lower rate, and then use that money to pay off the old higher-rate mortgage. Although such refinancing will result in lower monthly payments for the home owner, banks ordinarily charge a transaction fee to change the terms of a loan.

An adjustable-rate mortgage (ARM) has an interest rate that changes. As the market changes, interest rates go up and down. With an adjustable-rate mortgage, the interest rate can be changed periodically, usually at the end of six months or one year. If the market warrants higher interest rates, the rate on such a mortgage will increase, thereby causing monthly payments to increase. If rates drop, monthly payments would decrease. Typically, ARMs contain caps, a very valuable feature to the borrower, whereby the rate on the mortgage cannot rise above a certain amount, no matter the market rates.

The Internet and Mortgages

The Internet has streamlined the mortgage selection and approval process. In the past, a prospective buyer would have to call several companies to gather interest rate and fee information. Now, a prospective home buyer can simply enter some general information into a Web site, and within seconds, several quotes are returned on a single page with bank names and contact numbers.

Furthermore, once a mortgage company is chosen, the buyer can enter personal information (salary, existing debt, and employer, for example) onto the mortgage company's Web site to seek a preapproval. Usually within a day, the mortgage lender responds with a preapproval letter or a rejection notice; in the past, this process took several days. Eventually, through the proliferation of the Internet, a borrower will not even need to talk to anyone throughout the entire mortgage process.

Mortgages help people achieve their goals. A young couple wants to buy a first home. A company needs a building for office space. A contractor wants a plot of land on which to build a new townhouse development. Without a mortgage, these projects would be difficult, if not impossible.

Further Research
Mortgage Professor's Web Site
www.mtgprofessor.com
This Web site, managed by a former professor at the Wharton School of the University of Pennsylvania, is a comprehensive guide to mortgages and housing finance.

—David Korb and Andréa Korb

Mutual Funds

Mutual funds are investment vehicles managed by some investment companies. These companies pool money provided to them by individuals (as well as corporations and pension funds) and then invest that money in a portfolio of stocks, bonds, or other securities. Each individual who invests money in the fund purchases shares of the investment company. The price, or net asset value (NAV), of the shares is determined by the market value of all of the investment company's assets. The NAV changes daily as the prices of the underlying stocks and bonds fluctuate in the market. As shareholders, investors own a small piece of each asset that the investment company owns.

The term *mutual fund* has become common in the past few decades because of a period of spectacular growth in mutual fund investments since 1985. By 2008 more than 8,000 mutual funds were available to investors. These funds served a variety of personal financial objectives by means of investment in instruments that range from low-risk government bonds to high-risk technology funds. As the end of 2008 the Investment Company Institute estimated that 45 percent of all U.S. households owned mutual funds or other U.S.-registered investment companies,

Kinds of Mutual Funds

Kind	Characteristics
Aggressive growth funds	• Include riskier stocks that the manager believes will offer higher-than-average returns • Little or no dividend • May leverage assets by borrowing funds • May trade in stock options • High volatility
Growth funds	• Invest in larger stocks and industries with strong positions in their market, stable earnings, and good growth prospects • Generally surpass the S&P 500 during bull markets and do worse during bear markets • Volatile
Growth-income funds	• Invest in blue-chip stocks • Work to maximize dividend income while generating capital gains • More diversified than other kinds of funds
Income funds	• Invest in securities that pay both dividends and interest • Focus on high current income
Asset allocation funds	• Invest beyond the stock market, focusing on stocks, bonds, gold, real estate, and money market funds • Decrease reliance on one aspect of the economy
Bond funds	• Invest in corporate and government bonds • Seek high current income
Sector funds	• Invest in one sector, or industry, in the economy, e.g., biotech, communications • May underperform more diversified funds if the sector hits hard times
International funds	• Invest in foreign securities • Funds exist for individual countries or sections of the world
Precious metal funds	• Invest in gold, silver, and platinum • Generally move in opposite direction from stock market

including exchange-traded funds, closed-end funds, and unit investment trusts.

Some investment companies that manage mutual funds are also known as open-end companies because these mutual funds continually sell shares to, and buy (redeem) shares from, the investing public at NAV. Mutual funds do not have a fixed number of shares outstanding, and they continually issue new shares. The NAV of mutual funds is computed once a day, after the close of the U.S. stock exchanges. Therefore, when an investor submits a buy or sell order to a mutual fund during the trading day, the order is filled at the NAV computed at the end of the trading day. In contrast, closed-end mutual fund companies have a fixed number of shares outstanding, and these shares trade on exchanges—much in the way individual shares of stock trade on exchanges. The shares of closed-end funds trade continually throughout the trading day at prices determined by the supply and demand for the shares. Therefore, closed-end fund shares may trade for prices above or below their NAV.

Mutual funds can be categorized by a given fund's management. Passively managed funds, also known as index funds, use an index like the S&P 500. The S&P 500 index tracks the prices of 500 stocks that trade in the U.S. stock market. An index fund based on the S&P 500 owns the 500 stocks in the index, and the composition of the index fund changes only when the companies in the S&P 500 index change. Managers of actively managed funds buy and sell securities in an attempt to achieve high returns and outperform benchmark indexes like the S&P 500. Because of the frequent trading that occurs in actively managed portfolios, investors in actively managed funds typically face higher fees and higher taxes than investors in passively managed funds.

Mutual funds can also be classified by investment objective and by the kind of investment instrument selected to serve various objectives. Categories include stock funds, taxable bond funds, municipal bond funds,

Percent of Families Owning Mutual Funds 1998 – 2004	
1998, total	16.5
2001, total	12.3
2004, total	15.0
Age of Family Head, 2004	
Under 35 years old	12.2
35–44	8.3
45–54	12.3
55–64	18.2
65–74	18.6
75+	16.6
Income Percentile	
20–39.9	7.6
40–59.9	12.7
60–79.9	18.6
80–89.9	26.2
90–100	39.1

Note: Excludes money market mutual funds and funds held through retirement accounts or other managed assets.
Source: Survey of Consumer Finances, Federal Reserve.

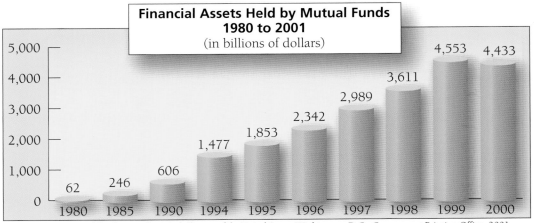

Financial Assets Held by Mutual Funds
1980 to 2001
(in billions of dollars)

Year	Amount
1980	62
1985	246
1990	606
1994	1,477
1995	1,853
1996	2,342
1997	2,989
1998	3,611
1999	4,553
2000	4,433

Source: U.S. Bureau of the Census, *Statistical Abstract of the United States,* Washington, D.C., Government Printing Office, 2001.

and stock and bond funds. Within each category, the objective of the fund is broken down further. For example, the stock fund category includes growth stock funds, utility stock funds, and international stock funds.

The Benefits of Mutual Fund Investing

The benefits of mutual fund investing include diversification, ease of use, liquidity (ease of converting mutual fund assets to cash), and professional management. The first two considerations are the most important for beginning investors.

When an individual invests $100 in a mutual fund, she becomes the owner of a certain number of shares of that fund and literally owns a small percentage of every asset that the mutual fund owns. Therefore, she has diversified her $100 investment across several companies rather than putting the entire $100 in the stock of a single company. Diversification is important because it decreases the risk associated with investing and helps to produce more reliable returns. Some experts suggest that investors who purchase individual stocks must have $100,000 in their portfolios to achieve adequate diversification. With mutual funds, each dollar invested is spread across many different companies.

Most individual stocks sell for $10 to $100 per share, and investors cannot initially buy fractional shares. Therefore, investing small amounts of money in individual stocks is difficult. However, investing small amounts of money in mutual funds is easy because mutual funds do sell fractional shares. Thus, investors can set up investment programs where they automatically invest as little as $50 per month in a mutual fund. If the mutual fund has a NAV of $10.50 per share on the day the $50 investment is made, for example, the investor will purchase 4.76 shares of the fund.

Individual mutual funds use a variety of fee structures. Most funds charge investors an annual fee to cover operating expenses, including fund manager salaries and advertising expenses. Annual fees are usually less than 3 percent. For example, if a fund returns 8 percent during the year and the expense fee is 2 percent, investors realize only 6 percent

Many mutual funds invest in a variety of stock strategies.

after annual fees have been deducted. In addition, some funds charge a commission, or front-end load, when the investor purchases the fund; others impose a redemption charge when the investor sells his shares. No-load funds impose no commission charges but may charge higher annual expense fees. Passively managed funds (index funds) are typically no-load funds, and they often have lower annual fees than actively managed funds.

Investors can create a strong portfolio by investing in a group of stock and bond funds with a variety of objectives. Successful investors choose funds with low annual expenses that have consistently performed well over a long period, and they monitor their portfolio at least annually to ensure that all investments remain appropriate to their situation and to the current state of the economy.

Further Research

Investment Company Institute

www.ici.org

The members of the Investment Company Institute, the national association of the U.S. mutual fund industry, manage over $9.8 trillion on behalf of 93 million shareholders. The organization compiles comprehensive statistics on the industry and provides investor guides.

Invest Wisely: A Guide to Mutual Funds

www.sec.gov/investor/pubs/inwsmf.htm

This guide to mutual fund investing, prepared by the U.S. Securities and Exchange Commission, includes practical advice on safe investing and a glossary of specialized terms.

—*Angeline Lavin*

Outsourcing

Outsourcing is the practice of obtaining a product or services from external providers. Parents outsource child care when they drop their children off at the day care center; office managers outsource maintenance when they contract for custodial services. The parents could stay home and take care of the children themselves, of course, and the office manager could mop the floors and empty the wastebaskets at night. By obtaining these services from others, however, the clients in each case expect to realize a number of benefits because the outsourcing arrangement enables them to focus on their core competencies—to spend more time doing what they do best. The benefits of outsourcing typically include improved efficiency and quality as well as reduced costs.

Widespread use of outsourcing is recent in the business world. Not long ago, the strategy in many industries was for businesses to seek economy and efficiency by consolidating many operations under one corporate roof. Late in the nineteenth

Vertical integration involves the consolidation of as many business operations as possible; outsourcing, on the other hand, involves a collection of relationships with subcontractors.

Vertical Integration vs. Outsourcing

Vertical Integration Model

Yesteryear Steel Corp. =

Mining fields

\+

Manufacturing facilities

\+

Distribution facilities

Outsourcing Model

Contemporary Steel Corp. =

Raw Materials Inc.

⟷

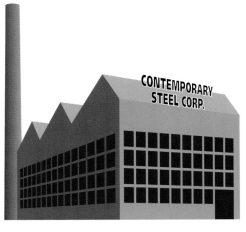

Contemporary Steel Corp.

⟷

Fastrack Shipping Co.

century, for example, John D. Rockefeller founded and managed the Standard Oil Company through an approach now known as vertical integration. Vertical integration allowed Standard Oil to own and operate not only its oil wells and refineries but also the storage facilities, railroad tank cars, barrel-making factories, and other units responsible for the production, marketing, and distribution of its products.

By the mid-twentieth century such corporate structuring was growing obsolete. Competitive pressures and consumer demand increasingly pushed suppliers of goods and services to control costs while offering special products and services and improved quality. Outsourcing helped many businesses to respond to these pressures, especially in their handling of administrative services, computer network support, and payroll operations. Even in the age of the Internet, for example, law firms and insurance companies still operate mail rooms to handle large volumes of incoming and outgoing U.S. mail. These firms could maintain their own staffs to operate their mailrooms, but the management and maintenance of mail services would divert resources from the practice of law or the writing, selling, and servicing of insurance policies. A lawyer whose specialty is mergers and acquisitions, for example, might need to spend some time every week supervising the mailroom staff, or supervising the mailroom supervisor. The firm would rather see that lawyer spend her time on her core competency—

Benefits of Outsourcing

- Cost reduction
- Personnel reduction
- Capital investment relief
- Better technology
- Improved quality
- Flexibility in delivery of service
- Extra management time

Source: Charles L. Gay, *Inside Outsourcing: An Insider's Guide to Managing Strategic Sourcing*, London, Nicholas Brealey Publishing, 2000.

handling mergers and acquisitions, not mail. As a result, the firm might contract with an outsourcing business to provide mailroom resources: labor, equipment, and industry expertise.

A successful relationship between a client firm and an outsourcing provider depends on two critical understandings. One has to do with costs; the other, with the client firm's ability to control its own products and services.

At first glance, the products or services provided by an outsourcing organization may seem costly, but appropriately designed outsourcing arrangements produce savings for many clients in the long run. Outsourcing organizations focus on providing a given product or service. By providing that product or service to law firms, insurance firms, and other companies having similar needs, outsourcing firms can achieve economies of scale that individual firms—even large, multinational firms—could never achieve. In focusing on mailroom services, for example, an outsourcing firm dedicates its resources to recruiting, hiring, and training mailroom workers, and to research and development in process engineering, equipment procurement, cost containment, and quality management. Client firms from any number of industries dependent on mailroom services benefit from the expertise and economies of scale produced by such specialization.

Outsourcing might seem to imply that a client firm would lose a measure of control over its operations. If somebody else is handling the payroll or delivery service, perhaps the client firm's own quality standards will not be met. In fact, however, a client firm can strengthen its control over key operations through contractual expectations for production, delivery, and application of a product or service consistent with its own business cycles.

Contractual arrangements geared to business cycles might result in a client firm not investing in labor or equipment needed only for a special, short-term project. Landscaping firms, for example, require different staffing levels at different times of the year, with peak demand often occurring in

Large firms frequently outsource their mailroom operations.

the spring. Outsourcing for additional, short-term labor from a temporary agency is one option for landscaping firms at such times. Temporary services are typically responsible for all costs associated with their employees. In contracting for temporary services, therefore, a client firm can avoid the costs that would be incurred in hiring workers for a short time and then releasing them when demand falls. Providing labor and specialty equipment is of interest to an outsourcing firm because other clients may need those same resources at different times of the year. The easy, flexible application of an outsourcing firm's resources can add significant value to the client–outsourcer relationship.

Not everyone likes outsourcing. Workers in traditionally integrated firms—for example the automobile industry—have objected to cost-cutting plans calling for the outsourcing of specific production or assembly tasks. Teachers' unions, similarly, have resisted some states' new legal provisions permitting school districts to contract with outsourcers for administrative and instructional services. In these disputes, each side claims to have consumers' interests in mind. Management claims that lower production costs and flexi-bility will translate into lower prices and better quality for consumers; organized workers claim that quality standards will yield to expedience in a corporate search for profits.

Although disputes of this kind will continue to arise, with resolutions influenced by political activity as well as market forces, outsourcing seems to be established in the economy. From the late twentieth century, there has been a marked trend toward outsourcing operations to countries with lower tax regimes, or to India, China, and the Philippines, with lower wage costs. Both skilled and unskilled jobs are subject to outsourcing. In 2008 more than two million people in India were directly employed in companies providing IT outsourcing, which provided $64 billion in revenues that year.

Further Reading

The Future of Outsourcing

www.businessweek.com/magazine/content/06_05/b3969401.htm
An article from Businessweek magazine explores outsourcing, looking at its pros and cons for the U.S. workforce.

—*John Western*

Patent

A patent is a legal instrument granting an inventor exclusive rights to use and benefit from his or her invention for a definite period of time. Patents are granted to encourage inventors to do their creative work.

Patents find their roots in Greek society. In his *Politics*, Aristotle referred to patents in discussing the need for a reward system for inventors. The city-state of Venice adopted the first patent law in the late 1400s. In the seventeenth century the British enacted a law that allowed for a review of all patents so that those not based on true inventions could be eliminated. Patents were introduced in the American colonies between 1640 and 1776 and were awarded at that time by individual colonies.

Modern patent law in the United States derives from the U.S. Constitution, adopted in 1789. To maintain uniformity in the granting of patents, the U.S. Constitution provides that Congress shall have the power to "promote the Progress of Science and useful Arts, by securing for limited Times to Authors and Inventors the exclusive right to their respective Writings and Discoveries." Congress passed the first Patent Act in 1790. Thomas Jefferson was an early administrator of the patent system and the author of the Patent Act of 1793. Current patent law is based on the 1952 Patent Act and its amendments.

A patent establishes the inventor's ownership of his or her invention. Ownership allows the inventor to exclude others from making, using, selling, or importing the invention for a definite term (length of time). In the United States, the term of a patent is 20 years (14 years for a design).

Under U.S. patent law, some inventions (a device that might threaten national security, for example) cannot be patented. Nor can patents be obtained on principles or laws of nature, on naturally occurring items, or inventions requiring only mental activity or processes. (Copyrights and trademarks protect inventions derived from mental processes.) The patents that may be issued in the United States are utility patents, design patents, and plant patents.

Utility Patents

Five classes of inventions may be the subject of a utility patent. One class is processes or methods—steps performed on a material, composition, or object, changing its nature or characteristics to produce a useful commodity. Examples include a process for making a chemical compound—paint, for instance—or for treating wool or linen.

Another class is machines—mechanical devices (with moving parts) that accomplish a task. Examples include a dishwasher, carburetor, lawn mower, or washing machine.

A third class is articles of manufacture—articles produced from raw or prepared materials that take on new forms, qualities, or properties. Such articles have no moving parts. Examples include a toothbrush, a table, a bench, or a golf ball.

Web Resources on Patents

www.uspto.gov is the home page for the United States Patent and Trademark Office.

www.nolo.com provides general information and resources on various legal concepts, including patents.

www.ipwatchdog.com/patent.html provides information and resource links for patent law.

www.micropat.com is a leading Web resource of searchable collections of patent and trademark information.

www.law.cornell.edu/topics/patent.html, a site maintained by the Legal Information Institute, offers information and resources on patent law.

www.bustpatents.com provides legal tools and information on Internet patents.

www.patentcafe.com offers a patent search, plus patent, trademark, and intellectual property information for inventors, attorneys, and entrepreneurs.

www.patentstorm.us is a free service that delivers full-text patents and patent applications from the U.S. Patent Office, supplying documents in pdf format. Its database of issued patents goes back to 1976.

www.younginventors.org is the home page of a nonprofit organization providing young inventors and innovators with support and information.

www.cipo.ic.gc.ca is the home page for the Canadian Intellectual Property Office and the Canadian patents database.

Patent certificates are displayed on the wall at the Bristol Labs in Syracuse, New York. The display shows patents from many different countries for many of the same compounds. Multiple patents may be necessary for international production and distribution.

A fourth class is composition of matter. The composition may be a chemical compound or a mixture of ingredients. Examples include formulations for toothpaste, shampoo, cleaning solution, or glue. The fifth class is any improvement to an invention from any of the first four classes.

Two new kinds of invention that may be patented as utility patents are computer software and biotechnology products. Recent court decisions allow computer software to be protected as machines, articles of manufacture, composition of matter, or processes. Biotechnology products involve subject matter relating to life—transgenic animals, for example, or amino acid sequences or genetic sequences. One court decision considered a new bacterium that broke down crude oil to be patentable as a composition of matter or article of manufacture.

To qualify for a utility patent, an invention must be novel, useful, and nonobvious. Novelty means that an invention must not have been known or used previously by someone in the United States or published or patented previously anywhere in the world.

To be considered useful, an invention must work, solve the problem it was

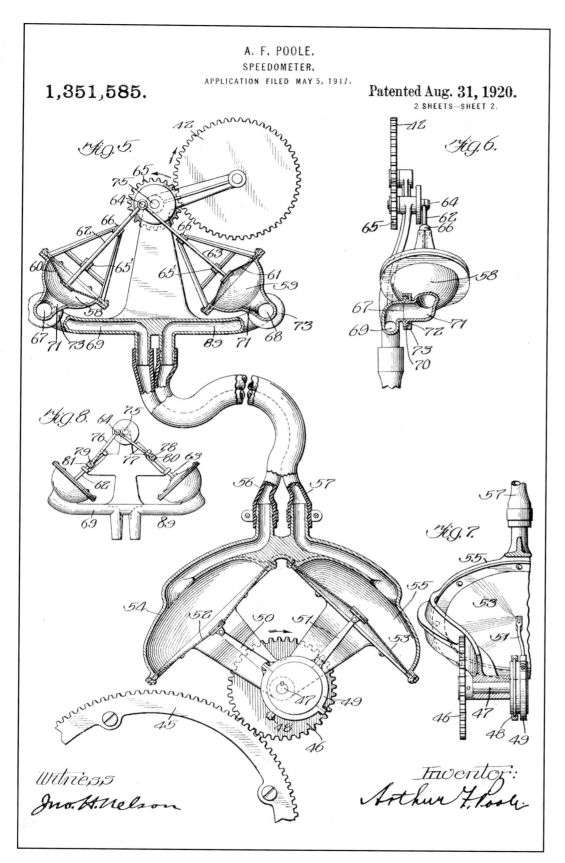

A. F. POOLE.
SPEEDOMETER.
APPLICATION FILED MAY 5, 1917.

1,351,585.

Patented Aug. 31, 1920.
2 SHEETS—SHEET 2.

Fig. 5.

Fig. 6.

Fig. 8.

Fig. 7.

Witness
Jno. H. Nelson

Inventor:
Arthur F. Poole

Patent applications are accompanied by technical drawings that illustrate the mechanics of the invention. This is one of several illustrations that accompanied a patent application for a magnetic speedometer for automobiles; inventor Arthur F. Poole filed the application in 1917 and the patent was granted in 1920.

designed to solve, and provide some benefit to society. Most inventions meet the usefulness requirement, although questions of interpretation do arise regarding its meaning. Some people believe, incorrectly, that an invention must be commercially successful to be useful. An invention does not have to be highly marketable or have outstanding performance characteristics to satisfy the usefulness requirement. If an invention is regarded as harmful to society, then the usefulness requirement is not met. For example, in 1897 a new invention known as a slot machine was considered harmful to society.

Nonobviousness is the most critical test for an item to be patented. An invention is not obvious if a person of ordinary skill in the field fails to deduce it from the prior art (public knowledge, prior publications, etc.). This area is often a major source of disagreement between patent applicants and patent examiners. In ruling on disputes arising from these disagreements, courts consider several factors, including whether an invention would be a commercial success; whether it successfully addresses some long-felt but unmet need; and whether it is something others have tried but failed to develop.

Patents 1980 to 2000
(in thousands)

	1980	1985	1990	1995	2000
Patent applications					
Inventions	104.3	117.0	164.6	212.4	295.9
Designs	7.8	9.6	11.3	15.4	18.3
Botanical plants	0.2	0.2	0.4	0.5	0.8
Reissues	0.6	0.3	0.5	0.6	NA
Total	113.0	127.1	176.7	228.8	NA
Patents issued					
Inventions	61.8	71.7	90.4	101.4	157.5
Individuals	13.8	12.9	17.3	17.4	22.4
U.S. corporations	27.7	31.2	36.1	44.0	70.9
U.S. government	1.2	1.1	1.0	1.0	0.9
Foreign (corporations and governments)	19.1	26.4	36.0	39.1	63.3
Designs	3.9	5.1	8.0	11.7	17.4
Botanical plants	0.1	0.2	0.3	0.4	0.5
Reissues	0.3	0.3	0.4	0.3	0.5
Total	66.2	77.3	99.2	113.8	176.0

NA = Not available.
Note: Covers patents issued to citizens of the United States and residents of foreign countries.
Source: U.S. Patent and Trademark Office.

Design Patents

A design patent protects the ornamental aspects of an article, or how the article looks. The design of an object may entail its configuration or shape; its surface ornamentation; and both its shape and surface ornamentation. However, a design patent does not protect the functional aspects of an invention.

A design patent consists in part of a series of drawings or photographs showing the ornamental features of an object. A design patent also includes a description of the object and its ornamental features. If drawings include too much detail, then somebody looking for a way to violate (infringe) the patent may have an easy task. The infringer could perhaps omit some small detail and contend that his or her invention is something new, falling outside the scope of the prior patent.

To qualify for a design patent, an invention must be novel and nonobvious. Such requirements are met if the shape, configuration, or surface ornamentation of the invention differs from and is not obvious in light of what is known publicly. Design patents remain in force for 14 years from the patent issue date.

An invention may receive both a design and a utility patent. The design patent protects the appearance of the article and the utility patent protects its functions. Examples of inventions that have been protected with both kinds of patents are tire treads, footwear, and flatware.

Plant Patents

The law also provides for the granting of a patent to anyone who has invented or discovered and asexually reproduced any distinct, new variety of plant. Asexually propagated plants are those reproduced by means other than seeding, for example, by the rooting of cuttings. Plant patents give the owner the right to exclude others from asexually reproducing the plant or selling or using the plant so reproduced.

Obtaining a Patent

To obtain a patent, an applicant submits a patent application to the U.S. Patent and Trademark Office. The application consists of a specification and claims, drawings (when appropriate), an oath or declaration by the applicant, and the filing fee. The specification is a written, technical description of the invention. The claims are one-sentence statements highlighting what it is that the inventor claims as an invention; these claims determine the property rights conferred by a patent. The drawings show features of the invention. Most mechanical and electrical patents have drawings, while most chemical and process patents do not. The specification, along with the drawings, must set forth the manner and process of making and using the invention. The oath or declaration is a statement by the applicant, asserting that he or she believes him- or herself to be the original inventor of the subject matter of the application.

After an application has been filed, it is assigned to a patent examiner who specializes in the subject matter of the application. The examiner does an initial study of the application to determine whether it follows Patent Office rules. One such rule is that each application may cover only one invention.

If the application passes the initial screening, the examiner does a detailed analysis for patentability. This includes a "prior art" search of all U.S. patents, foreign patents, and technical publications in the field to determine whether the subject matter is novel and nonobvious to those skilled in the field. After the prior art search, the patent examiner rules on the application and sends

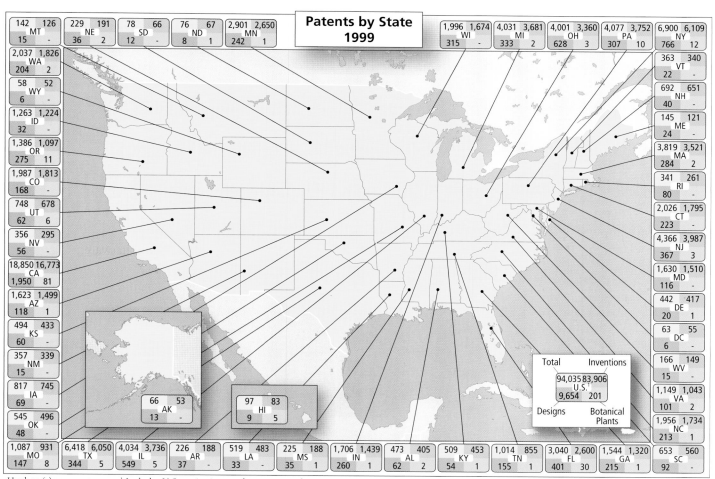

Patents by State 1999

Hyphen (-) represents zero. [1] Includes U.S. territories not shown separately.
Note: Includes only U. S. patents granted to residents of the United States and territories.
Source: U.S. Patent and Trademark Office, Technology Assessment and Forecast Database.

Dr. Ananda Chakrabarty poses in front of the U.S. Supreme Court. He was the first scientist to receive a patent on a life-form that resulted from his experiments with a recombinant-DNA-created oil-spill-eating bacteria. A 1983 Supreme Court decision validated the issuance of patents on life-forms created in the lab.

this decision, in writing, to the applicant or his patent lawyer or agent. If the application is denied, the applicant is provided time to ask for reconsideration of their applications.

After a reconsideration, the examiner's decision is again sent in writing to the applicant. Usually the second decision is final; however, if the second decision is negative, the applicant may appeal to the U.S. Patent Office Board of Appeals, a judicial body within the Patent Office. Adverse decisions from the Board of Appeals can be reviewed by the Court of Custom and Patent Appeals or by the district court of the District of Columbia.

An inventor who wishes to obtain patent protection in countries other than the United States must apply for a patent in each of the other countries. Almost every country has its own patent law, and a person desiring a patent in a particular country must make an application for patent in that country.

The Paris Convention for the Protection of Industrial Property is a treaty relating to patents that is adhered to by 172 countries, including the United States. The treaty provides that each signator guarantees to the citizens of other countries the same rights in patent matters that it gives to its own citizens. On the basis of a regular patent application filed in one of the member countries, the applicant may, within a certain time, apply for protection in all the other member nations.

Patent infringement occurs when any person or business makes, uses, or sells a patented invention without permission. The patent holder has redress and can file a civil lawsuit in any federal district court asking for damages and an injunction to prevent further infringement. Any district court decision may be appealed to a circuit court of appeals; in some cases, appeals reach the U.S. Supreme Court. Patent holders must mark their invented products as patented; failure to do so may prevent them from obtaining money damages in an infringement suit.

Further Research

Paris Convention for the Protection of Industrial Property
www.wipo.int/treaties/en/ip/paris/trtdocs_wo020.html
The full text of the treaty, first issued in 1883, and its amendments.

Thomas Jefferson and the Patent Act of 1793
etext.virginia.edu/journals/EH/EH40/walter40.html

Software Patents

Patents are an important part of any technology corporation's property; software companies are especially reliant on patents. Software creation requires a significant investment of programming time and talent; however, it does not require the infrastructure needed by, for example, an automobile manufacturer. New software producers have relatively few barriers to entering the market and producing software applications. Therefore, the industry has attempted to find means of enforcing ownership over certain software processes.

Initially, patents appeared to offer little protection to computer programmers. A Supreme Court decision in 1972, *Gottschalk v. Benson*, determined that a computer algorithm was not subject to patent protection. Computer algorithms are procedures a programmer creates to perform particular tasks. A method for more quickly sorting a list of names into alphabetic order, for example, would be considered an algorithm. The Court determined that algorithms are more like mathematical formulas, abstract ideas, or natural laws: they are discovered rather than invented.

Gottschalk effectively made software unpatentable; however, the Court opened the door a bit to software patents almost a decade later in *Diamond v. Diehr*. The Court still maintained that many kinds of software were not patentable, but stated at the same time that the mere inclusion of a mathematical formula or an algorithm did not mean that an invention could not be patented. This position was cemented for software in *Whelan v. Jaslow* in 1986. This warming to software patents was further reinforced in the 1998 *State Street v. Signature* case, whose ruling did away with the exclusion of "business process" patents, allowing processes for services and sales techniques, which had become increasingly important on the Internet, to be patented.

Since the *State Street* case, a number of software patents have come under harsh criticism. In a few cases, the patents have even been reexamined and overturned. Some of these patents, if enforced, would make the World Wide Web impossible. British Telecommunications, for example, has attempted to enforce an older patent that appears to give it ownership over the idea of hyperlinking, and Unisys has begun to enforce its patent on the GIF picture-file format. Amazon.com's patents for "one-click" shopping (ordering and paying for a product with a single mouse click on a hyperlink) and for affiliate advertising have been criticized by many in the software industry.

Some, like members of MIT's League for Programming Freedom and Harvard University Law School professor Lawrence Lessig, see the rise of software patents as impeding innovation in software design. According to those who argue against software patents, many patents are used as leverage between large corporations, which force one another to share the use of a collection of patents to mutual benefit. As a result, individual programmers or small companies are unable to compete without worrying about infringing on one of the thousands of existing software patents. On the other hand, some believe that companies that invest in the research to create new software should be able to reap the benefits of that research.

—*Alexander Halavais*

This article from *Essays in History* examines Jefferson's involvement with early patent legislation in the United States.

World Intellectual Property Organization
www.wipo.org
Home page of the United Nations' specialized agency dedicated to protecting intellectual property.

—*Carl Pacini*

Pricing

Economics may seem abstract, but everyone knows what a price is. The Consumer Price Index, a compilation of prices of common goods and services, is the subject of as much media attention as the unemployment rate. Rising prices can decimate a nation's economy; falling prices can do even worse damage. Governments regularly intervene to manipulate prices, either directly through price controls or indirectly by altering interest rates to control inflation.

How are prices actually set? In theory, pricing is simple: companies want to charge as high a price as they can because that increases profits, while consumers want to pay as little as possible. The price set is a compromise, affected mainly by the scarcity of the item.

The real world, however, is much more complicated. According to the law of demand, demand for a product should go up when the price is reduced. In reality, sales of certain products will actually increase if the price is raised—the exact opposite of what the law of demand predicts. Indeed, the best-selling brands of a particular good are usually priced somewhat higher than competitive brands. Under the right circumstances, people under no duress will pay more for the same product that is readily available elsewhere for less. Not surprisingly, psychologists have as much to say about pricing as economists.

Setting Prices

Setting the right price is a balancing act. Companies want to charge as much as possible; however, if prices are set too high, not enough customers will buy the product for the company to be profitable. If the company sets prices too low, the company will receive less for the item than it cost to produce—and the more people buying the item, the more money lost.

The cost of production is sometimes the main consideration in pricing. For example, a traditional regulated utility has a monopoly on a vital service—for example, providing electricity in a particular state. To protect consumers, state regulators set the prices the utility may charge customers. Those prices are usually based on the cost to the utility of providing electricity, plus a profit. If the utility wishes to raise rates, it must convince regulators that its costs have increased or will soon do so.

In most cases, cost is only one consideration when a company sets a price; often cost is far from the most important factor. The cost of producing a good usually serves as a lower limit to its price, but sometimes a company will deliberately set prices below the cost of production and lose money on sales. Often this step is taken as part of a larger strategy to raise cash, enter a new market, or undermine competitors.

The competitive environment often has a much larger effect on pricing than does the cost of production. If two companies are offering two very similar products, one business may decide to undercut the other on price. That action may trigger what is called a price war, with competitors cutting prices until all are selling the product for less than it cost to produce. Like a real war, the object of a price war is usually to kill the enemy; whichever company is in better financial shape will survive.

When many companies offer essentially the same product, price wars are common, and prices generally settle at a level that is only slightly above the cost of making the product—a situation called

Factors Involved in Pricing		
Market factors	Customer behavior and preferences	
	Competitive environment	
	Cost	
Corporate factors	Product positioning	
	Marketing strategy	
	Regulation and taxes	

commodity pricing. When commodity pricing becomes the norm in an industry, weaker competitors tend to go out of business, merge, or get bought by stronger companies. The shakeout produces a few strong players who control most of the market and thus have more power to raise prices. Profits in commodity businesses, nevertheless, tend to be small.

Prices can be set higher, however, if a single company, a monopoly, takes over the entire market. A monopoly has no competitors to undercut its prices, so it can keep prices high and be very profitable. Higher prices do not benefit consumers, however, so the monopolies can run afoul of antitrust laws, which are designed to ensure competition. Whether a monopoly has legal trouble depends on the market it controls and how it responds to attempts by other companies to enter that market.

An equally effective method of preventing commodity prices from declining is for companies to collude to keep prices high, a practice called price fixing. Price fixing is illegal in the United States; nonetheless it occurs regularly—surrepti-

tiously within the country and openly outside of it. The OPEC oil cartel, for example, is a group of oil-producing nations that meet periodically and agree on how much oil they will produce, which essentially fixes the price of oil (although some OPEC nations cheat and produce more oil than they have agreed to—a common problem among price fixers).

Companies that become monopolies or fix prices may run afoul of the law. However,

Ministers of the Organization of Petroleum Exporting Countries (OPEC) meeting at OPEC headquarters in Vienna.

Effect of Commodity Pricing

Many companies offer same product.

⬇

Price wars ensue.

⬇

Price settles slightly above cost (commodity pricing).

⬇

Weaker competitors fail, merge, or are bought.

⬇

A few strong players emerge.

⬇

The few players raise prices.

a completely legal method to avoid the downward spiral of commodity pricing exists: prevent the product from becoming a commodity. A good example is personal computers (PCs). IBM-compatible PCs, which are made by many different manufacturers, are all very similar and have, in pricing terms, become a commodity. Personal computers made by Apple remain expensive. Unlike PCs, Apple computers are made only by Apple, and they differ in many ways from PCs, which insulates Apple from price wars in the PC market. For example, Apple computers are considered easier to use than PCs, which makes them popular with schools. They also handle graphics well, which makes them popular with design professionals. Educators and design professionals who believe that Apple computers are better than PCs are willing to pay more, so Apple can keep its prices high.

Apple Computer CEO Steve Jobs shows off the Macbook Air in 2008. Apple's small but devoted fan base and its one-of-a-kind products make Macs somewhat price insensitive.

This approach has drawbacks. Apple is a relatively small company with only a small share of the personal computer market; Apple must be relentlessly innovative to justify its higher price and keep customers loyal. Nonetheless, Apple's approach has helped it to survive for more than 20 years, a significant achievement in the volatile computer industry.

The Psychology of Pricing

What keeps Apple viable is that consumers, under the right circumstances, will pay higher prices and in some cases would rather pay more. Why people will pay more, who will pay more for what, and how much more they are willing to pay are subjects that keep countless marketers, advertisers, psychologists, and economists gainfully employed. Successful companies find the right mix of intangibles that make people willing to accept higher prices, and then set prices at the appropriately higher level.

Whether consumers will find a particular price acceptable can be hard to predict. The way prices are presented can make a difference. Retailers tend to use odd pricing—pricing a good at $3.99 rather than $4.00—which makes consumers more likely to think they are getting a bargain. Likewise, consumers are more willing to find a price acceptable if they believe it has been discounted from a higher price. Consumers are more accepting of high prices for optional items like desserts and fancy shoes than for necessities like electricity. Even the same goods—soda or candy, for instance—can command vastly higher prices in an entertainment venue like a movie theater than in an ordinary setting like a grocery store.

One of the reasons people do not always seek the lowest price is that most people do not really know exactly what prices they pay for goods—even goods they buy fairly regularly. People tend to think in terms of price ranges. They have an upward limit of what they would be willing to spend for a particular item, and they also have a downward limit—if an item is priced below that limit, people tend to assume something is wrong

with it. The acceptable price range for a product can shift over time to reflect, for example, inflation or the falling price of aging technology.

Customers may also be willing to pay a higher price for a good if they believe they are receiving more value. What is perceived as value depends on the individual buyer. However, groups of people tend to share similar attitudes about what constitutes value. Such a group is known as a market segment or market niche, and successful products and brands usually target a particular segment very carefully.

One kind of value is convenience. For example, people will pay a good deal more for food that has already been prepared and cooked than for food that they must prepare and cook themselves. Drugstores have increased revenues by expanding the kinds of goods they carry to include items like

Psychological Factors in Pricing

- Quality
- Convenience
- Value
- Social status in luxury goods

Pricing Airline Tickets

Until the late 1970s the airline industry in the United States was heavily regulated, not only for safety but also in all aspects. Federal regulators set ticket prices, and the vast majority of travelers paid the full fare. That is no longer the case: ticket prices vary widely, and the vast majority of travelers get some form of discount. Prices and profit margins on different routes vary considerably, usually depending on how many carriers fly the route.

Ticket prices can vary widely even for the same route. Fly tourist class from New York City to London in January, and a round-trip ticket could cost less than $400. Fly the same route business class, and the ticket could cost more than $6,000.

Market segmentation is one cause of this price differential. Tourists, by definition, do not need to fly to London—they could go anywhere. Consequently, the price of the flight must be low, otherwise very few people will choose to vacation in London and the flight will have lots of empty seats. Businesspeople, on the other hand, travel because they must, and, as their company is paying the price of the ticket, they are far less sensitive to price. Businesspeople are also far more likely than tourists to need to travel at the last minute and to stay in their destination for only a few days. The tourist, who buys well in advance and stays longer, benefits from the airline's need to plan because the airline will offer cheaper fares in return for certain profit.

The Internet Browser Price War

In the spring of 1996, Netscape's Navigator was king of Web-browsing software, which allows users to access the World Wide Web. Navigator controlled almost 90 percent of the market largely because of an innovative pricing strategy that Netscape executives called "free, but not free." Navigator was available as a free download from the Internet for 90 days. After that, users were supposed to pay. Many casual users never did, but corporate users, who wanted technical support along with the software, usually did pay. In addition, wide distribution of Navigator promoted sales of Netscape's lucrative server software.

However, Microsoft, which makes the operating systems used on the vast majority of PCs, began giving away its own browser, Explorer, for free when people purchased the Windows operating systems on a new computer that had Windows already installed. For most users, Navigator was also free from a monetary standpoint, but it had another cost—the time and effort spent to download it.

Navigator began to lose market share rapidly, and in early 1998 Netscape made it truly free. The loss of revenues from this policy hurt Netscape financially, and the company failed to upgrade its browser. Netscape was acquired in late 1998 by America Online, but its browser effectively became obsolete, leaving Explorer to dominate the market.

groceries. Milk may cost more at a drugstore than at a grocery store, but many people will pay the premium if it saves them a trip to another store.

A broad market segment values quality. Quality, like value, means different things to different people, but generally it guarantees that an item will last, will not break, and will effectively do the job it is designed to do. As most people equate higher price with higher quality, people who value quality expect to pay higher prices. Most best-selling brands market themselves as providing better quality for a slightly higher price.

Sometimes the higher price itself is the appeal because some people want the social status that is attached to being able to buy something very expensive. Luxury brands that sell to such status-oriented people must be priced very carefully to ensure that their prices do not become too low, or they will "go downmarket" and alienate their core market segment.

If a maker of luxury goods does not protect its brand from going downmarket, its goods might get caught between market segments, which is never good. Say the House of Swank makes hand-embroidered silk shirts that are sold at high-end boutiques for $600 and are coveted by socialites and social climbers everywhere. The House of Swank does not pay too much attention to distribution, and pretty soon Swank shirts are available at outlet malls for $200. Word gets around that Swank shirts might not cost as much as previously believed. Soon wearing one becomes a faux pas among the status-conscious, and, as no one else is willing to shell out $600 for a shirt, sales of Swank in high-end boutiques grind to a halt.

The market share that shops in outlet malls, however, is still the wrong crowd for House of Swank. Outlet-mall shoppers are looking for bargains—$20 shirts, not $200 ones. Swank shirts are thus too cheap for the status-conscious and too expensive for the budget-minded. Swank cannot sell in the boutiques, it cannot sell in the outlet malls, and pretty soon the House of Swank, a victim of poor pricing, is out of business.

Pricing remains more of an art than a science and will probably always have an element of unpredictability. Indeed, the prices people are willing to pay are so difficult for others to predict that some economists point to auctions as a sort of ultimate solution to the quandaries of pricing. Instead of having marketers, regulators, and economists attempt to determine a good price, auctions allow consumers to set their own price, and their reasons for picking that price remain their own.

Further Research
Consumer Price Index
www.bls.gov/CPI

The Consumer Price Indexes (CPI) program, part of the U.S. Bureau of Labor Statistics, produces monthly data on changes in the prices paid by urban consumers for a representative basket of goods and services.

Pricing Strategy
www.netmba.com/marketing/pricing

An article from the Internet Center for Management and Business Administration presents a clear outline of the topic.

Professional Pricing Society
www.pricingsociety.com

The home page of the association of pricing professionals offers links to case studies and to the association's blog.

—*Mary Sisson*

Product Development

Product development is the process of turning science into business or market research into market share. An individual or company takes an idea and turns it into a salable product. Products can be breakthrough products, for example, Apple's original computer, which was the first mass-marketed personal computer. It is considered a breakthrough product because it spawned a whole new market and way of life. Others, the wide-mouth toaster, for instance, are upgrades or improvements to existing products. Still others might be existing products in a new package, for example, pantyhose that comes in a plastic egg, or next-generation products like the change from cordless to wireless in telephones.

Product Development Cycle

Depending upon the product, various kinds of research are necessary to even begin thinking about creating a new product. Research is an information-gathering mission. Some very basic questions are: Will anyone want this product? Does the product solve a problem or, if it is a new product, will it improve quality of life? Two basic categories of research are market research, for example, questioning consumers about the proposed product or about problems with existing products, and scientific research, for example, finding a way to produce higher-quality sound recordings. Ideas for products can come from both.

The design phase, which follows scientific and market research, is the beginning of serious decision making. Who is the target market? Should the product be aimed at a high-end market willing to pay for superior quality or should it be aimed at the low-end market using the lowest-cost materials with mass production in mind? Will its price–value relationship turn a profit? How many ways can this product outperform the competition? How will the product be distributed? Will the product idea be licensed or will the inventor start a new business? Is it a stand-alone product or is it part of a product line? Does the product idea actually work in the real world? A good design process looks at the product and its potential from all angles.

Once the project is determined to be feasible, which may be as early as the research phase or as late as the end of the design phase, the planning and execution of a project plan begins. With the individual inventor, a project plan may be as basic as a notebook filled with notes, ideas, sketches, and statistics. With a large project in a corporation, it will be managed with project management software complete with phases, deadlines, and deliverables plus a full marketing plan. Project management software helps the project manager keep track of all phases of the process and tracks progress against deadlines.

Missed deadlines may indicate a bigger problem in product development—requirements creep. If the research and design phase was incomplete when the project began, often new requirements will crop up and will have to be addressed in the middle of the product's development. This can be a costly process in terms of time, money, and other resources. For example, when a product is seasonal and misses its production schedule, then the product is unlikely to achieve its greatest potential. Colored sunscreen is an example. Although it was intended for both summer fun outdoors

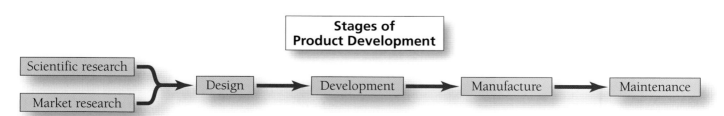

Stages of Product Development

Scientific research / Market research → Design → Development → Manufacture → Maintenance

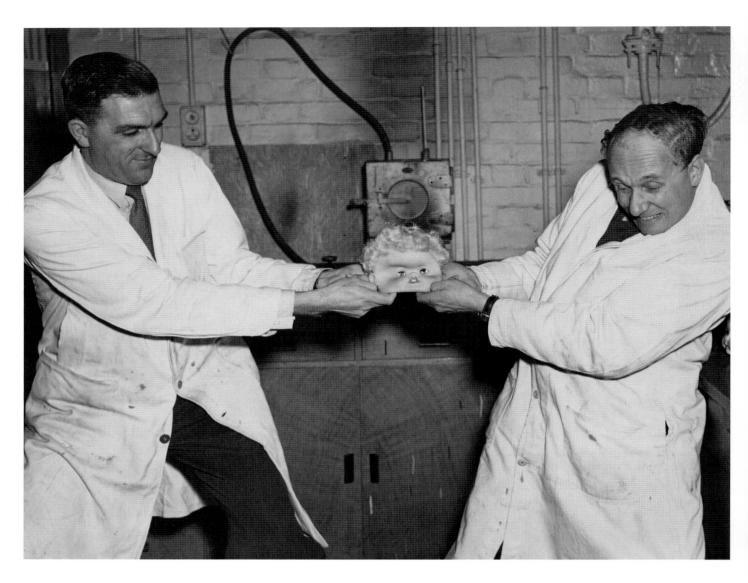

and for winter skiing, the product was released late and missed its first window of opportunity.

Going from the design phase into production is more than a simple progression from the drawing board to the manufacturing plant. Manufacturing, distribution, and marketing all must be addressed simultaneously. Marketing and distribution are closely aligned—marketing makes the public aware of the product and distribution gets it to the right place at the right time. If the product is not shipped immediately upon completion through distribution channels, then the manufacturer must pay to store it. The ideal is to have the marketing campaign in place during manufacture, with distribution channels established before the product is completed.

Once a product is delivered to the consumer, another step in the product development process, depending on the product, may come into play. Some products provide warranties or require ongoing maintenance. Warranties can originate with the manufacturer or can be offered by wholesalers or distributors. Full-function wholesalers and distributors actually purchase the product from the manufacturer, and then resell it with a standard markup. In that case, the wholesaler or distributor may offer a warranty through its own stores. Other products, for example, appliances or electronics, may require maintenance. Even though the manufacturer does not typically service these products, the product development plan must include a plan for servicing those items.

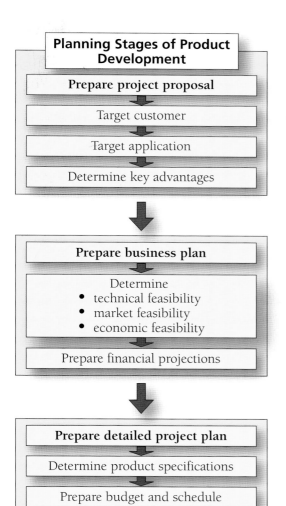

Planning Stages of Product Development

- **Prepare project proposal**
  - Target customer
  - Target application
  - Determine key advantages

- **Prepare business plan**
  - Determine
    - technical feasibility
    - market feasibility
    - economic feasibility
  - Prepare financial projections

- **Prepare detailed project plan**
  - Determine product specifications
  - Prepare budget and schedule

Source: Preston G. Smith and Donald G. Reinersten, *Developing New Products in Half the Time,* New York, Wiley, 1998.

Entrepreneurs

Entrepreneurial inventors face different issues than do big corporations in product development. First, they must have an idea that comes across as a sure winner right from the start. Unless inventors have enough money to manufacture, distribute, and market their products, they have to rely on other kinds of funding.

Family members might invest in a product without fully believing in the product if they believe in the inventor. However, most other investors require a convincing product and marketing plan before they will put up any money. A good idea is a good idea only if it works and if someone is willing to pay for it—both in the production phase and in the marketplace.

When individual inventors have ideas that they can make into salable products, they must decide either to create a business to produce and sell that product or to license that product to another company to make and sell for them. Licensing the product and letting someone else manufacture, market, and distribute it may seem easier. However, most companies are not willing to purchase a license unless they are quite sure the product will be successful. If a large company will buy the license and put its marketing and distribution power behind the product, that can be very helpful to the individual inventor.

If the inventor tries to set up his or her own business, then the product must meet a few basic criteria. First, it must have some significant advantage over the competition. Second, that advantage must be easily shown or demonstrated on the packaging, particularly if little money is available for advertising. For example, an individual invents a power tool for woodworking that requires both precise handling and lots of instruction. Without a major advertising campaign to explain the tool's value to consumers, the tool will probably fail. Most consumers scan store shelves for purchases. If the product's value is not obvious on the package or from advertising, then consumers are unlikely to purchase.

Protecting an Idea

A patent is the most common method of protecting a scientific discovery or an idea for a new invention or improvement to an existing one. Although a patent offers some protection against those who would copy or steal the idea, it is not always the best route to take. The U.S. Patent Office works under an exchange system. The Patent Office grants exclusive use of a patented product or process for 20 years. In exchange, the content of the patent is put into a public repository where anyone can view it. The risk is that someone will take a patented idea and make changes or improvements. With enough change to the original idea, that person can then patent the new idea.

Software Development Cycles

Software development differs slightly from other product development. The manufacturing process is actually the coding process. The manufacturing cost of developing software lies in the expertise, labor, and computers that develop it and test it. Parts are not purchased, and the majority of actual product production costs are concentrated in the cost of documentation and disks or CDs. In the case of downloadable software, even those costs are eliminated.

The software development cycle includes the research phase, which is broken down into planning, then analysis. Both product and software development have a design phase, then a construction phase (called the development phase in product development). The implementation phase in software development is simply product distribution.

The maintenance phase is completely different in software development. Almost all software requires some kind of maintenance in the form of upgrades. Even if the product itself never changes in function, it must be updated to keep up with new technology or it will be relegated to the growing pile of obsolete software. Software also requires maintenance in the form of fixes (called patches) to correct any problems inherent in the software or with its compatibility with other products.

In some cases, a patent is not appropriate. For example, KFC has not patented its "12 secret herbs and spices" because it wants to keep the recipe a secret. Instead, it works under a trade secret agreement where manufacturers of the spice mix agree not to reveal the recipe.

Trademarks can become a form of idea protection. If a certain product is associated with a particular name, consumers will lean toward that brand, protecting it from theft. For example, RollerBlades are a trademarked product (the generic name is inline skates). The same is true of Kleenex.

Collaboration

The individual inventor is not completely extinct, but the individual is being replaced by collaborative teams who work together to bring products to market. Increased competition makes every day count in the consumer market. Product cycle times are decreasing with advances in technology and business processes. Cheap labor in some parts of the world puts intense pressure on U.S. companies to find lower-cost methods of producing competing products. Lightning-speed advances in technology make it difficult for one company or product development team to keep up with all the changes. Accordingly, companies are beginning to collaborate on product development.

A large, multinational corporation may have engineers and designers in the United States, manufacturers in Taiwan, and marketing professionals worldwide working together to bring a product, for example, computer disk drives, to market. This kind of development effort requires focused project management and well-defined communication channels and structures. On a smaller scale, collaboration may be necessary among a company's scientists, engineers, marketers, managers, suppliers, sales force, and retailers; pharmaceuticals are an example.

Software product development becomes a major collaborative effort when working

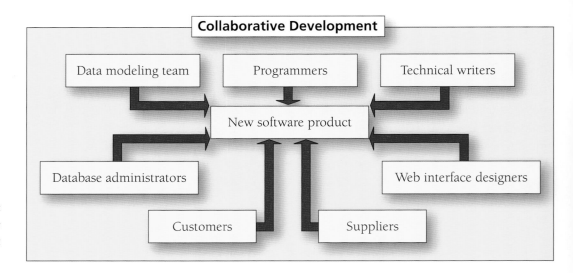

The collaborative development process for a new software product involves many different participants.

In a graphics studio, designers work on packaging for a new product.

on a product like an enterprise information base that can be accessed through the Internet. Some of the technical professionals involved in such an effort are the data modeling team to design the database, the programmers to write the code, technical writers to document the system and create online help, Web interface designers, network engineers, and the database administrators who maintain the information stored in the database. Nontechnical individuals involved might be customers and suppliers who will use the database and their contacts inside the company. All of these teams must work together to bring a major software product to market.

Whenever the idea for a new or improved product begins—with an individual inventor working in a basement or a team of scientists working in a sophisticated lab—product development requires time, talent, and financial backing. The foundation of a successful product is thorough research coupled with a useful product idea. Developing that idea into a marketable product requires understanding what people want, determining the price–value relationship, and making the public aware that the product is available and that it is better than anything else they have access to today.

Further Research
Entrepreneurs Organization
www.eonetwork.org
The mission of the Entrepreneurs Organization, a global network of business owners, is to encourage learning and growth.
Product Development and Management Association
www.pdma.org
The association provides up-to-date resources and information on new product development.
United States Patent and Trademark Office
www.uspto.gov
This government agency issues and regulates patents. Among the resources available from its home page are links to explanations of patents, copyright, and the legal issues surrounding them.

—*Stephanie Buckwalter*

Recession

A recession is a downturn in a nation's economy. More precisely, it is a decline in a nation's gross domestic product (GDP)—a nation's total expenditure on all goods and services produced in its economy—for six months or more. Ten recessions have occurred in the United States since 1950, including one that began in 2008.

An expanding economy, one in which the GDP is growing, creates jobs, rising wages, and steady prices. These conditions give a sense of stability, confidence in the future, and optimism, encouraging people to invest their resources and engage in productive activity. Society benefits as goods and services become cheaper while wages increase. Recessions reverse these positive conditions. In recessions, unemployment increases, wages fall, and overall confidence suffers.

The causes of upturns and downturns in the economy are not well understood. One theory postulates that they result from events that affect specific companies or industries initially but then, through a "ripple effect," have broader impact. For example, in the early twentieth century Henry Ford perfected techniques for the mass production of cars, which created jobs as new workers were needed to both produce and subsequently maintain those cars. Other industries, including steel, road construction, and oil production, expanded because of the new technology, creating yet more jobs. The new jobs increased the earning power of workers and their ability to buy new goods and services; they produced economic growth.

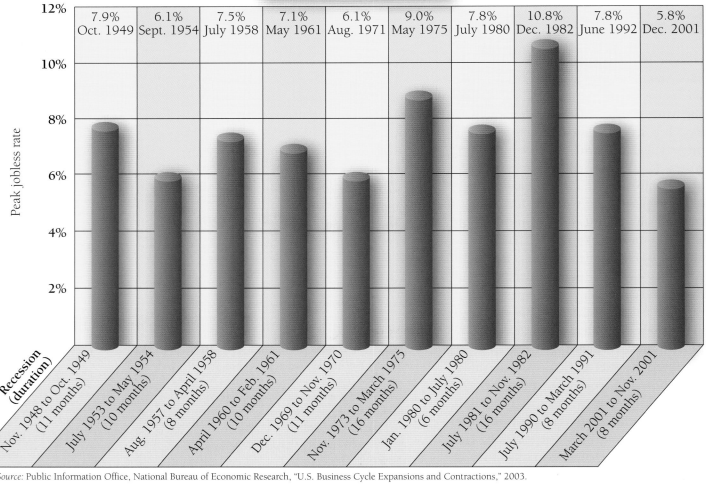

U.S. Recessions 1950–2001

Peak jobless rate

7.9% Oct. 1949	
6.1% Sept. 1954	
7.5% July 1958	
7.1% May 1961	
6.1% Aug. 1971	
9.0% May 1975	
7.8% July 1980	
10.8% Dec. 1982	
7.8% June 1992	
5.8% Dec. 2001	

Recession (duration)

Nov. 1948 to Oct. 1949 (11 months)
July 1953 to May 1954 (10 months)
Aug. 1957 to April 1958 (8 months)
April 1960 to Feb. 1961 (10 months)
Dec. 1969 to Nov. 1970 (11 months)
Nov. 1973 to March 1975 (16 months)
Jan. 1980 to July 1980 (6 months)
July 1981 to Nov. 1982 (16 months)
July 1990 to March 1991 (8 months)
March 2001 to Nov. 2001 (8 months)

Source: Public Information Office, National Bureau of Economic Research, "U.S. Business Cycle Expansions and Contractions," 2003.

This process may also operate in reverse. If workers and company owners in a particular industry suffer a setback causing widespread losses of earnings and jobs, they will cut back on spending, and the ripple effect might push the economy toward or into a recession. One such recession occurred in 1973. Overseas oil producers colluded to increase prices dramatically. Demand for goods that used petroleum products dropped in response as the price for these goods rose. American car manufacturers were forced to reduce production of low-mileage vehicles that consumers no longer wanted. Hundreds of thousands of workers became unemployed in the automobile industry and in related industries; the entire economy went into a recession.

Another theory, developed by John Maynard Keynes, holds that recessions occur when people begin to spend less of their income. Events like the terrorist attacks in the United States on September 11, 2001, reduce optimism. Consumers lose confidence, saving more and spending less. Businesses react by reducing investment and employment. Unemployment then rises, wages fall, and the economy enters a recession. In these cases a recession might be said to occur because people acted as if one would occur.

The Great Depression of the 1930s is an excellent example. (A depression is a deep, prolonged economic downturn.) The decade of the 1920s was generally a period of optimism in the United States. People invested heavily and spent willingly on new consumer products. Businesses expanded, building new factories and hiring more workers, because consumers were willing to spend. The mood changed when the stock market crashed on October 29, 1929. Many investors suffered heavy losses and were unable to repay loans. Consequently, many banks were forced to close; many depositors lost their savings because their accounts were not insured. In the panic that followed, unemployment soared, spending dropped sharply, and the economy shrank dramatically. Government efforts to fix the

The gas crisis of the 1970s pushed the U.S. economy deep into recession.

economy did not work, and employment rates and consumer confidence remained low until the United States entered World War II in 1941.

The U.S. government uses several methods to try to prevent recessions. First, it serves as a guarantor of economic stability. It protects the value of currency, acts as a lender of last resort to banks, and guarantees (through a program of federal insurance) the security of bank deposits. All of these measures foster economic confidence

Gray's Papaya hot dog stand on New York City's Upper West Side.

The government may also use fiscal policy—decreasing taxes, increasing spending, or both—in its efforts to stimulate a faltering economy. When the government increases spending (as it did in the buildup for World War II, for example), the demand for goods and services rises. This rise in demand increases employment and stimulates economic growth. Tax cuts are intended to work in a similar way: consumers who can keep an increased share of their income can presumably spend more. Fiscal policy changes may also fail, however. The necessary legislation may come too late to make a difference. New spending programs may be insufficient; tax cuts may be too small, or they may be targeted to benefit constituency groups for reasons unrelated to overall economic growth.

Government efforts to ensure economic stability and growth are also complicated by the degree to which national economies throughout the world have become interdependent. As world trade has increased, economic problems in one country can easily spread to others. For example, a nation in recession will be less able to purchase goods and services from other nations. The decrease in demand can cause job losses in other countries as producers of trade goods cut back. Similarly, economic shocks related to political instability or war can also have destructive ripple effects. In efforts to address international economic problems, many national governments now participate in cooperative efforts carried out through institutions like the International Monetary Fund and the World Bank.

and optimism. Second, through the Federal Reserve system, the government monitors the economy and takes action to limit recessions when they do occur. It does this primarily through monetary policy. Monetary policy decisions made by the Federal Reserve Board of Governors have the effect of controlling the money supply. If a recession appears likely, the Fed has the power to purchase securities and to reduce the interest rates charged when banks borrow money at Federal Reserve district banks. These actions are intended to get more money into circulation, thus encouraging lending and giving businesses and consumers a greater incentive to spend and invest. The stimulus provided by increased spending and investment may then reignite economic growth.

Adjusting monetary policy does not always work. Six months or more may be needed for policy actions to take effect. To take timely, effective action, therefore, policy makers must try to predict future economic events. Often they are unable to provide accurate forecasts and, accordingly, fail to act in time to prevent a recession. Increases in the money supply can also overheat the economy—causing inflation and thus introducing a new set of economic problems.

Further Research

National Bureau of Economic Research

www.nber.org/cycles.html

A database of business cycles and contractions.

Recession

Recession.org

This site, founded in 1999, compiles news and research on topics relating to economic recession in the United States.

—*David Long*

Savings and Investment Options

Almost everyone dreams about becoming financially independent and retiring young. Most people do not fulfill that dream because they do not take control of their finances. The hardest part of saving money is the discipline required to do so regularly, but setting goals and developing a financial plan can provide the motivation necessary to be a successful, disciplined saver.

The question that lurks in the minds of many potential investors is "When should I start saving?" The practical answer is "yesterday." Consider the following example (shown in the chart on compound interest). Beginning at age 18, Julie contributes $1,000 per year for 10 years to an investment account that earns 10 percent interest. Julie's twin brother, John, decides to wait until he is 28 to begin saving. He contributes $1,000 per year to an account earning 10 percent from age 28 until age 65. Who will have more money at age 65? Julie will have accumulated $596,129 by age 65 even though she contributed a total of only $10,000 to her account. John will have contributed $38,000, but his account will be worth only $364,043 at age 65. Why the difference? Julie started earlier and enjoyed the benefit of more years of compound interest. As this example illustrates, the cost of waiting to begin investing is significant.

Financial Securities

The first step to successful investing is understanding the available investment choices. Investments are often referred to as financial assets or securities. Financial securities, which provide cash return, can be divided into two categories: nontradable and tradable securities. Nontradable securities include savings accounts, certificates of deposit (CDs), and other accounts offered by banks and brokerage firms. Investors can put money into and withdraw money from these accounts on demand, but they cannot sell their ownership in these accounts to another investor. Nontradable accounts are usually very low risk because they are insured by the government (Federal Deposit Insurance Corporation [FDIC]) or through private investment insurance (Securities Investor Protection Corporation).

Stocks and bonds are tradable securities; they can easily be bought and sold in public markets like the New York Stock Exchange or the Nasdaq market. Stocks, also known as equities, represent ownership in a publicly traded company. An investor who owns stock in Coca-Cola, for example, literally owns a piece of the company, has the right to vote at the company's annual meeting, and can claim a proportionate share of the company's net income. Stockholders receive their share of the company's net

Analysts say it is never too soon to start saving.

The Impact of Compound Interest						
	Period of savings	Annual contribution	Total contribution at age 65	Annual interest	Age of account	Value of account
Julie	10 years	$1,000	$10,000	10%	47 years	$596,129
John	38 years	$1,000	$38,000	10%	37 years	$364,043

Although Julie saved less money over a shorter period of time than her twin brother, John, she ends up with far more money than John at age 65, because her savings earned compound interest over a longer period of time.

income as dividends. Equities (stocks) are the savings vehicle of choice for many investors. According to Equity Ownership in America, a 1999 study commissioned by the Investment Company Institute and the Securities Industry Association, 48 percent of U.S. households owned stock in 1999, up from only 19 percent in 1983.

Investors who own bonds are lenders, not owners; they lend money to the company that issues the bonds in return for a fixed series of combined interest and principal payments. Bondholders do not have voting rights, nor do they have a claim to the company's earnings. Bonds are referred to as debt securities.

Mutual funds, another kind of investment, became very popular in the last two decades of the twentieth century. According to the Investment Company Institute, the number of U.S. mutual funds has grown from 371 funds in 1984 to more than 8,000 funds in 2008. Mutual funds collect money from many investors and pool the money to purchase shares of stock in many different companies. Investors in mutual funds own shares of the fund. Each share represents ownership of a small piece of every company that the mutual fund owns. Mutual funds are ideal investment vehicles for beginning

investors because they allow for small contributions (as low as $25 per month) and provide immediate diversification (ownership of stock of companies in many industries).

Some mutual funds also invest in bonds. Money market mutual funds have become a popular alternative to savings accounts. They purchase short-term government securities, such as Treasury bills (T-bills), which are relatively safe. Unlike savings accounts, money market mutual funds are not insured by the FDIC, but they do provide higher returns than savings accounts.

Risk and Return

The return on an asset can be divided into two components, capital gains and dividends or interest. Companies pay interest to their bondholders to compensate them for lending money to the firm. Some companies distribute a portion of their earnings to stockholders (owners) by paying dividends. Capital gains occur when an asset (a stock or bond) is sold for more than its original purchase price. Bondholders receive most of their income through interest payments, but they may achieve capital gains as well. Because not all companies pay dividends, stockholders receive most of their return in the form of capital gains. Dividends, interest,

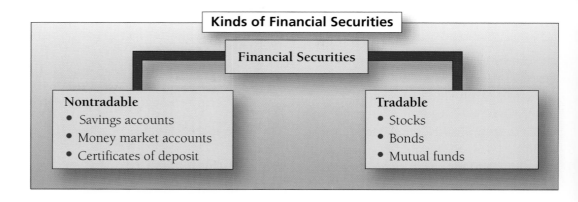

Kinds of Financial Securities

Financial Securities

Nontradable
- Savings accounts
- Money market accounts
- Certificates of deposit

Tradable
- Stocks
- Bonds
- Mutual funds

and capital gains are all taxed, but capital gains are usually taxed at a lower rate. Furthermore, the tax on capital gains is not due until the asset is sold; the tax on interest and dividends is due every year.

Different financial assets offer different amounts of return and risk, but what is a realistic return? The return that investors earn depends on the kind of security in which they invest. For example, savings accounts, which are insured by the FDIC, are virtually risk free and usually provide a return of less than 2 percent per year. To earn higher returns, investors must be willing to take on more risk. The table on the right shows average annual returns and standard deviations (in this case, a measure of risk) in 2006 for several kinds of tradable U.S. financial assets.

The return is the reward that investors receive for bearing the risk (standard deviation) associated with each asset. More risk gives more uncertainty about future returns—the chance of losing money is greater. Assets that provide higher rates of return are usually riskier. Small-company stocks, the asset class with the highest standard deviation, provide the greatest potential reward, while T-bills, the asset class with the lowest standard deviation, provide the least potential return.

In *Stocks for the Long Run*, noted economist Jeremy Siegel asserts that stocks are unquestionably riskier than bonds or T-bills in the short run. However, investing in common stocks for the long term provides a very different risk profile. Siegel studied returns from 1802 to 1997 and found that if stocks are owned for at least 10 years, they perform better than do bonds or T-bills. Furthermore, Siegel's analysis shows that for 20-year holding periods, stock return rates have never fallen behind inflation, while bonds and T-bills fell behind inflation at an average rate of 3 percent per year over 20-year periods. This evidence suggests that stocks are the safest long-term investment for investors who hope to maintain and increase their purchasing power.

To reduce risk, investors should diversify their portfolios (their array of investments).

Average Returns and Risk Premiums 2006

Asset	Average Annual	Risk Premium
Large-company stocks	12.3	8.5
Small-company stocks	17.4	13.6
Long-term corporate bonds	6.2	2.4
Long-term goverment bonds	5.8	2.0
Short-term goverment bonds (T-bills)	3.8	0.0

Source: Ibbotson Associates Inc. Note: Risk premium refers to the extra return on a risky asset compared to the risk-free rate.

Diversification occurs when investors divide their money among many different kinds of investment. The most basic level of diversification is buying stock in many companies rather than just one. Investors can diversify even more by purchasing different kinds of stocks, including international stocks, and adding bonds to their portfolios.

Developing a Savings and Investment Plan
Investors have the opportunity to participate in many different kinds of savings plans, either through their jobs or on their own. For example, anyone with earned income can open an Individual Retirement Account (IRA) and make annual contributions to that account. In 2009 investors under the age of 49 were able to contribute $5,000 per year to IRA accounts. The money invested in an IRA can be used to purchase many kinds of financial assets, including stocks, bonds, and mutual funds. IRAs are of two kinds: the Roth and the Traditional IRA. The Roth IRA provides tax-free earnings, while the Traditional IRA provides tax-deferred earnings; in some cases, Traditional IRA contributions are tax deductible.

Many investors also have the opportunity to participate in retirement plans at

Qualities of Successful Investors

1. **Disciplined:** Pay themselves first.
2. **Diversified:** Divide money among many different kinds of assets.
3. **Patient:** Leave money invested in the stock market for the long term.
4. **Proactive:** Do not wait to start investing.

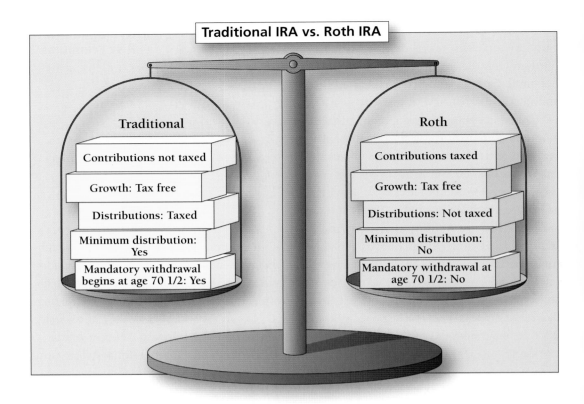

Traditional	Roth
Contributions not taxed	Contributions taxed
Growth: Tax free	Growth: Tax free
Distributions: Taxed	Distributions: Not taxed
Minimum distribution: Yes	Minimum distribution: No
Mandatory withdrawal begins at age 70 1/2: Yes	Mandatory withdrawal at age 70 1/2: No

work, including plans known as 401(k) and 403(b) plans. Contributions to these plans are tax deductible, and the earnings they generate are tax-deferred until the money is withdrawn. In many cases, the employer will offer to match some of the employee's contributions to the plan, which effectively increases the employee's annual salary. Contributions to these plans are usually invested in mutual funds.

Successful investors are disciplined, diversified, patient, and proactive. Disci-plined investors pay themselves first by having money deducted from every paycheck and deposited directly into their retirement plans, IRAs, or other investment accounts. Diversified investors understand that dividing their money among many different kinds of assets reduces risk and stabilizes return. Patient investors leave their money invested in the stock market for the long term. They do not try to "time the market"—pulling their money out when the stock market begins to decline. Proactive investors do not wait until next month or next year to start investing; they start now to get the maximum benefits of compound interest.

Further Research

Siegel, Jeremy. *Stocks for the Long Run: The Definitive Guide to Financial Market Returns and Long Term Investment Strategies.* New York: McGraw-Hill, 2007.

www.jeremysiegel.com

The Motley Fool

www.fool.com

Motley Fool's Web site features investment data and advice, discussion boards, and portfolio-tracking features.

—*Angeline Lavin*

Web Resources on Savings and Investment

www.oag.state.ny.us/bureaus/investor_protection provides general information from the New York State Office of the Attorney General on establishing a solid financial plan to ensure the ability to save and invest earnings.

www.urbanext.illinois.edu/ww1 is a woman's guide to saving and investing, from the University of Illinois.

www.sec.gov/investor/pubs/roadmap.htm is the Security and Exchange Commission's Web page providing general information regarding savings and investments.

www.morningstar.com is the home page of Morningstar, a provider of mutual fund, stock, and variable annuity investment information.

Small Business

The Small Business Administration Act defines a small business concern as a business that is independently owned and operated and is not dominant in its field of operation. For example, an agricultural enterprise is considered a small business if its annual receipts do not exceed $500,000. A study conducted by Joel Popkin and Company found that small businesses make up approximately 68 percent of services, 65 percent of wholesale and retail trade, and 27 percent of mining and manufacturing enterprises. Small business has continued to be an important part of the U.S. economy even through less stable times for larger businesses.

Brief History of Small Business

Before the Industrial Revolution, small business was the dominant form of economic enterprise in the United States. The production of textiles and food products as well as metal, wood, and leather goods was, in most cases, handled by small, family-based operations using local raw materials and serving their immediate communities. Scholars believe the early entrepreneurial spirit of small business owners helped create a recognizable business culture in America that continues to exist—a culture based on idealism, individualism, and the desire to be one's own boss.

The nineteenth century saw unprecedented growth in American small businesses, especially in the most common small business, the retail store. In 1814 the U.S. government issued more than 46,000 retail licenses (during the short time during which licensing was federally mandated). An additonal 12,000 retail stores were logged in the census of 1840, and that number grew to 720,000 by 1869. These general stores were often the hub of commerce during this era, especially in smaller towns. Meanwhile, peddlers—the quintessential one-person operation—traveled from town to town selling their wares. In 1850 more than 10,000 peddlers were on the road; by 1860, nearly 17,000. These general stores and peddlers carried out the distribution of goods and services in America well into the 1870s.

The grocery store of Fred Gower, in Baltimore, circa 1920.

A shrimper and his staff outside his store in Bayou La Batre, Alabama.

nesses was growing as well. By the turn of the century, nearly two-thirds of all American workers were employed by small businesses.

As big business came to dominate the economic landscape, the federal government stepped in to help small businesses survive. America's first antitrust laws, the Sherman Act in 1890 and the Clayton Act in 1914, were passed mainly to protect small business. After nearly 110,000 businesses failed during the Great Depression, the government responded with the Robinson–Patman Act of 1936 (also known as the Anti-Chain-Store Act) and the Miller–Tydings Act of 1937 (also known as the Fair Trade Act), both of which sought to protect smaller retail firms from unfair pricing practices by national chain stores. After World War II, when small businesses found they could not compete with the large businesses that had dominated wartime production, the federal government stepped in once again, establishing the Small Business Administration (SBA) in 1953.

Scholarly interest in small business and small business history grew in the 1970s and 1980s, sparked, in part, by economic encroachment of foreign competition. Over the next several decades, most business schools and universities throughout the nation began to offer courses on developing and operating small businesses, and bookstore shelves began to fill with titles on small business management. Contemporary small businesses continue to struggle to compete with large chain stores, but economists and entrepreneurs alike look to small businesses for innovation, flexible production, and specialization.

Starting a Small Business

The SBA offers major assistance in the starting of a small business. The SBA is the nation's largest single financial backer of small business. Before starting a small business, SBA recommends that entrepreneurs evaluate their personal and business goals, including completing a sound business plan. Before developing a plan, entrepreneurs should list the reasons that they are interested in starting a business and then

In the 1870s the rail system in the United States opened up the local markets dominated by small business, allowing big business access for the first time. Advances in technology created economies of scale for larger companies, allowing for previously impossible efficiencies. Nevertheless, the number of smaller businesses continued to grow. They existed in the niches neglected by big business, for example, in local markets, producing specialized goods and often offering high levels of craftsmanship. Small businesses enabled skilled workers to survive in the face of unskilled assembly line work, and they provided service—in the old-fashioned sense of face-to-face contact and first-name-basis encounters. At this time, the absolute number of small busi-

ask themselves which kind of business would be right for them based on interests, skills, and time available to run the business. Prospective entrepreneurs may wish to evaluate themselves on such characteristics as stamina, level of organization, and the business's effect on their family.

In addition, a potential entrepreneur should conduct some research to determine market potential in the geographic area. Prospective business owners should try to identify competitors and plan the niche that their business will fill in the market. Profitable and competitive prices for services and goods are determined by analyzing production costs, including materials, labor, and overhead. Setting prices can be complicated, thus new business owners are advised to seek the advice of an expert.

A decision must be made about whether to start the business as a sole proprietorship (the easiest and least expensive method), to develop a partnership, or to incorporate. The structure of the business should take into consideration the kind of business operation, legal restrictions, liabilities, capital needs, number of employees, and tax

advantages. The SBA suggests that a tax accountant or attorney assist in making these decisions.

Prospective business owners should draw up a business plan. Included in the plan are a current and pro forma balance sheet, an income statement, and a cash flow analysis. Assistance in planning is available through SBA and also through the Service Corps of Retired Executives (SCORE) and Women's Business Centers (WBCs). In addition, resources are available through procurement center representatives at each major military installation and through more than 2,700 chambers of commerce located across the United States.

Once a plan is developed, information about licenses, zoning laws, and other regulations can be obtained through the local SBA or chamber of commerce. Entrepreneurs need to investigate the local, state, and federal governmental regulations that would apply to the business. For example, a certificate of occupancy will be needed if planning to occupy a new or used building. Businesses that use a name other than the owner's must register the name with the county according to the Trade Name Registration Act. State

Sarah of Sarah's Kitchen in Ruston, Louisiana.

Estimates of Business Wealth by Firm Size 1990 to 2000
(in billions of dollars)

Year	Corporate wealth (small firms)	Corporate wealth (large firms)	Noncorporate wealth	Total business wealth	Total small business wealth	Small business share of corporate wealth (%)	Small business share of total business wealth (%)
1990	909	2,328	2,478	5,716	3,387	28.1	59.3
1992	1,764	3,214	2,404	7,381	4,168	35.4	56.5
1997	3,920	7,876	3,176	14,972	7,096	33.2	47.4
1998	3,751	10,026	3,508	17,285	7,259	27.2	42.0
1999	5,369	11,827	3,757	20,953	9,126	31.2	43.6
2000	4,288	11,108	4,039	19,434	8,327	27.9	42.8

Note: Market value of corporate wealth and new worth of noncorporate business.
Source: Small Business Administration, "Estimate of Business Wealth by Firm Size," *Small Business Research Summary,* September 2002.

and local government offices can provide more information about this regulation. Depending on the kind of business, owners may wish to investigate trademarks and copyrights, which can be registered through the state or federal government (U.S. Department of Commerce).

In estimating financing needs, a business owner should have enough money on hand to cover operating expenses for at least a year, after building and equipment expenses are covered. This includes the owner's salary and money to repay loans. An accountant can help estimate cash flow needs. In addition to committing personal funds, entrepreneurs may wish to consider a partner for additional financing. Banks are one source of financing; other sources include commercial finance companies, venture capital firms, local development companies, and life insurance companies.

Taxes should be taken into consideration when starting a new business. Business owners must contact the U.S. Internal Revenue Service (IRS) to obtain information about taxes that need to be withheld. Many publications are available from the IRS. The Social Security Administration can provide information on FICA. Information on sales tax and unemployment insurance tax can be obtained from the state government.

Other information must be gathered before starting a small business: benefits and state labor laws concerning employees

should be investigated; health and safety standards can be obtained through the Federal Occupational Safety and Health Administration (OSHA). The U.S. Department of Labor provides information on minimum wage.

A successful business usually includes sound management practices, industry experience, technical support, and planning ability. The availability of many resources and the innovations of entrepreneurs enable small businesses to continue to be an important part of the business world.

Further Research
Canadian Chamber of Commerce
www.chamber.ca
The home page of the Canadian organization.
Entrepreneurs Organization
www.eonetwork.org
The home page of the Entrepreneurs Organization, a global network for entrepreneurs, with members in more than 38 countries.
Internal Revenue Service
www.irs.gov/businesses/small/index.html
Tax advice tailored to small businesses.
Small Business Administration
www.sba.gov
The mission of the SBA is assist and protect the interests of small business concerns, to preserve free competitive enterprise, and to maintain and strengthen the overall economy. Its Web site provides a wealth of useful resources.
United States Chamber of Commerce
www.uschamber.org
The home page of the U.S. organization.

—Denise Davis and Laura Lambert

Stocks and Bonds

The financial markets have become prominent in ongoing news stories; watching television or reading the newspaper almost invariably brings a story on stocks and bonds to our attention. This popularity is attributable in part to the varying cycles of bull markets (a period of rising stock prices) and bear markets (decreasing prices): the bear market of 2009 returned share prices to pre-2000 levels, after a bull market that saw the Dow-Jones index of stocks rise over 10,000 for the first time. Interest in financial securities has increased substantially since the mid-1970s as more Americans have gained access and exposure to the market through mutual funds, 401(k) and 403(b) retirement plans, and Individual Retirement Accounts (IRAs). In 2005, the Investment Company Institute (ICI) and the Securities Industry Association estimated that half of U.S. households owned stock, up from just 19 percent in 1983.

Although the surge in participation in financial markets is a relatively recent phenomenon, the roots of today's financial markets can be traced to the early 1790s. At that time, the U.S. government began issuing debt (bonds) to pay the debts it had incurred in fighting the Revolutionary War, and it sold 10 million shares of stock to finance the creation of the first U.S. bank. More banks followed, and investors became more interested in investing in stocks and bonds. This increase in demand for financial securities spurred transportation and manufacturing companies to issue their own stock. The U.S. economy has grown through the issuance of debt and equity (stock) by businesses and the purchase of those financial instruments by investors. For more than 200 years, U.S. businesses have benefited from access to one of the most developed capital markets in the world.

Since the 1970s the global financial market has been changing dramatically. Prior to 1970 the U.S. stock and bond market made up about 65 percent of all financial securities available in the world. In 2001 the U.S. stock and bond market made up less than 50 percent of all securities available worldwide. This shift in the markets has occurred because many developing countries are growing quickly and are using debt and equity to fund economic growth.

Stock and Bond Basics

Businesses require capital (money) to grow—to develop new products, build new plants, expand internationally, and invest in technology. Owners of small businesses may choose to use their own savings to start or maintain their business, or they may seek a loan from a bank. Large businesses, corporations like Wal-Mart, General Motors, and Coca-Cola, require large amounts of capital from a variety of sources to fund their growth. Rather than borrowing great sums of money from banks, large businesses often enter capital markets directly by selling stocks or bonds to individual investors.

Stocks and bonds differ fundamentally. Common stock represents ownership of a company. If an investor owns 100 shares of Coca-Cola, he or she owns a minuscule piece of that company and has the right to vote on important issues at the company's annual meeting. With this ownership comes a certain amount of risk because stockholders are not guaranteed a return on their investment. Some companies, for instance, Coca-Cola, distribute a portion of their earnings each year to shareholders in the form of dividends. Other companies, including Microsoft, have not traditionally paid annual dividends. Many investors buy stock regardless of dividends because they believe that the value of the company will increase, thereby increasing the value of the individual shares.

Bondholders, on the other hand, are not company owners. A bond is a loan: the individual who buys the bond lends a certain

The floor of a modern stock exchange.

amount of money, called the principal, to the company that issues the bond. Bondholders do not have the opportunity to vote on issues facing the firm because they do not own a piece of the company. They have simply lent capital to the firm, and they receive periodic interest payments in exchange for that loan.

Bond interest payments, unlike stock dividends, are guaranteed. Investment in bonds is, accordingly, less risky than stock investments. Bonds issued by corporations like GM and Wal-Mart are referred to as long-term corporate bonds while bonds issued by the U.S. government are referred to as long-term government bonds. When a firm or government issues a long-term bond, the intention is to borrow money for 10 to 30 years. The U.S. government also issues Treasury bills (T-bills) to borrow money for short periods, usually less than one year.

Risk and Return

If stocks are more risky than bonds, what induces investors to buy stocks? In general, risk and reward go hand in hand. Stock investors, who are willing to bear more risk,

generally receive a higher return than bond-holders, who wish to bear less risk. The average annual return on stocks of large companies (Coca-Cola and Microsoft, for example) is much larger than the average annual return on bonds. The difference between the returns is referred to as a risk premium, which measures the extra reward that investors may earn for bearing the additional risk associated with investing in common stock.

The risk of each asset class is measured by the standard deviation. Both the average return on large-company stocks and the standard deviation risk of large-company stocks are more than twice as high as the respective numbers for long-term corporate bonds. Risk and return generally move in the same direction: with greater risk comes greater reward. The only exception is the long-term government bonds; corporate bonds provide a slightly higher return than government bonds although they have have slightly less risk.

The return on T-bills is only marginally higher than inflation. As inflation erodes the

A trader in the Nasdaq 100 Stock futures pit at the Chicago Mercantile Exchange signals a trade.

purchasing power of money, investors who invest large sums in low-risk T-bills do not enjoy much increase in purchasing power. To enjoy increased purchasing power through time without bearing the risk of an investment portfolio containing only common stock, investors must diversify their portfolio across asset classes, allocating money to stocks, long-term bonds, and T-bills, as well as alternative asset classes such as real estate. Furthermore, studies show that investors should have a portion of their portfolio invested in international securities. The exact allocation of money across asset classes depends on the individual investor's risk tolerance, age, financial goals, and constraints.

Issuance and Trading

When a company wishes to sell equity or borrow money by issuing bonds, the firm typically employs an investment banker, also known as an underwriter, to assist with the

A shareholder speaks out at a Walt Disney Company shareholders' meeting. Shareholders can use their equity stakes in companies to put pressure on management. Shareholder activism is on the increase worldwide.

issuance process. Security issuance is an involved process because the companies that wish to issue securities must disclose a significant amount of information about their company to potential investors. This information is assembled in a prospectus, a document that must be approved by the Securities and Exchange Commission (SEC). The SEC was created by Congress in 1934 to regulate securities trading and protect the interests of current and potential investors. The prospectus contains information about the company's financial prospects and business operations. Before investing in any securities, investors should study the prospectus carefully.

When a company issues stocks and bonds and subsequently receives the proceeds from the sale of the stocks or bonds, the transaction is referred to as a primary market transaction. After the primary market transaction, investors can trade securities among themselves through the secondary market. The firm itself does not receive any money from secondary market transactions. In 2005 the average trading volume on the New York Stock Exchange (NYSE), which is a secondary market, was more than 1.6 billion shares per day. The largest trading day was September 19, 2008, when 2.99 billion shares were traded. These recent volume numbers are even more impressive considering that prior to 1960, volume averaged less than 3 million shares per day.

The bond market is small compared with the equity market. In 2007 bond trading averaged just under $10 million per day on the NYSE. For both stocks and bonds, the majority of this volume originates in secondary market transactions (investors trading with each other). Very few transactions involve the sale of new stock or bonds by a firm.

To buy bonds or individual shares of stock, investors typically must have an account with a financial institution, usually a brokerage firm that owns a seat on a U.S. securities exchange. Brokerage firms that own one or more seats on an exchange have trading privileges on that exchange and can buy and sell securities on the floor of the exchange. When an investor wishes to buy or sell, he or she places an order with a broker. The order is entered into the brokerage firm's computer system, travels to company headquarters, and enters the exchange's vast computer network. The order then proceeds to the trading floor where it is executed, and confirmation of the trade is sent to the investor. On average, less than 22 seconds are needed to process a trade because of the advanced technology that has been put in place by the stock exchanges. The NYSE alone has spent more than $2 billion on computer technology.

Technology and the Amateur Investor
The increased use of technology to facilitate stock trading has coincided with the growth of the Internet as a tool of commerce. In the mid-1990s several online discount brokers arrived on the trading scene, offering low-cost stock trades. Full-service brokers provide investment advice combined with trading; discount brokers only execute trades. The arrival of online discount brokers also coincided with the beginning of an incredible up-trend in the stock market. From 1995 to 1999, U.S. stocks returned more than 20 percent per year; prior to that run, the market had had no more than two years of back-to-back 20 percent increases.

This five-year period of incredible returns gave many investors unfounded confidence in their stock selection abilities and enticed them into trading for themselves through online discount brokers. Some investors became so interested in the market that they began day trading. Day trading goes against the traditional theory of long-term investing because it involves buying shares of stock and holding them only long enough to earn a quick profit. Some day traders earned large sums; others lost large sums when they bought stocks that decreased in value. By mid-2000 the popularity of day trading had begun to wane as the market started to tumble.

The bull market that essentially began in 1982 ended in 2000, when the U.S. stock markets were actually down for the year, a trend that continued in 2001 and 2002. Another bull market beginning in 2003 was followed by a bear market starting from 2007, triggered by the subprime mortgage crisis; the bear market continued into 2009.

Money lubricates the gears of the U.S. system of free enterprise, and the stock and bond markets provide an efficient way to transfer money from investors to businesses. The financial markets in the United States are some of the most developed markets in the world and are constantly evolving and changing to meet the needs of businesses as well as individual investors. Although the global capital market has more than $50 trillion invested in stocks, bonds, real estate, and cash, stocks and bonds remain the financial securities held by the vast majority of investors.

Further Research
Bloomberg.com
www.bloomberg.com
Online information service provides market data, business and finance news, and analysis.
New York Stock Exchange
www.nyse.com
Home page of the NYSE offers news, finance and investment information, and market analysis.
—*Angeline Lavin*

Taxation

Taxation is the generation of revenue from fees imposed on the purchase of goods, services, property, and membership (in the case of a tax on persons, such as a head tax). A country's tax system is the primary means by which governments extract revenues from the economy needed to pay for the government and its programs. Taxation has a considerable effect on business decisions, which affect the overall health of an economy. Economists generally characterize a tax system by how well it addresses four objectives: fairness, simplicity, efficiency, and sufficiency of revenue generation.

Fairness is normally measured by ability to pay, distribution of income, and beneficiary of service (or good). Ability to pay implies that taxpayers should not be taxed to the point where they will be unable to support themselves. Distribution of income deals with the effect that taxes have on different income groups. A progressive tax, such as the U.S. income tax, places a greater burden on people with higher incomes; a progressive tax will ideally redistribute income from the wealthier sections of the economy to the poorer. Sales taxes are sometimes described as regressive because the same tax burden is placed on everyone who purchases the good, regardless of the economic condition of the purchaser. The concept of beneficiary of service (or good) calls for taxpayers to pay directly for a

Objectives of the U.S. Tax System

- Fairness
- Simplicity
- Efficiency
- Sufficiency of revenue generation

service that they use. A toll charge on a road is an example: only people who use (benefit from) the road are subjected to the toll.

Simplicity in a tax considers the degree to which a tax is computable by both taxpayers and tax collection authorities. Ideally, the amount of tax owed should be easily known. Businesses in the United States spend vast sums of money each year to determine their income tax obligations. Simplifying the nation's income tax system would reduce the complexity and number of forms required to file tax returns. Thus, simplicity ultimately reduces the compliance cost of the tax.

Efficiency looks at how tax-influenced decisions affect the economy. Every business is concerned with making regular and sustainable profits. For a tax to be efficient, its existence should not persuade a business to invest in office buildings when it might have more usefully invested in a factory. From the perspective of a particular businessperson, the well-being of her business takes precedence over the well-being of the overall economy. For example, if a corporation decides to close a production plant because of the expense of a corporate income tax (a tax imposed on corporations' profits), the average amount that the plant would have earned is considered a loss to the economy. The decision to close the plant may be bad for the economy, but from the individual company's perspective, the decision is sound because operating with the corporate income tax would not be profitable.

In addition to the question of economic efficiency, the previous example also raises the issue of incentives. Economists study how a tax system induces individuals and firms to purchase or not purchase capital (human-made goods used to produce other goods and services) by offering various tax-saving

Effect of Insufficient Tax Revenue

Tax system produces insufficient revenue.

⬇

Government borrows funds, competing with business.

⬇

Added demand for funds raises interest rates.

⬇

Higher interest rates reduce capital investment.

⬇

Future growth potential lowered.

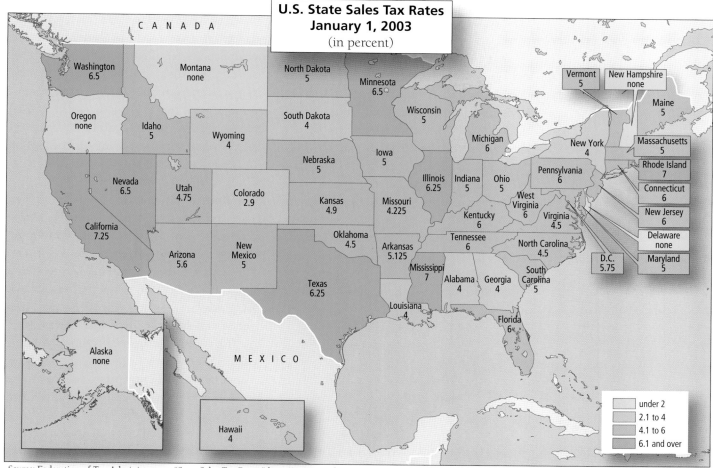

**U.S. State Sales Tax Rates
January 1, 2003**
(in percent)

Washington 6.5	
Montana none	
North Dakota 5	
Minnesota 6.5	
Oregon none	
Idaho 5	
Wyoming 4	
South Dakota 4	
Wisconsin 5	
Michigan 6	
Vermont 5	
New Hampshire none	
Maine 5	
Nevada 6.5	
Utah 4.75	
Colorado 2.9	
Nebraska 5	
Iowa 5	
Illinois 6.25	
Indiana 5	
Ohio 5	
Pennsylvania 6	
New York 4	
Massachusetts 5	
Rhode Island 7	
California 7.25	
Arizona 5.6	
New Mexico 5	
Kansas 4.9	
Missouri 4.225	
Oklahoma 4.5	
Kentucky 6	
West Virginia 6	
Virginia 4.5	
Connecticut 6	
New Jersey 6	
Delaware none	
Texas 6.25	
Arkansas 5.125	
Tennessee 6	
North Carolina 4.5	
D.C. 5.75	
Maryland 5	
Mississippi 7	
Alabama 4	
Georgia 4	
South Carolina 5	
Louisiana 4	
Florida 6	
Alaska none	
Hawaii 4	

CANADA
MEXICO

Legend:
under 2
2.1 to 4
4.1 to 6
6.1 and over

Source: Federation of Tax Administrators, "State Sales Tax Rates," http://www.taxadmin.org/fta/rate/sales.html (February 3, 2003).

incentives (deductions, exceptions, and so on). Economic distortions are created when firms are persuaded by tax considerations to hoard cash surpluses or enter into dubious mergers and acquisitions rather than pay greater dividends to stockholders.

Even sales taxes enter into pricing decisions. A sales tax is imposed on the consumer at the point of sale. The seller receives the price paid by the consumer minus the sales tax (which is paid to the government). Production decisions are made based on this lower price. Thus, buying decisions are made at one price and production decisions at another price, which results in an inefficiency to the economy at large.

The final characteristic to consider about tax systems is whether the system generates sufficient funds for the government. A tax system that does not generate enough revenue will cause the government to borrow funds. Government borrowing affects business by competing for limited funds in the financial markets. The added demand by the government for funds results in higher interest rates on capital investments (assuming all else remains the same). Higher interest rates cause business to reduce capital investments and thus reduce future growth potential.

Taxation is an important consideration in the making of business decisions. A tax imposed by the government offers possible gains and losses to a business; management must incorporate the tax code into the bottom line. The government must consider the impact of taxation on business decisions in the designing of the tax system.

Further Research
Taxworld
www.taxworld.org
Comprehensive information on tax regimes around the world, as well as a section on the history of taxation.

—*James K. Self*

Trademark

Trademarks are the images, words, signs, and symbols that corporations use to represent the products and services they offer. Trademarks began with the brands, marks, and tattoos that identified the livestock of a farm or ranch. Such marks of identity, ownership, and origin go back more than five millennia to the great empires of the Middle East. Royal marks, heraldry, and monograms identified the owners of public and private property and certified the origin of products.

As trade grew in the Mediterranean region and beyond, these marks came to include the marks found on ancient ceramic artifacts. The first true trademarks were in use by the time of the Roman Empire, where they identified the oil lamps manufactured by such early multinational firms as Fortis and Stroboli. In time, watermarks, quarry gang marks, mason guild marks, hallmarks, assay marks, and furniture marks all came to serve the twin functions that trademarks serve today.

The Role of Trademarks

The first function is to inform the public that a specific organization or individual makes a product or provides a service. Public law protects trademark rights as a form of intellectual property. Trademark law enables those who invest in providing goods and services to protect their investment by securing the sole right to be identified with their own products and services. This encourages enterprise, increases the flow of investment, and increases the opportunities for profit.

The second function of trademarks is to signal the attributes and level of quality that can be expected of the product or service offered. It constitutes a form of public information and helps to regulate markets. By permitting trademarks to function as quality guarantees, this aspect of the law increases the transparency of markets. In this way, the law helps to secure the rights of investors, firms, and consumers.

A trademark is an information artifact. As a tag or marker, it has no true value apart from its connection to a good or service. The good or service could exist without the trademark, but the trademark would not have the same meaning without the good or service with which it is associated. Nevertheless, the value of a trademark is so closely connected to the good or service it represents that many trademarks take on a special value of their own.

Repeated and consistent use of a respected trademark endows it with the significance of the underlying products and services that the trademark represents. Customers who prefer a product or service

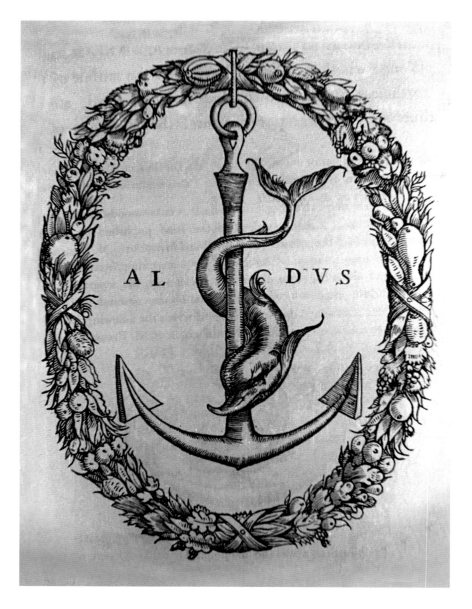

A fifteenth-century trademark belonging to Aldus Manutius, a Venetian printer.

Trademarks 1980 to 2001 (in thousands)	1980	1985	1990	1995	1997	1998	1999	2000	2001
Applications filed	46.8	65.1	127.3	188.9	234.6	246.6	328.6	296.5	232.9
Trademarks issued	24.7	71.7	60.8	92.5	145.2	136.1	191.9	115.2	133.8

Source: U.S. Patent and Trademark Office, "Statistical Reports Available for Viewing Calendar Year Patent Statistics," http://www.uspto.gov/web/offices/ac/ido/oeip/taf/reports.htm (April 5, 2003).

seek it out, creating market value for the provider. This market value is called brand equity. Brand equity and the value of a trademark constitute part of the intellectual capital of an organization.

In some circumstances, the significance of a trademark can take on value in its own right. The organization that owns a trademark can legitimately use it to extend meaning and guarantee the quality of other related products and services. Used illegally, the trademark can be attached to products or services from other providers. This activity—known as piracy or counterfeiting—allows those who have not invested in the development of a trademark to take the profits that the trademark represents, usually at a lower cost than the costs of the true trademark owner.

For individual firms and organizations, counterfeiting represents an immediate cost, a loss of business, and a threat to markets. This form of piracy once mostly concerned specific firms or trademark owners. The international flow of goods and services is now so great that it has become an issue of international concern. Trade flows in trademarked goods and services constitute a massive part of the global economy. These flows affect huge portions of the trade balance of every industrial nation. Accordingly, trademark law is now a matter of international treaty.

Organizations of all kinds use trademarks. Manufacturers and service firms, public agencies, governments, and non-profit organizations use them along with universities, professional associations, and churches. Trademarks identify tangible products and immaterial services. They help consumers to recognize the information products and virtual services of the knowledge economy.

Further Research

International Trademark Association

www.inta.org

The organization, with members in 190 countries, provides educational resources.

Overview of Trademark Law

cyber.law.harvard.edu/metaschool/fisher/domain/tm.htm

A briefing put together by Harvard Law School's Cyberlaw Clinic, which provides high-quality, pro-bono legal services to individuals, small start-ups, non-profit groups, and government entities regarding cutting-edge issues of the Internet, new technology, and intellectual property.

United States Patent and Trademark Office

www.uspto.gov

The USPTO reviews trademark applications for federal registration and determines whether an applicant meets the requirements for federal registration. Its Web site contains information on trademarks in the United States.

—Ken Friedman

Trademark Symbols		
Mark	**Definition**	**Use**
TM	A word, name, symbol or device that is used in trade with goods to indicate the source of the goods and to distinguish them from the goods of others	Alerts public of claim of rights in a mark
SM	Same as a trademark except that it identifies and distinguishes the source of a service (banking, dry cleaning, transportation, house painting, etc.)	
®	Registered trademark	May be used only after the U.S. Patent and Trademark Office registers the mark

Source: U.S. Patent and Trademark Office, "What Are Patents, Trademarks, Servicemarks, and Copyrights?" http://www.uspto.gov/web/offices/pac/doc/general/whatis.htm (March 18, 2003).

Unemployment

Unemployment occurs when a person is not currently working but is able to work and is actively seeking employment. A low level of unemployment is a sign that an economy is strong and healthy, while high levels of unemployment can indicate serious problems in many areas of an economy. For any country as a whole, high levels of unemployment indicate that the productive potential of workers is being lost. For the government, periods of high unemployment result in a loss of tax revenue because workers and families pay fewer taxes when their income is lower.

Unemployment can create a vicious cycle. For unemployed workers and their families, unemployment usually results in a dramatic loss in the wages needed to buy goods and services. Because of this decline in income, unemployed workers are usually forced to cut spending, thus hurting businesses that would have benefited from their patronage. If unemployment becomes widespread, the spending cutbacks can become dramatic, and these businesses may, in turn, be forced to lay off even more workers.

Governments collect data about unemployment in an effort to measure and understand its varied effects. The most important indicator is the unemployment rate. The unemployment rate is the percentage of people in the labor force who are considered unemployed. The labor force is all who are employed or not employed and want to work. People who are not working but also not looking for a job are considered to be out of the labor force. (In some cases, people may be out of work for long periods and give up looking for work; they are called discouraged workers.) The U.S. unemployment rate has varied widely. On a monthly basis, the lowest rate was 2.5 percent in May 1953 and the highest was 10.8 percent in November and December 1982.

Data are also collected on many characteristics of people who are employed and unemployed, including geographic location, industries and occupations, age, sex, and race. Do unemployed people live in a household alone or with children and spouse? Whether unemployment is increasing or decreasing is a key indication of an economy's improvment or decline. All these measures help analysts understand the nature of the unemployment trends in the economy.

Unemployment and the Economy

The unemployment rate is the most widely cited measure of labor market conditions. People often refer to the labor market as tight or loose. A tight labor market has few people who are unemployed; most people who want to find work can do so quickly and employers often have difficulty locating and hiring qualified people. A loose labor market has many people who are unemployed; finding a job can be difficult, and employers can easily fill open positions. Historically an unemployment rate of 5 percent was considered tight and a rate of about 7 percent was considered loose.

One of the most important ways that unemployment affects the economy as a whole is by increasing or decreasing inflationary pressures—the prices of goods and

Unemployment Rates by Industry 1980 to 2000 (in percent)					
	1980	*1985*	*1990[1]*	*1995[1]*	*2000[1]*
All unemployed [2]	7.1	7.2	5.6	5.6	4.0
Industry: [3]					
Agriculture	11.0	13.2	9.8	11.1	7.5
Mining	6.4	9.5	4.8	5.2	3.9
Construction	14.1	13.1	11.1	11.5	6.4
Manufacturing	8.5	7.7	5.8	4.9	3.6
Transportation and public utilities	4.9	5.1	3.9	4.5	3.1
Wholesale and retail trade	7.4	7.6	6.4	6.5	5.0
Finance, insurance, and real estate	3.4	3.5	3.0	3.3	2.3
Services	5.9	6.2	5.0	5.4	3.8
Government	4.1	3.9	2.7	2.9	2.0

Note: Rate represents unemployment as a percent of labor force in each specified group.
[1] Data not strictly comparable with data for earlier years. [2] Includes the self-employed, unpaid family workers, and persons with no previous work experience, not shown separately. [3] Covers unemployed wage and salary workers.
Source: U.S. Bureau of Labor Statistics, *Employment and Earnings,* January issues, 1980 to 2000.

A protest against unemployment in New York City in 1909.

services. When unemployment is low and the market is considered tight, workers are not only more likely to have a job but also more able to demand pay increases in the jobs that they have, and employers are less able to resist. In response, businesses often raise the prices of their goods or services to be able to pay the higher salaries. Similarly, as more workers are employed and those who have jobs are more able to demand wage increases, they are better able to pay increasing prices.

By contrast, when unemployment is high, workers are less able to demand higher wages because they are glad to have any job. Similarly, as more people are unemployed, they are less able to spend on consumer goods. Businesses are forced to keep prices steady.

Generally this market dynamic for unemployment seems to hold true. However, some periods seem to be notable exceptions. For example, during the 1970s, both inflation and unemployment rates were high. During the 1990s, unemployment was quite low, but upward pressure on prices was absent.

Types of Unemployment

Economists have identified four types of unemployment: frictional unemployment, cyclical unemployment, structural unemployment, and seasonal unemployment. These each have different qualities and different causes.

Frictional unemployment (because transitions between jobs are rarely smooth) is thought to be relatively short-term unemployment when workers find themselves between jobs. Individuals can lose a job by being fired, being laid off, quitting, or for other reasons. When any of these happens, some time may be needed to find a new job. Short delays are considered friction in the labor market. Some amount of frictional unemployment is always present as some people always experience short delays between jobs.

Cyclical unemployment is caused by a deeper downturn in the economy as a whole. It affects a large number of people who may face a longer period of unemployment. When the business cycle turns downward, demand for goods and services drops as a result, and workers are laid off. Because the entire economy is suffering, workers often have difficulty finding new jobs.

Structural unemployment results from a mismatch between the skills of workers and the skills needed by employers. This can occur in a particular geographic area or during a specific time. Technological advances, for example, often cause businesses to need workers with new skills to take advantage of the technology. People without those skills can find themselves unemployed. Structural unemployment can also affect a geographic area where a plant or business closes down or moves and lays off its workers.

Seasonal unemployment primarily affects workers in the agricultural and construction industries. In the winter months, for example, jobs associated with fruit harvesting and new home construction disappear in some regions until the weather improves. Students often look for work during their summer vacations. If they do not find jobs, they are also usually considered seasonally unemployed.

Employment and Government Policy
Workers who lose their jobs through no fault of their own can receive unemployment

Unemployment by Occupation 1990 to 2000

	Number (in thousands)			Unemployment rate		
	1990	1995	2000	1990	1995	2000
Executive, administrative, and managerial	350	420	356	2.3	2.4	1.8
Professional specialty	316	460	369	2.0	2.5	1.7
Total, executive, managerial, and professional	666	880	725	2.1	2.4	1.7
Technicians and related support	116	113	97	2.9	2.8	2.2
Sales occupations	720	795	684	4.8	5.0	4.0
Administrative support, including clerical	804	836	684	4.1	4.3	3.5
Total, technical, sales, and administrative support	1,641	1,744	1,464	4.3	4.5	3.6
Private household	47	99	58	5.6	10.7	6.9
Protective service	74	86	65	3.6	3.7	2.6
Service except private household and protective	1,018	1,193	900	7.1	7.9	5.6
Total, service occupations	1,139	1,378	1,023	6.6	7.5	5.3
Mechanics and repairers	175	182	129	3.8	4.0	2.6
Construction trades	483	501	312	8.5	9.0	4.9
Other precision production, craft, and repair	202	177	113	4.7	4.2	2.8
Total, precision production, craft, and repair	861	860	554	5.9	6.0	3.6
Machine operators, assemblers, inspectors	727	629	455	8.1	7.4	5.9
Transportation and moving occupations	329	329	253	6.3	6.0	4.4
Handlers, equipment cleaners, helpers, laborers	657	660	520	11.6	11.7	8.7
Total, operators, fabricators, and laborers	1,714	1,618	1,228	8.7	8.2	6.3
Farming, forestry, and fishing	237	311	215	6.4	7.9	6.0
Total unemployed[1]	7,047	7,404	5,655	5.6	5.6	4.0

[1] Includes persons with no previous work experience and those whose last job was in the armed forces.
Source: U.S. Bureau of Labor Statistics, *Employment and Earnings,* January issues, 1990 to 2000.

benefits from their state. These payments cover a percentage of the worker's previous salary. However, a particular worker is not necessarily eligible to collect unemployment. Eligibility is keyed to an employee having worked a minimum number of weeks, which varies widely by state. The amount of the benefit, which is subject to a cap, is based on a percentage of the employee's salary earned over a specified period. The employer supports the insurance program through premiums based on its payroll. Workers can typically receive unemployment checks for up to 26 weeks, except in times of recession when the federal government may allow states to provide extended benefits, as happened in 2009. To continue to receive benefits, unemployed workers must demonstrate that they are actively seeking work but have not been able to find a job.

Unemployment insurance (UI) principally provides some financial cushion to people who lose their jobs. Without unemployment insurance, workers who face even short periods of unemployment may become impoverished. UI also helps the economy as a whole by enabling people to continue to spend money and fuel business activity.

When looking at government policies on unemployment and employment, economists are often interested in evaluating their effect on labor market flexibility. A flexible labor market is one in which people move easily in and out of jobs. For UI, economists seek a balance between providing a financial cushion for unemployed workers and providing so much money that workers will have little incentive to find a new job. If unemployed workers are provided substantial UI checks over a long period, the fear is that they will simply live off their unemployment checks and not try hard to find new employment. Thus UI is sometimes considered to be a barrier to a flexible labor market. Policy makers can have very different opinions about how to strike a balance between supporting workers' income and creating incentives for them to find new work.

Measuring Unemployment

In the United States, unemployment-related data are primarily collected by the Bureau of Labor Statistics (BLS), a division of the U.S. Department of Labor. On the first Friday of every month, BLS releases the results of its survey. These data include the total number of employed and unemployed persons for the previous month.

The data are gathered from a monthly survey, *Current Population Survey* (CPS), which has been conducted every month since 1940. The survey consists of responses from 60,000 households in the United States. The sample is selected to be representative of the entire population of the United States.

The survey asks about the employment status of each person in the household over the age of 15. People are considered employed if they did any work during that week for pay or profit, worked 15 hours or more as an unpaid worker in a family business, or were temporarily absent from a job. People are considered unemployed if they do not have a job, have actively looked for work in the prior four weeks, and are currently available for work. Actively looking for work is defined as any of the following:

- contacting an employer
- having a job interview
- meeting with a public, private, school, or university employment counselor
- talking with friends or relatives about job possibilities
- sending out resumes or filling out applications
- placing or answering advertisements
- checking union or professional registers
- some other means of active job search

For workers who have jobs, a balance must be struck between protecting them from sudden changes in the economy or unfair treatment from employers, while providing employers the flexibility to have the best workers when they are needed. In some countries, and in some industries, employers face barriers to firing employees whose performance is substandard or employees whose skills are no longer required. These are sometimes considered signs of an inflexible labor market. Here, too, policy makers differ widely on where to strike the right balance.

Further Research

Bureau of Labor Statistics: Current Population Survey

www.bls.gov/cps

The CPS is a monthly survey of households conducted by the Bureau of Census for the Bureau of Labor Statistics. It provides a comprehensive body of data on the: labor force, employment, unemployment, and persons not in the labor force..

—Carl Haacke

Venture Capital

For a business to expand, business owners need money. Usually the amount of money needed is much larger than the business owner alone can provide. Public companies can sell stock, but for a private company, especially a small private company, finding investors can be difficult. Small business owners can borrow money from friends and family, take out bank loans, vie for any available government grants. Although enough money might come from those sources to sustain a business or fund a small expansion, it is usually not enough to fund aggressive growth. Venture capital fills this need.

Kinds of Venture Capital

In its most general sense, venture capital is money and resources provided by investors to small businesses that wish to become large businesses. Providing venture capital is a high-risk game—very few small businesses actually become large ones. However, venture capital's impact on the economy at large is substantial because it enables entrepreneurs with new ideas and new technology to turn those ideas into substantial businesses.

In a sense, what is now called venture capital is very old. Throughout history wealthy people and institutions have funded entrepreneurs in hopes that their ideas would turn into successful businesses.

These days individuals who give money to new businesses are called angel investors; they invest in a new business in exchange for an ownership stake in the company. An angel investor is usually a seasoned businessperson who also provides advice, expertise, and useful business contacts. Angel investors tend to focus on start-up businesses or businesses that are very small—generally those that could use more management expertise and do not require huge amounts of capital.

Some large corporations, especially in the high-tech field, will fund start-ups they believe may produce products that could be useful to their core product. Intel, for example, which makes computer microprocessors, has funded start-ups developing technology that could make microprocessors faster. Such corporations also have in-house research and development departments, but start-ups are generally more likely to have innovative ideas and to take bigger risks in developing technology. Corporations sometimes take ownership stakes in the start-ups in return for the funding they give, but generally speaking, corporations are more interested in obtaining exclusive access to the new product once it is developed.

Businesses that are just starting out can also obtain assistance from incubators. Like an angel investor, an incubator provides more than just money—in fact, nonprofit incubators sometimes provide no cash at all. Instead, incubators provide facilities like

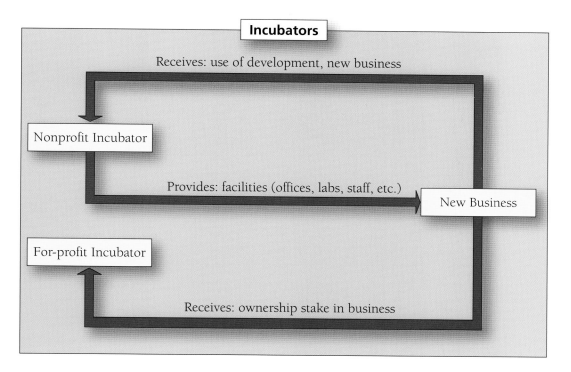

Incubators

Receives: use of development, new business

Nonprofit Incubator

Provides: facilities (offices, labs, staff, etc.)

New Business

For-profit Incubator

Receives: ownership stake in business

offices, high-speed Internet access, and support staff at little or no cost. Incubators can be run as a for-profit business, in which case the start-up provides the incubator with an ownership stake in return for use of the facilities. Many incubators are not-for-profit and are run by universities or municipal governments, which may also give tax breaks to the businesses in the incubators. With nonprofit incubators, start-ups do not always give an ownership share. Instead, a business might agree to let a university use any technology it develops free of charge. A municipality might not get anything at all in return for use of its incubator—except a slew of new businesses that are more likely to locate in the area once they are established enough to leave the incubator.

Probably the best-known providers of venture capital are venture capital firms—indeed, when people talk of the venture capital industry, they are usually referring to the firms, not angel investors or incubators. Venture capital firms run venture capital funds, which are generally set up as limited partnerships. The venture capital firm (or firms, as it is not uncommon for firms to join forces) is the general partner (the firm actually manages the fund and has also invested money into the fund). The limited partners,

who are the investors, provide the fund with money (usually a good deal of money—investing in a venture capital fund is beyond the means of most) and expect returns. In addition to providing money, the firm behind the fund offers management expertise and connections to other financiers and companies. A venture capital fund has a given lifespan, usually five to seven years. At the end of that period, the firm and the investors take their profits or losses, and the fund is disbanded.

Unlike angel investors, venture capital firms are a relatively new phenomenon. American Research and Development, a now-defunct Boston company established in 1946, is generally considered to have been the first venture capital firm. For decades, the industry was very small and clubby, and such firms generally dealt only with extremely wealthy families and institutions. Boston remains a center for the venture capital industry, but what is now known as Silicon Valley in California began to grow prominent in the industry in the 1960s. At the time, companies were beginning to develop expensive high-technology products, but most of the traditional financing firms were located on the East Coast, so West Coast financiers began to form venture

Venture Capital Commitments by Industry 1998–2008
(in million dollars)

Industry	1998	2000	2002	2004	2006	2008
Biotechnology	1,583	4,250	3,237	4,267	4,594	4,500
Electronics / Instrumentation	227	770	317	362	682	573
Financial services	822	4,201	348	524	468	534
Healthcare services	935	1,404	373	363	399	195
Industrial/energy	1,445	2,535	749	777	1,956	4,651
IT services	1,096	8,644	1,105	706	1,321	1,832
Media and Entertainment	1,829	10,541	736	976	1,641	2,039
Medical Devices and Equipment	1,187	2,474	1,860	1,936	2,924	3,460
Networking and Equipment	1,462	11,730	2,685	1,507	1,054	645
Semiconductors	643	3,642	1,573	2,181	2,162	1,651
Software	4,505	24,528	5,311	5,421	5,028	4,919
Telecommunications	2,896	16,774	2,357	1,915	2,649	1,688

Source: PriewaterhouseCoopers / National Venture Capital Association MoneyTree Report, Data: Thomson Reuters.

capital firms to help raise money for local businesses. Backing successful technology companies like Intel and Apple helped raise the profile of Silicon Valley venture capitalists, as well as the venture capital industry as a whole. The majority of West Coast venture capital firms are located in northern California, and most money in venture capital funds flows to the high-tech companies located there.

In the 1960s and 1970s the federal government became more involved in the venture capital industry with the creation of small-business investment companies (SBICs). SBICs received loans from the U.S. Small Business Administration to match funds raised privately for investment in small businesses; many venture capital firms organized as SBICs to gain access to these loans. In 1978 changes to the law made investing in venture capital funds by pension funds easier. By 2003, pension funds accounted for 42 percent of total venture capital investment.

Exit Strategies
Some venture capital funds specialize in start-ups, but generally speaking, a company must already be fairly well established to attract money from a venture capital fund because the fund has a limited life span. When its time is up, investors and venture capital firms want to be able to cash out and to have more money than they put in. Consequently professional venture capitalists are very focused on what is known as the exit strategy. The exit strategy is the way in which the small companies that the venture capitalists have invested in are going to generate lots of cash for the venture capital fund. This is also known as a liquidity event, because it turns all of the value in the small company into liquid assets, usually cash or stock in a publicly traded company.

One kind of liquidity event is the sale of a small, private company to a much larger company. Say a venture capital fund invests in a small software company that is making an exciting new product used on desktop computers. The fund's investment and advice helps turn the company into a medium-sized software company that attracts a lot of media attention. It also attracts the attention of the software giant Microsoft Corporation, which buys the privately held company with a combination of cash and Microsoft stock. Cash is already liquid, and as Microsoft is a public company, its stock can easily be sold, so the venture capitalists have achieved a liquidity event and can cash out. Around one-third of the companies funded by venture capital between 1991 and 2000 were acquired by another company; another 14 percent went public; 18 percent are known to have failed; and the remainder may have quietly failed, according to the National Venture Capital Association.

Another kind of liquidity event is to turn the private company into a public company and hold an initial public offering (IPO) of that company's stock. An IPO also makes the value of the company liquid, as its stock can be readily sold. In addition, going public makes shares of the company available to many more investors. If those investors are excited about the company, they will bid up the stock price, permitting the venture capital fund to sell its shares at an even greater profit.

Generally speaking, a company needs to be fairly large to attract either a buyer or enough investor interest to hold an IPO. As most companies that venture capital funds invest in are small, and the fund must achieve a liquidity event in a fairly short time, venture capitalists invest in companies that they think can expand very quickly. A company that wants to offer a service only in a specific locality is of no interest to venture capitalists, no matter how profitable that business might be, because that company

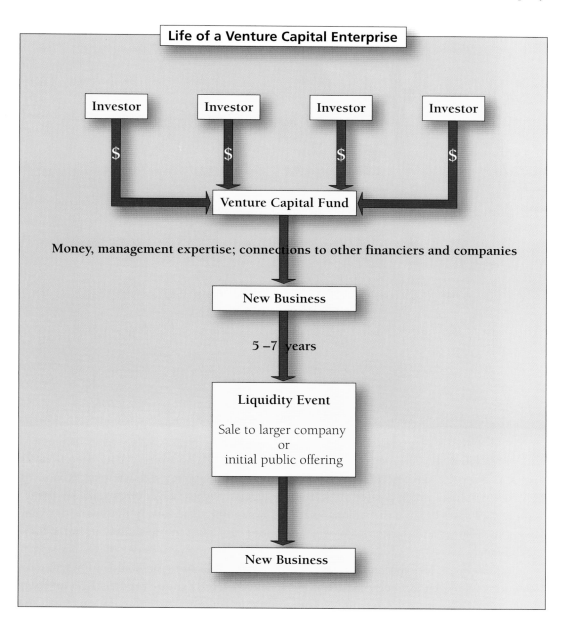

Life of a Venture Capital Enterprise

Investor   Investor   Investor   Investor

$ $ $ $

Venture Capital Fund

Money, management expertise; connections to other financiers and companies

New Business

5–7 years

Liquidity Event

Sale to larger company
or
initial public offering

New Business

Angus Davis, cofounder of Tellme Networks, Inc., poses in an English telephone booth at his company's offices in Palo Alto, California, in 1999. Davis announced that he and his partners at Tellme had received $47 million in funding from leading high-tech investors at rival venture capital firms. Unlike many venture capital–based companies founded in the late 1990s, Tellme Networks weathered the dot-com crash. It was acquired by Microsoft in 2007 for around $800 million.

will never grow very big. A company that wants to offer the same service nationally, however, will be of much greater interest to venture capitalists because the national market is much larger and the company will be much bigger.

This emphasis on expansion can lead to tremendous conflicts between the management of a small company and the venture capitalists who invest in it. A company's management may not want to expand as aggressively as the venture capitalists desire. Expanding aggressively may help the venture capitalists in the short run, but a company's management may believe that such a strategy will hurt the company in the long run. Because venture capitalists get an ownership stake in the company in return for their investment, they may be able to oust a company's existing management and replace it, which is rarely good for employee morale. On the other hand, as venture capitalists need the company to succeed to make money, they are often willing to dedicate a great deal of time, money, and effort to helping the company thrive. As a result, small companies that receive backing from venture capitalists are more likely to survive and grow than those that do not.

Boom and Bust

The majority of companies that venture capitalists invest in never make much money. A study of 1,765 investments in companies by venture capital funds from the mid-1980s to the mid-1990s found that fully 677 of the investments either lost money or broke even. Nonetheless, the amount of money invested overall increased tenfold because 89 companies returned more than 25 times the amount of money invested. The very small group of high-performance investments more than made up for the much larger group of bad investments.

The rule of thumb among venture capitalists is that only one of ten companies they invest in will really pay off. However, the payoff can more than compensate for the flops. Kleiner Perkins Caulfield & Byers, a venture capital firm, saw its investment in the online bookseller Amazon.com increase 6,000 percent. The investment of the three venture capital firms that backed the Internet-advertising company DoubleClick increased 9,930 percent. In 1997 the venture capital firm Benchmark Capital invested $5 million in the online auctioneer eBay for a share of the company that was worth $2.5 billion two years later—a return of 49,900 percent.

Such lavish returns are possible only if a liquidity event occurs, and that requires not just the right company but also the right business environment. Large corporations and small investors must be willing to buy the companies venture capital firms are selling. As a result, the venture capital industry is highly cyclical: when the economy is doing well, venture capital takes off; when the economy is doing poorly, venture capital crashes.

A spectacular boom-and-bust cycle began in the late 1990s; Internet companies like Amazon.com, DoubleClick, and eBay were red-hot, with investors gladly snapping up shares in IPOs. Many venture capital funds were generating very high returns, so investor money poured in and new funds and firms were established. In 1995 venture capital firms closed 60 funding deals with IT companies; in 2000 they closed 680.

In April 2000 the market for Internet stocks crashed. The bust wiped out many publicly held Internet companies, but more important for venture capitalists, it made offering an IPO impossible—investors simply were not interested in putting their money into a crashing sector. For the rest of 2000 no Internet company was able to raise money through an IPO, cutting off what had become the major exit strategy for venture capitalists. Many firms shut down funds or went out of business altogether, and those that remained became much less willing to invest. In 2001 venture capital firms closed only 321 funding deals with IT companies.

Although the bust certainly hurt the industry, many observers argue that in the long run a more conservative atmosphere encourages venture capitalists to do what venture capital is supposed to do—fund worthwhile business ideas. It is notable that during the stock market boom in 2007 and 2008, total venture capital funding rose, but not as astronomically as it had in 2000: in 2005, $23.2 billion was invested, compared to $30.9 billion in 2007 and $28.3 billion in 2008. Finding companies worth funding remains challenging but can also generate tremendous rewards, both for the venture capitalists and for the economy as a whole.

Further Reading
National Venture Capital Association
www.nvca.org
The NVCA represents U.S. venture capital.

—*Mary Sisson*

Glossary

accounts receivable Debts owed to a business by its customers.

antitrust Process of encouraging business competition.

asset Something of value.

asset management Process of managing money and other items of value to make them grow in value.

audit Review of the finances of publicly owned companies.

bankruptcy Legal process that allows a company or individual to restructure debts.

bear market Period of declining stock prices.

benefits Noncash items of value provided, in part, by employers to employees, including insurance, pension plans, and so on.

best practice Standard of comparison used in businesses that takes companies or individuals who operate most efficiently as a benchmark.

blue chip Well-established company (or the stock of such company) considered to be a leader in its industry.

bonds Certificates stating that a firm or government will pay the holder regular interest payments and a set sum on a specific maturity date.

brand Distinct symbol or phrase that distinguishes a good or service from competitors.

brand equity Value represented by a consumer's preference for a specific company's good or service.

branding Creating an image for a person or product.

brokerage Business that sells investment vehicles and advice.

bull market Period of rising stock prices.

capital Money or wealth that is put at risk to fund a business enterprise.

cash flow analysis Process of examining the financial effects of different decisions.

collateral Assets used to guarantee the payment of a debt.

commodity Any natural resource or good that is traded.

compensation What a business gives employees in exchange for their labor.

compound interest The money earned on the original principal and on interest reinvested from prior periods.

conglomerate A company that grows by merging with or buying businesses in several different industries.

consumer debt Debts incurred by the purchase of consumable goods that have little or no lasting value once purchased; food and cloths are examples.

consumer price index (CPI) Measure of the overall price level of goods.

copyright The exclusive ownership rights of authors, artists, or corporations to their works.

corporation Company owned by stockholders.

cost-benefit analysis Evaluating the monetary and nonmonetary gains and losses that ensue from making various choices.

credit A promise to pay.

credit rating Assessment of the likelihood of an individual, company, or government repaying its debts.

demand Amount of a good or service consumers will purchase at different prices at a given time.

demographics The study of groups within a population, subdivided by age, gender, income, or other factors; related to marketing, the groups studied are buyers of specific products and services.

deposit insurance Insurance to protect depositors in financial institutions against loss if the financial institution fails.

distribution channel Choices that producers have for reaching consumers; this includes catalogs, commercials, or stores, and so on.

diversification Allocation of money among different kinds of assets to minimize risk and maximize long-term results.

dividend The part of a corporation's profits paid to its stockholders.

economies of scale Declining average cost of production that results from increasing output.

elasticity Sensitivity of supply and demand to changes in a good's price.

entrepreneur Person who combines different resources to make goods or services available to others.

exchange rates Price of one currency in terms of another.

expense Cost of doing business.

fair use Legal doctrine allowing limited use of materials under copyright to encourage the spread of knowledge.

Federal Reserve Central bank of the United States; it is responsible for the orderly operation of the banking system, monitoring the economy, and conducting monetary policy.

fixed costs Charges to a business that are not directly affected by the amount of goods or services sold.

401(k) plans Method of saving for retirement in the United States that allows workers to set aside a portion of each paycheck for investment; no tax is imposed on the invested money or interest earned until withdrawal.

franchise License to operate a business that is part of a larger chain.

globalization Process of world economic integration driven by a combination of free trade and information technology.

gold standard Basing a currency on a set amount of gold.

gross domestic product (GDP) Total output of goods and services in a country in one year.

gross national product (GNP) Estimate of the value of goods and services produced by a country over a given period, including those goods and services produced by national entities outside the nation's physical boundaries.

inflation Period of rising prices.

initial public offering The first time a company sells stock to the public.

intellectual property Creations of the mind, for example, literary works and graphic designs.

interest Cost of borrowing money.

inventory The supply of goods held by a business.

investment bank Financial entity that provides expertise in assisting companies selling stock to the public.

IRA Acronym for Individual Retirement Account; a tax-advantaged account in which money is invested until withdrawn at age 59 or older.

joint venture Two or more businesses cooperating to produce a good or service.

liabilities Debts of a business or individual.

liquidity The ease with which assets can be converted into cash without a decline in value.

market research The attempt to gain an understanding of customers in order to sell them products or services.

market segmentation Marketing method that focuses on groups of consumers who share specific characteristics, for example, age, sex, or income.

market share Percentage of all dollars spent on a product or service that a specific company earns for that product or service; the proportion of a particular market dominated by a specific company.

mission statement Written statement that identifies the purpose of a business.

monopoly Type of market that involves only one seller.

mortgage a loan in which the borrower uses the title to real estate, such as a home, as security for the loan. If the borrower fails to pay back the loan according to agreed terms, the lender can claim (foreclose on) the property.

partnership Business structure with two or more individuals as owners.

patent Exclusive rights to a new product or invention for a set period.

payroll A business's accounting of what it pays its employees.

pension A retirement savings plan.

price fixing One or more businesses colluding to charge prices higher than the normal market would determine.

productivity Amount of work that can be completed in a given time.

public relations Process of creating a favorable public opinion of a person, product, concept, or organization.

qualitative research Market research using in-person contact with the consumer; interviews and demonstrations are qualitative research.

quantitative research Market research using mathematical or statistical methods; questionnaires are an example.

recession Period in which overall economic output declines.

revenue Income earned during a specific period from the operations of a business.

reverse engineering Determining how to reproduce a product by studying an existing version.

secondary market A stock exchange; the New York Stock Exchange is a secondary market.

securities Stocks, bonds, and other financial instruments.

small business An independently owned and operated business that is not dominant in its field of operation.

stock Part ownership in a corporation.

subsidy Financial payment from government to support a business endeavor.

supply Amount of a good or service producers will provide at different prices at a given time.

trademark Legal ownership of a unique symbol or design associated with a product or service.

venture capital Private funds used to start or expand a business.

vision statement Description of a business as it will exist at some point in the future.

yield Return on an investment.

Index

YA 332.024 P432D
Personal finance :

APR 0 9 2010